# ENHANCING SELF-CONCEPTS
# AND ACHIEVEMENT OF
# MILDLY HANDICAPPED STUDENTS

# ENHANCING SELF-CONCEPTS AND ACHIEVEMENT OF MILDLY HANDICAPPED STUDENTS

## Learning Disabled, Mildly Mentally Retarded, and Behavior Disordered

*By*

### CARROLL J. JONES, PH.D.

*Associate Professor of Special Education*
*Lander College*
*Greenwood, South Carolina*

CHARLES C THOMAS • PUBLISHER
*Springfield • Illinois • U.S.A.*

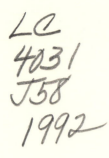
*Published and Distributed Throughout the World by*

CHARLES C THOMAS • PUBLISHER
2600 South First Street
Springfield, Illinois 62794-9265

© *1992 by* CHARLES C THOMAS • PUBLISHER

ISBN 0-398-05760-5

Library of Congress Catalog Card Number: 91-27886

*With* THOMAS BOOKS *careful attention is given to all details of manufacturing
and design. It is the Publisher's desire to present books that are satisfactory as to their
physical qualities and artistic possibilities and appropriate for their particular use.*
THOMAS BOOKS *will be true to those laws of quality that assure a good name
and good will.*

*Printed in the United States of America*
*SC-R-3*

**Library of Congress Cataloging-in-Publication Data**

Jones, Carroll J.
    Enhancing self-concepts and achievement of mildly handicapped
students : learning disabled, mildly mentally retarded, and behavior
disordered / by Carroll J. Jones.
        p.   cm.
    Includes bibliographical references (p. ) and index.
    ISBN 0-398-05760-5
    1. Handicapped students—United States.   2. Learning disabled
children—Education—United States.   3. Problem children—Education—
United States.   4. Self-perception.   I. Title.
LC4031.J58   1991
371.9'046—dc20                                              91-27886
                                                            CIP

*In Memory of*
*David Wesley Johnston*

# FOREWORD

We have long been aware that unless we, to some degree, appreciate and understand ourselves, it is most difficult to relate to the world around us. This is no less true of exceptional than nonhandicapped learners. The author of this book has given us a wonderfully complete window of insight into this most tenuous of human aspects, the self-concept.

Dr. Jones has given us a broader frame of reference as she reviews self-concept theory, globally, examining it from a chronological and developmental perspective, and relating the impact of self-concept on academic functioning. This she does within a normal child development framework.

When the reader is comfortable with the idea of self-concept from a theoretical perspective, only then does Dr. Jones introduce it as it relates to various categories of mildly handicapped students—learning disabled, mildly mentally retarded, and behavior disordered. Specific attention is given to the interaction of the characteristics of exceptionality with self-concept, and the resulting affect on academic achievement and learning. In addition to giving the reader an ear into the thoughts of mildly handicapped students about themselves, the author concludes with specific directions and recommendations for the teacher intent on strengthening the self-concepts of exceptional students. She has provided a veritable array of approaches and techniques the teacher might choose, including interventions which are metacognitive, behavioral, social, or academic in nature.

Indeed, Dr. Carroll Jones, in her characteristically complete way, has succeeded in giving us a valuable review of what are current best practices for understanding and intervening on behalf of mildly handicapped learners with emotionally fragile self-concepts.

Virginia J. Dickens, Ph.D.
*Area Coordinator, Special Education*
*Fayetteville State University*

vii

# PREFACE

The passage of P.L. 94-142, The Education for All Handicapped Children Act in 1975, focused national attention on the education of handicapped children. Individualization of academic programming and the enhancement of the self-concept were mandated as educational goals. An explosion of self-concept related research including that of the author contributed enormously to the understanding that the self-concept was multifaceted, and that having a caring teacher in a smaller less stressful classroom environment was not, by itself, enough to raise the self-concept of children who had a history of academic failure.

Currently, sixteen years after the passage of P.L.94-142, enhancement of the self-concept as a curricular objective is not usually programmed into the Individual Education Program (IEP) with specific goals and objectives, though there is a focus on social skills development. Frequently, affective characteristics are ignored altogether.

At present a void exists in providing understandable information to regular and special education teachers regarding the social, emotional, and self-concept development theory, and self-concept research. *Enhancing the Self-Concept and Achievement of Mildly Handicapped Students* was designed to fill this void with readily understandable information synthesized from the fields of sociology, psychology, and education regarding normal social, emotional, and self-concept development, and to explain differences exhibited by mildly handicapped students. Additionally, this book was designed to provide a basis and means for including the improvement of the self-concept as a curricular goal in the Individual Education Program.

The book was organized into three major units as follows: Unit One: Self-Concept Perspectives; Unit Two: Categorical Perspectives, and; Unit Three: Curricular Perspectives. Unit One: Self-Concept Perspectives provides an overview of self-concept theory (Chapter 1), the social and emotional development of nonhandicapped children during infancy and early childhood (Chapter 2), middle childhood (Chapter 3), and

ix

adolescence (Chapter 4), and the impact of the self-concept on academic achievement (Chapter 5).

Unit Two: Categorical Perspectives discusses the definitions, characteristics (academic, cognitive, social), sense of personal control (metacognition, motivation, attributions), general self-concepts and self-concept of academic achievement of learning disabled (Chapter 6), mentally retarded (Chapter 7), behavior disordered students (Chapter 8). Unit Three: Curricular Perspectives concerns the assessment of social, emotional, and self-concept behaviors of mildly handicapped students (Chapter 9), and methods, procedures, and strategies for enhancing the self-concept and achievement (Chapter 10).

Special acknowledgements to my colleague and friend at Fayetteville State University, Dr. Virginia Dickens, Coordinator of Special Education, who provided continuous encouragement and read rough drafts. Thanks to Julian Butler, Jr., Director of Special Education in Scotland County, Laurinburg, N.C. and some of his special education teachers for sharing self-enhancement techniques.

Thanks always to my family: Merrell, Andrea, and Camille for unfaltering faith and support in all of my projects.

The book is dedicated to the memory of David Wesley Johnston, my nephew, an exceptionally gifted young man, who greatly enriched the lives of all who knew him.

C.J.J.

# CONTENTS

xi

# ENHANCING SELF-CONCEPTS
# AND ACHIEVEMENT OF
# MILDLY HANDICAPPED STUDENTS

# Unit One
# SELF-CONCEPT PERSPECTIVES

# Chapter One

# SELF-CONCEPT THEORY: AN INTRODUCTION

*. . . . the self-concept has an aura of mysticism about it appearing not far removed from the concept of a soul (Epstein, 1973, 404).*

---

"One can neither see a self-concept, nor touch it, and no one has succeeded as yet in adequately defining it as a hypothetical construct" (Epstein, 1973, 404). Although the importance of the self-concept is an established fact, "the concept continues to be elusive" (Yamamoto, 1972, 81).

## DEFINITIONS OF SELF-CONCEPT

The self-concept, traditionally, has been regarded as a "single pervasive entity" (McNelly, 1972, 21) that included the entirety of the personality. Over the past few decades researchers have typically approached self-concept investigation from that point of view.

Representative of the all inclusive definitions of the self-concept is Jersild's (1951) definition which states:

A person's self is the sum total of all he can call his. The self includes among other things, a system of ideas, attitudes, values, and commitments. The self is a person's total subjective environment; it is the

5

distinctive center of experience and significance. The self constitutes a person's inner world as distinguished from the outer world consisting of all other people and things (9).

Phenomenologists including Combs, Snygg, and Rogers consider the self-concept to be the most central concept in all of psychology, since it provides the only perspective from which an individual's behavior can be understood (Epstein, 1973). Phenomenologists and many current researchers, however, view the self-concept as a complex multi-faceted "perceptual organization" including numerous separate self perceptions (Combs, 1965). Individuals may simultaneously have positive and negative self perceptions regarding various aspects of their personality and their abilities to function in their world.

According to Rogers (1951) four of the primary propositions of personality provide the foundation for theory relating to the self-concept. (1) The self-concept is a result of a person's interaction with the environment. (2) The self-concept may incorporate the values of others. (3) The self-concept strives for consistency. (4) The self-concept changes as a result of maturation and learning.

Many definitions of self-concept include one or more of Rogers' four propositions. A number of self-concept definitions propose that the self-concept is the resultant effect of an individual's interaction with the environment. These definitions specify that a person is not born with a self-concept but forms one as a result of experiences within the environment (Battle, 1982). The self-concept is described as a picture the individual forms of himself from his interaction with experiences within his environment.

A number of definitions of self-concept reflect the perspective that the self-concept may incorporate the values of others. Self-conceptions are learned and the evaluative reactions of others play a significant part in the learning process (Videbeck, 1960). The self-concept may be molded not only by direct communication from others, but also, by observations of other persons which have implications for self-labeling (Gergen, 1971). Thus, a child forms his self perceptions by observing the reactions of others toward him.

Additionally, self-esteem is the set of evaluative attitudes that a person applies to himself (Fontana, 1966). As one matures s/he learns to use this evaluative component to evaluate his/her own performance (e.g. actions, behaviors) in various situations and in relation to peers, parents, and academic performance; and in accordance to an "ideal" which is dictated by the superego (Battle, 1982, 25). According to this definition, self-concept suggests more than a picture of ones' self, but includes the individual's evaluation of that picture as good or bad (Roessler & Bolton, 1978).

A third perspective of self-concept reflected in many definitions includes the striving of the self for consistency. The self-concept is a self theory which each individual constructs about himself out of his experiences, and the stability is determined by his ability to derive pleasure from life, to assimilate experience and to maintain self-esteem (Epstein, 1973, 407). The self-concept, especially the general self-concept, tends to be stable and fairly resistant to change, an enduring personality characteristic (Battle, 1982). It has been suggested that a unified core of self-relevant experiences is crystallized into a core self or sense of identity and remains stable over time and across diverse circumstances (Gergen, 1977, 140).

The fourth property of self-concept described by Rogers was the self-concept changes as a result of maturation and learning. The self-concept takes shape as the child develops and interacts with significant others, and learns about his environment and himself (Battle, 1982). Self-concept change is a cognitive process by which a person defines appropriate behavior in a particular situation (Brookover & Erickson, 1962). Specific self perceptions depend on the circumstances of the social role which changes as the personality and social requirements evolve throughout the lifespan (Gergen, 1971).

Utilizing Rogers's (1951) primary propositions of personality as a framework, the following definition of self-concept was developed: The self-concept is the set of evaluative attitudes comprising a stable core self, that each individual constructs of his or her self, which changes and evolves throughout a lifespan based on social interactions, observations, reactions, experiences with others, and the environment.

## PHENOMENAL SELF

Phenomenology is a philosophical system which asserts that reality lies not in the event, but in the individual's perception of the event (the phenomenon). The phenomenological perspective was embodied in the "third force" in psychology referred to as humanistic psychology, as distinguished from Freudian psychology and behavioristic psychology (Campbell, 1984, 91). The phenomenological point of view strives to understand behavior from the perspective of the individual based on the individual's unique perceptions of themselves and the world in which they live, and the meanings things have for them (Combs & Snygg, 1959). Rogers, Combs, Snygg, and Maslow, major proponents of the humanistic approaches to education, were "interested in how the affective (emotional and interpersonal) aspects of behavior influence learning" (Biehler & Snowman, 1986, 385).

> Self perception is the most important variable determining behavior because the way we view ourselves determines how we respond to the demands of our environment. An individual's behavior, therefore, may be considered to be irrelevant and irrational to the outsider, but, to the behaving individual, the behavior is relevant, purposeful, and pertinent to the situation as the individual understands it (Battle, 1982, 13–14).

The phenomenal (conscious) self is the self we consider our personality. The phenomenal self is the self of whom we are aware, the self who is our constant companion, the self who judges our behaviors and performances and compares their outcomes to the "ideal" self. Current behavior judgements and outcomes evaluated by the phenomenal self influences future behavior.

Each person is constantly seeking to maintain and develop the conscious self into an adequate self, one that is capable of effectively and efficiently dealing with the problems of life. All behavior of an individual is targeted at the satisfaction of the need for adequacy (Combs & Snygg, 1959). "From birth to death the defense of the phenomenal self is the most pressing, most crucial, if not the only task of existence" (Combs & Snygg, 1959, 58).

Phenomenologists assume that an individual's verbal statements accurately reflect his phenomenal reality, his conscious self perceptions (Battle, 1982, 14). The phenomenal (conscious) self-concept is usually measured by administering self-reporting instruments, such as The Piers-Harris Children's Self-Concept Scale.

## NONPHENOMENAL SELF

The nonphenomenal self includes the unconscious aspects of our personality (Wylie, 1961). Perceptions lying hidden in the nonphenomenal (unconscious) self are often motivations for certain behaviors that are unexplainable to the phenomenal (conscious) self. The nonphenomenal self, also, is our constant companion, but one that does not interact on a conscious level with our reasoning. We do not have a direct conscious access to our nonphenomenal self. Kruger (1979, 104) indicates, "The unconscious is that aspect of our inner life which cannot be brought to consciousness by ordinary introspective methods. Secondly, the unconscious is the area of primary process thinking."

The nonphenomenal self reveals itself through projective tests and measures which require a trained psychologist or counselor to interpret. Some projective techniques utilized include human figure drawings, sentence completion, pretend situations, and immediate response situations. "When used with clinical skill and sensitivity, the projective techniques are the most effective instruments for penetrating the deeper recesses of the personality. They provide a method of studying personality and conflict through an unstructured medium" (Siegel, 1987, 85).

## DEVELOPMENT OF THE SELF-CONCEPT

The development of the self-concept begins in infancy and continues throughout one's lifetime, constantly undergoing modification in response to the environment (Lerner & Shea, 1982). By the time the child is six months old, s/he has begun to give evidence of having formed some more or less definite concepts about himself. These self concepts or awareness of self characteristics are predicated upon the interactions of numerous factors including the following: (1) Body Awareness, (2) Recognition of Attention, (3) Body Image, and (4) Concept of Child's Own Capabilities (Self-Concept Factors) (Jones, 1988).

### Self-Awareness

"The self develops gradually as the child matures, and becomes fairly stable about age ten" (Battle, 1982, 30). "Body image is essential in the development of a sense of self" (Battle, 1982, 31). The process of developing an accurate body image begins with body awareness which initially is manifested as total body responses to sensory stimulation and movement. Gradually, the child becomes aware of his/her body through visual exploration of self; sensory exploration with hands and mouth (e.g. sucking fingers, playing with toes); and studying himself/herself in the mirror. The concept of body image develops concurrently with cognitive, and fine and gross motor skills. The child develops an understanding of object concept and is able to discriminate himself/herself from objects and others (Jones, 1988, 252). Body image continues to develop as the child uses locomotion (e.g. crawling, walking) to move through space and become aware of directionality. Body image and concepts of maleness and femaleness begin to develop as the young child identifies with the same sex parent and imitates them and their sex role during play activities (Jones, 1988).

Related to the development of negative or positive concept of self is the child's initial recognition of attention to him/her by others. The baby is an egocentric being and thrives on attention by adults and other children, not only to satisfy physical needs, but also for social attention (e.g. tickling, playing simple games, tummy kissing). As the sensorimotor stage child learns to interpret emotions through the intonation system, s/he begins to understand, attend to, and obey "No" when paired with appropriate intonation. The young child learns to differentiate positive and negative attention and may cry when scolded and laugh when praised. Thus, as the awareness of self emerges, a need for positive self-regard develops out of the association of satisfaction or frustration during experiences with significant others (Battle, 1982).

## Self-Concept Aspects

As the individual matures, a portion of his experience is differentiated into a conscious perception of self-as-object or self-concept, which once formed influences the perceptions, thoughts, and memories of the individual (Rogers, 1959). Since the individual is a product of both physical and psychological (emotional) properties, the self-image is representative of both of these dimensions and possesses physical and psychological components (Battle, 1982, 32). A number of factors are involved in the development of the child's concept of his/her own capabilities, including the following: athletic skill, personal physical attractiveness, social attractiveness, special aptitudes, intelligence, academic performance, peer acceptance, moral code, and leadership qualities. These self-concept factors are not of significant importance to the sensorimotor stage child (birth to two years of age), but are crucial to the self-concepts of elementary school-aged children and adolescents.

## Athletic Skill

The athletic skill differences among preschoolers is not significant as they generally are involved in free play or noncompetitive activities of short duration (Biehler & Hudson, 1986). Fine motor skills and eye-hand coordination are not well developed even among primary grade children (grades 1, 2, 3), thus, proficiency in athletic activities involving these skills is at a rudimentary level. Some primary grade children begin getting actively involved in T–Ball and Little League softball, though the level of competitiveness in such sports is determined by parental expectations. By third grade ideas about who are the "best players" is well established, and when children choose up teams certain children who are labeled as "poor players" are consistently chosen last. However, at this level children are still eager to please the teacher, so will select the "poor players" without too much complaining as long as each team has an equal number of nonathletes. Athletic competition is not generally stressed during the primary grades due to short attention span and interest, and to lack of skill development. Thus, athletic skill at the primary grade level is generally not significantly important to the development of the self-concept.

From the intermediate grades (grades 4, 5, 6) through high school, athletic skill is considered very important in our culture for both boys and girls with competitiveness emphasized in intramural and intermural sports, as well as leisure time activities after school and during the summer. Athletic teams more than any other group serves to rally school support among students and patrons. Athletic teams always have the greatest financial support of any extracurricular activity. Successful athletes are held in high regard even though they may be poor scholars. Children and adolescents who are not athletes may experience severe discrimination unless they are able to achieve in other areas or to develop an athletics-related skill that is held in high regard. For example, a nonathlete may experience high regard by others by being a valued member of the pep band or of the marching band that performs at half-time at football games or as an athletics team manager or a school journalist who writes about the games and knows all of the "stats". Handicapped children and adolescents frequently experience difficulties with fine and gross motor skills, eye-hand coordination, eye-foot coordination, following directions, remembering the rules, taking advantage of competitive "gift" situations, and playing as a member of a team, thus, they usually are not outstanding in athletics.

## Physical Attractiveness

Physical attractiveness includes not only physical beauty, but also, involves good grooming and posture, attractive and stylish dressing, acceptable hair styles and make-up, and a good feeling about one's looks. In our society, physical attractiveness is emphasized from the cradle to the grave. Billions of dollars are spent annually on grooming aids, diets, exercise equipment and clubs, famous-label clothing, and surgery to enhance one's appearance; and on beauty contests for males and females from infancy through senior citizens. Physically "beautiful" persons hold a high and privileged status, and are given special consideration from that extra cookie as a youngster to a special, perhaps undeserved, job assignment as an adult.

> Not unexpectedly, it has been shown that a primary determinant of how we are perceived by others is our physical appearance. A large number of research studies support the conclusion that the impression we make is influenced by physical attractiveness and neatness of dress and grooming, plus a number of other immediately obvious characteristics such as the wearing of glasses (Lanyon & Goodstein, 1982, 17).

Dion, et. al. (1972) found that physically attractive people are seen by others as more exciting, more sociable, more interesting, more sensitive, and kinder than less attractive people. Individuals at all ages who do not fit the picture of the "ideal person," may experience significant distress. The greater the person's deviance from the "ideal" (ie., physically handicapped, disfigured, "ugly") the more difficulty the individual experiences in accepting their body image and in developing a positive self-concept.

## Social Attractiveness

Social attractiveness involves a wide range of attributes including temperament, emotional stability, pleasantness, sense of humor, use of manners appropriately in various social situations, true concern for others, enjoyment of life, and being liked by members of ones own and opposite sex. Temperament, generally reflected as social attractiveness, begins to be important almost from birth as adults and children prefer to interact with a pleasant, easy-going person.

During the preschool years, socially attractive children learn to control anger outbursts, and to solve disagreements by means other than hitting and aggressiveness. Children do not like to play with a child who is "mean." Primary grade children are very sensitive to criticism, ridicule, and failure. Socially attractive children have begun to develop a sensitivity to the feelings of others and are learning to be friends by avoiding criticism and ridicule.

The discrepancy between socially attractive students and social deviants becomes most noticeable during the intermediate grades when the referral for special education consideration due to behavior disorders is the most prevalent. Socially attractive students show respect both for teachers and other students, learn to cooperate and negotiate, begin to automatically use perspective-taking when attempting to understand a situation, remain calm during disputes, and try to avoid verbal and physical conflict situations.

Social attractiveness is a valuable attribute during adolescence when peer group membership is of primary importance. An aversive personality may serve to repel the very persons with whom the adolescent most wants to associate. Many handicapped students experience difficulty with interpreting affective cues, voice intonation, and facial expressions; in understanding teasing, flirting, sarcasm, and body language. Handicapped adolescents may experience significant difficulty in social situations and in conducting themselves verbally and physically in appropriate manners because they are never quite sure of the "real" dynamics of a situation. Social attractiveness is a very important aspect of social acceptance which dramatically impacts the development of the self-concept.

## Special Aptitudes

Special aptitudes include any of the areas of "gifted and talented" abilities in which a student's skills are considered exceptional and any abilities or activities which are valued within the community. Students who excel in traditional areas of art, music, dancing, and drama which bring glory and accolades to the school are held in high regard. Students who have received acclaim for extracurricular or community activities — volunteer hospital work, community competitive sports (e.g. YWCA swimming team, golf, tennis, bike racing), community arts programs (e.g. writing contests, speech contests, civic symphony and/or chorus, ballet, civic theatre productions) — earn high regard for their individual successes.

Students who have special hobbies or abilities such as motorcycle or dirt bike racing, rodeo competition, mountain climbing, flying airplanes, building model rockets earn status because of their unusual abilities. Special skills and abilities may be valued based on regional differences, for example, students who live near the beach may gain esteem from their abilities in surfing, shagging, scuba diving; while students who live in the mountains may gain regard from abilities at rappeling, mountain climbing, skiing, driving in the snow; and students in rural areas may gain esteem from abilities involving crop growing or owning a pickup truck and for homemaking skills (e.g., sewing, cooking, canning food). Students may also gain esteem from activities involving teenage music, such as, playing and/or singing in a rock 'n roll band; demonstrating and/or teaching the new dances.

Students sometimes gain special regard based on their parents' acquisitions (e.g., own a beach house or cabin) and willingness to sponsor or allow parties; parents' activities (e.g., sponsor various community activities, serve as fund raisers for valued activities); parents' occupations (e.g., influential positions in the community, unusual jobs or hobbies such as astronaut, test pilot, hot air balloonist).

Special abilities may be extremely important in developing a positive self-concept in students who are unable to be successful in traditional school sponsored and valued areas; and who are unable to enhance their self-esteem through athletic prowess, physical beauty, academic achievement, sense of humor, or specialized skills.

### Intelligence, Academic Performance, and Leadership Qualities

During the primary grades students are engaged in initial experiences with school learning. Most early primary grade students initially approach school with an excitement and eagerness to learn to read and write, and participate in the various school-related activities. Toward the end of the primary grades, differences in learning styles and abilities, and rates of learning become obvious. Children are divided into groups based on academic performance and functioning levels. Since academic performance and intelligence are considered to be highly related, students begin to form opinions about their intelligence based on their academic performance. Their first experiences in groups and committee experiences provide their first experiences as leader or follower.

By the intermediate grades, the differences in knowledge and skills of the fastest and slowest learners is quite apparent. The transition at the 4th grade level from "learning to read" to "reading to learn" changes the focus of academics and exaggerates the differences between students functioning on grade level and those below grade level. During the intermediate grade years, the referral rate to special reading and special education is at its peak. Handicapped and slow learners are sent to "special rooms" for "special help" and the differences between them and their achieving peers becomes extreme. The intermediate grade students show sex differences in specific abilities and overall achievement with girls evidencing superiority in verbal skills and earning higher grades, and boys showing superiority in mathematical and spatial abilities. The differences between the intermediate grade intellectually competent and remedial student becomes very obvious as the brighter or more successful students begin cognitively to deal with abstractions and generalizations, and begin to understand and use metacognitive skills. Leadership, frequently, is based on academic performance and/or athletic performance.

By the end of adolescence, students are aware of the significance of academic ability, and the importance/relationship of grades and levels of academic achievement to career choices. The majority of students are cognitively capable of logical thought, but may not use it consistently; of understanding abstractions; of forming and testing hypotheses; of consistently using metacognitive skills.

Early maturing males in Junior and Senior High School who are self-confident and possess high degrees of self-esteem are likely to be chosen as leaders (Biehler & Snowman, 1986). During adolescence students who excel in the various self-concept factors (e.g., athletics, personal physical attractiveness, social attractiveness, special aptitudes, intelligence, and academic performance), especially those who hold the most status, are the most likely to be chosen as leaders.

School is the major arena in which adolescents earn status. For students who are handicapped and low achieving in academics, slow learners, and elective underachievers, school is not an arena for earning status. Many authorities have stressed that repeated academic failure almost always leads to a damaged self-concept at least in the areas of perceptions of own abilities in intelligence, academics, and leadership.

## Peer Acceptance

During preschool and kindergarten most children have one or two best friends, but these friendships change rapidly as preschoolers are quite flexible socially and are usually willing to play with most of the other children in the class (Biehler & Snowman, 1986). Favorite friends tend to be of the same sex, but there are many friendships between boys and girls.

Primary grade children are more selective in their friends. They usually have a special or best friend and often have an "enemy." Primary grade students quarrel frequently when involved in organized games because they may be overly concerned with rules. By the end of the primary grades most children are able to assume a self-reflective role taking perspective, and begin to understand the importance of processing social information in determining role taking (Biehler & Snowman, 1986).

During the intermediate grades the peer group becomes powerful and begins to replace adults (e.g., parents, teacher, club leader) as the major source of behavior standards, and for recognition of achievement. Intermediate grade children begin to form "private" clubs which require initiation rituals. Though intermediate grade children can analyze their own behavior and that of others by engaging in multiple role taking (Selman, 1981), they can be very cruel to those who are not accepted into their peer group.

During adolescence the peer group becomes the general source of rules and behavior. Each high school generally has several identifiable peer groups, and according to my teen-aged daughter, at her school the groups include the following: the "nerds" (nonathletic intellectuals), the "jocks" (athletes and cheerleaders), the "geeks" (weird, strange people generally considered outcasts), the "heads" (long haired, like hard-rock music, who may also use drugs), "trendies" (trend setters in clothing, music, etc.), "transients" (accepted marginally by all groups but not in the inner circle of any particular group).

In order to function in a peer group, the adolescent must adopt the subgroup's standards and moral values. They must assume the group's common mode of behavior and become proficient in speaking the common language. Their dress, make-up, and hair style must follow group dictates. Adolescents must listen to and know the music sanctioned by their chosen peer group. They must frequent the accepted social hangouts. In these ways adolescents create a "we" status of group membership and an identity for themselves in a very unsure period of their lives. Adolescents are greatly concerned about what others think of them and the reactions of friends are very important.

**Moral Code**

During preschool and kindergarten rules are viewed as unchangeable edicts handed down by those in authority (Biehler & Snowman, 1986). Young children obey rules to avoid the physical consequences or punishment that comes from misbehavior rather than viewing their intentions as wrong. Primary grade children continue to obey rules to avoid punishment, but they also expect that obeying the rules should bring a benefit or reward in return. They experience difficulty in understanding how and why rules may need to be adjusted to special situations (Biehler & Snowman, 1986).

The intermediate grade and junior high school aged students are concerned with cooperation. They view rules as flexible mutual agreements for most of their organized games, but "official" rules should be obeyed out of respect for authority or to impress others (Biehler & Snowman, 1986).

During high school years, adolescents for the first time must determine a personal moral code. They must make personal value decisions regarding the use of drugs and alcohol, premarital sex, and a code of ethics, and be willing to accept the consequences for their decisions. Most people reach the conventional level of moral development during adolescence. The conventional level is characterized by the ability to internalize or identify with the rules prescribed by social groups and with the expectations of others especially authorities (Kohlberg, 1976). Adolescents who do not progress to the conventional level of morality do not take responsibility for their actions, do not understand that laws benefit society, and are frequently in "trouble" with authorities.

Thus, the development of the self-concept begins shortly after birth through body awareness, recognition of attention, and body image. The self-concept is a complex entity composed of the individual's conceptions of his/her own capabilities in athletic skill, personal physical attractiveness, social attractiveness, special aptitudes, intelligence, academic performance, peer acceptance, moral code, and leadership qualities. Though the self-concept changes and evolves throughout a lifespan, it possesses a stable core composed of evaluative self attitudes which are resistant to change. "The self, once established, motivates the individual to choose objectives and goals which are consistent or congruent with it" (Battle, 1982, 44).

# POSITIVE SELF–CONCEPT

## (Adequate Personality)

Adequate personalities have been described as those who perceive themselves in essentially positive ways, accept themselves and others, and perceive themselves as closely identified with others. Individuals possessing an adequate personality view themselves realistically, neither overevaluating nor undervaluing the perceived self. They have achieved a considerable degree of self-enhancement and self-maintenance, and perceive themselves as liked, acceptable, and worthy (Combs & Snygg, 1959).

A phenomenal self becomes adequate by being accepted. The more adequate a person feels, the more acceptant s/he becomes, with increased ability to feel compassion and empathy for others. Persons with adequate personalities can accept their own human nature inspite of discrepancies from the ideal self-image without feeling significant concern (Maslow, 1954).

Persons possessing adequate personalities behave in more effective and efficient manners than inadequate personalities. This type of behavior stimulates the learning of new things, the retention of learnings, and the solving of new problems. Successful students, adequate personalities, are generally seen to have positive self-concepts (Combs & Snygg, 1959).

The conclusion that successful students are likely to see themselves in essentially positive ways has been verified by a host of studies (Purkey, 1970). Achievers are characterized by self-confidence, self-acceptance, and positive self-concept. A composite portrait of the successful student would show s/he has a relatively high opinion of her/his self and is optimistic about the future. Coopersmith (1967, 41–42) indicates the following factors are characteristic of individuals who possess high self-esteem: (1) Effective, active and assertive in meeting environmental demands; (2) Demonstrate confidence in abilities to succeed and deal with events; (3) Participates in more exploratory and independent activities; (4) Possess self-respect, pride, self-acceptance, and self-love; (5) Popular with peers; (6) Defends themselves well against threats and demeaning attempts by others; (7) Slow to arouse anxiety.

In one research study a statistically significant positive correlation was found between self-concept and perceived evaluations of significant others, general performance in academic subjects, and achievement in specific subject matter fields (Brookover et. al., 1964). Other researchers have reported the more positive the self-concept, the higher the achievement level (Snyder et. al., 1965). High achieving boys and girls report significantly higher self-concepts than low achieving boys and girls (Farls, 1967).

> Self-expectations and the expectations of others exert a powerful influence upon the level of performance achieved. Higher estimates of our own powers lead to higher expectations of success which appear to evoke greater efforts and focus, eventuating in higher levels of performance (Coopersmith, 1959, 242).

## NEGATIVE SELF-CONCEPT

### (Inadequate Personality)

Individuals possessing a negative phenomenal self or inadequate personality view themselves in essentially negative ways. They feel unworthy, unwanted, unacceptable, and unable to deal with the changes in life. Inadequate personalities are unable to achieve need satisfaction, unable to enhance the self, and perceive themselves in constant danger from external events (Combs & Snygg, 1959, 266). The level of self-esteem is of primary importance in determining one's actions and if the self-esteem is inadequate, various forms of maladaptive behavior may be anticipated (Purkey, 1970, 140).

Persons with negative self-concepts lack confidence in their abilities, feel despair because they cannot find a solution for problems, and believe that most attempts will result in failure (LaBenne & Greene, 1969, 122). Inadequate personalities are unable to cope with life because they feel continuously threatened and in constant danger from external events. Threatened people almost always overreact and behave in exaggerated ways that produce the very reactions in others which verify their own already existing beliefs. "The inadequate self may find it necessary to live a life of continuous, aggressive seeking for self-enhancement to protect himself from destruction" (Combs & Snygg, 1959, 267).

Research results indicate persons of low self-esteem do not protect themselves from negative evaluation, so they are more likely to evaluate a failure as a very poor performance and a success as a small success (Wagner, 1980). Given equal competence at a task, a person with low self-esteem would be expected to evaluate his own performance less favorably than a person with high self-esteem (Ziller et. al., 1969).

Inadequate personalities do not possess strong feelings of identification with others. The inability of a person to accept themselves is strongly correlated with the inability to accept others. People with little feeling of identification with other people are unlikely to be concerned about them. A low self-opinion is likely to be associated with fear and distrust of others (Combs & Snygg, 1959).

General characteristics of individuals with low self-esteem include the following: (1) Passive and nonassertive in adapting to environmental demands and pressures; (2) Indecisive and tend to vacillate when dealing with problems; (3) Demonstrate feelings of inferiority, timidity, lack of personal acceptance, submissiveness; (4) Exhibit high levels of anxiety, psychosomatic symptoms, and feelings of depression; (5) Experience difficulty forming friendships; (6) Conform more readily to social pressures; (7) Unwilling to express contrary opinions even if correct; (8) React strongly to criticism; (9) Prone to emitting self-defeating responses and behaviors; (10) Pessimistic in views concerning the future (Coopersmith, 1967 Battle, 1982).

## ANXIETY

The self-image serves as a reference point from which to evaluate new experiences. If a person has unclear or negative perceptions of the self, they are prone to be anxious. Anxiety may be defined as a feeling of threat from unknown sources (Hansen & Maynard, 1973). Anxiety and its accompanying tensions are the inseparable partners of inadequacy feelings. "Anxiety is the apprehension of not being a worthwhile, esteemed person" (Campbell, 1984, 38). The anxiety feelings experienced by the individual may be more or less clearly attached to some perception, phobia, or may be vague and unattached to any perceptions, "free-floating anxiety," (Combs & Snygg, 1959, 286).

Anxiety prone individuals have chronically low self-esteem; consider themselves less desirable than their peers; experience more guilt, daydream more, and appear less curious than their peers (Levitt, 1980). "Anxiety is an interpersonal phenomenon that occurs when an individual expects to be or is indeed rejected or demeaned by himself or others" (Coopersmith, 1967, 32). Those who have low self-esteem are very sensitive to criticism (Horney, 1950). Other researchers suggest that low self-esteem creates anxiety and that people with low self-esteem experience enormous amounts of anxiety because of a shifting self-esteem (Coopersmith, 1959).

For many individuals, school becomes a threatening situation producing anxiety. Anxiety arises from the school situation as a result of what is valued by the child and/or the parents. If the child comes from an environment in which scholastic success is valued, failure in school will bring about a sense of personal failure and anxiety from disapproval (Kaplan, 1970, 75).

The literature contains a considerable amount of evidence in support of the hypotheses that anxiety interferes with intellectual functioning. Anxiety interferes with accuracy, spontaneity, and expressiveness (Silverstein, 1966). "Experimental investigations indicate that anxiety detrimentally affects various cognitive processes such as problem-solving, incidental learning, and verbal communication skills. Under extreme stress, human problem-solving falls from its lofty cerebral level and resembles the performances of infrahuman mammals" (Levitt, 1980, 122).

The effect of anxiety on intelligence test performance seems to be related to whether the test is timed. Anxiety seems to have a detrimental effect on intelligence measures that are timed, but inconsequential effect on untimed tests (Levitt, 1980). The effects of anxiety appear to be related to the degree or amount of anxiety the student perceives. Moderate anxiety may energize the student and improve performance (Levitt, 1980).

"It is almost impossible to escape strong feelings of anxiety by conscious effort" (Levitt, 1980, 36). Individuals experiencing anxiety may react in a number of ways to protect the self-concept. Conscious avoidance of the stimuli or situations or circumstances that are anxiety provoking is one of the most common methods of defending against anxiety (Levitt, 1980, 34).

Avoidance may also be used unconsciously, however, this is most likely to occur when the cause of the avoidance is socially unacceptable (Levitt, 1980, 122).

The employment of defenses (unconscious processes which defend against anxiety) is the most common method used by individuals in their attempts to rid themselves of anxiety. Defenses, although protective, tend to deny, falsify, or distort reality and—as a consequence—are basically maladaptive (Battle, 1982, 19).

## SUMMARY

Though the self-concept seems to be elusive and numerous professionals have attempted to define it from many perspectives, no one has ever denied its existence. The self-concept, according to the phenomenological point-of-view, provides the only perspective from which an individual's behavior can be understood.

According to Rogers, four of the primary propositions that provide the foundation for theory relating to the self-concept include the following: (1) Results from interaction with the environment; (2) Incorporates the values of others; (3) Strives for consistency, (4) Changes as a result of maturation and learning. Many definitions of self-concept incorporate one or more of these four propositions. Utilizing Rogers' propositions as a framework, a definition of self-concept was developed. The self-concept is the set of evaluative attitudes comprising a stable core self that each individual constructs about himself which changes and evolves throughout a lifespan based on his social interactions, observations, reactions, and experiences with others and the environment.

Adequate personalities, those described as having a positive self-concept, have achieved a considerable degree of self-enhancement and view themselves as liked, acceptable and worthy, and approach tasks with confidence. Inadequate personalities, those possessing a negative self-concept, have been unable to enhance the self. They feel unliked, unacceptable, lack confidence in abilities, and expect failure.

Anxiety has been defined as a feeling of threat and fear from unknown sources, or as feelings which are the result of being rejected or demeaned or in some way made to feel inadequate and not worthwhile. Anxiety interfers with intellectual functioning, accuracy, problem-solving, and verbal communication.

The self-concept has generally been measured from one or two aspects—phenomenal (conscious) self-concept or nonphenomenal (unconscious) self-concept. The phenomenal self-concept is generally measured through the use of self-reporting devices, while the nonphenomenal self-concept is analyzed by utilizing projective techniques. Using a multiple measures approach results in a more accurate assessment of the self-concept.

# Chapter Two

# INFANCY AND EARLY CHILDHOOD
# SOCIAL/EMOTIONAL DEVELOPMENT

*Experiences that a little girl or a little boy has not only mold that child's self-concept, they also play an active role in shaping the later experiences in which the child will engage (McDonald, 1980, 51)*

---

In studying children we frequently compartmentalize their skills into categories such as fine and gross motor skills, cognition, communication, etc. and consider these developmental areas as discrete skills. "In reality, however, we cannot separate a child into individual components. Social and emotional growth and development are closely linked with all aspects of child development into a synergistic relationship," (Jones, 1988, 241). However, "... human behavior develops in a highly patterned way. It seems quite possible to describe rather clearly the more or less predictable stages through which any kind of behavior—motor, language, adaptive, personal-social—develops (Ames & Ilg, 1976a, Foreward).

# SENSORIMOTOR-STAGE
# SOCIAL/EMOTIONAL DEVELOPMENT

Physical, mental, social, and emotional developmental behaviors are interdependent behaviors whose composite is the personality, or overall behavior pattern at any stage of development. The major areas of social/emotional abilities of children functioning within the sensorimotor stage include the following: (1) Normal social and emotional development: An overview, (2) Interactions with adults, (3) Interactions with children, (4) Interactions with the environment, (5) Self-awareness development, and (6) Play skills development.

## Normal Sensorimotor Social/Emotional Development: An Overview

Newborns have few ways of expressing their feelings or emotions and show limited discrimination of people and situations or social behavior. The infant's social and emotional behavior depends to a great extent on whether his/her physiological needs are met. By the age of three months, the infant has begun to be a social individual, smiling in response to mother's or caregiver's face, voice, and/or smile. S/he responds to person-to-person contact with adults and other children. The three-month-old infant has begun to develop an emotional repertoire, including the ability to express joy and delight; distress; frustration or pain; surprise and interest.

After the age of three months, the child's smiling and crying begin to take on social meaning. The child realizes that both crying and smiling can produce desire results in adults—attention. The four-to-nine-month-old child enjoys being near people and responds gaily to attention and play. The child continues to be very self-centered and uses many means to attract attention to himself, including those considered positive by adults (e.g. cooing, laughing, smiling) and those considered negative by adults (e.g. crying and shouting). The child soon learns that both negative and positive behaviors gain him/her the desired attention (Jones, 1988).

By about eight months of age, the child begins to display stranger anxiety, responding differently to strangers than to familiar people, displaying timidity and shyness with strangers. The eight-to-nine-month-old child begins exhibiting more influence over his/her environment by shouting for attention, loudly (vocally) rejecting confinement in the playpen or confined area, and even fighting for a disputed toy. The nine-month-old child is beginning to learn empathy and may cry if another child cries. His/her emotional repertoire is becoming more sophisticated to include enjoyment, protest, fear, anger, humor, teasing, and shyness.

By the time the average child is one-year old, s/he has made enormous strides in growth and development. The year-old child cognitively understands imitation, a prerequisite to language acquisition and other refined developmental skills; understands anticipation and object permanence, major sensorimotor stage accomplishments. The twelve-month old child has developed the pincer grasp and uses it to remove objects from a container, can feed himself finger foods, and pick up his/her cup. Gross motor skills of the year-old child include crawling, pulling up to stand, and walking with help. Communicatively, the year-old child has mastered the adult intonation system which, paired with gestures and one understandable word or gibberish, convey his/her primary thoughts and wants/needs (Jones, 1988).

It is within this increasing ability to effect his/her environment that the year-old child continues to develop socially and emotionally. The year-old child is learning to cooperate and responds to different tones of voice. S/he recognizes herself/himself as an individual apart from mother, although mother continues to be very special and the year-old child may suffer separation anxiety when mother is gone. The child may even use protest or persuasion to attempt to alter mother's plans to leave. The year-old child is beginning to participate in social activities, actively seeking to maintain interactions with an adult, and attempting to play with another child.

The one-year-old is able to interpret the emotional expressions of familiar adults, and s/he feels guilty at wrong doing. The year-old child is also developing a sense of humor, and teases and tests parental limits. S/he fears strangers and new places. The year-old enjoys demonstrating affection, but also, periodically reveals increased negativism. Emotionally, the year-old's repertoire of emotions is very wide ranged from delight, joy, affection, and humor to anxiety, fear, protest, guilt, and negativism.

Imitation plays an important role in the development of a child's emotional behavior. Gradually, the child's emotional behavior develops from generalized expressions of emotionalism to focusing emotions on the person or object responsible for causing the emotional response. A child learns to respond to adult attitudes toward his emotional behaviors.

The child of emotionally well-balanced parents usually learns early to control his/her emotions. The developing child soon learns that temper tantrums are not tolerated by adults or by other children.

The year-old child has gradually developed feelings of affection for his/her parents and/or those who care for him/her and play with him. The receiving of affectionate attention by others is very important to emotional growth as the child learns to transfer some of the affection from his/her family to other children and adults outside the home.

By the time a child is two years old, s/he has an almost complete store of emotional expressions. The one-to-two-year-old child is developing socially and in individual personality characteristics. The two-year-old recognizes himself/herself in a mirror or picture, and refers to himself by name. S/he is developing trust and confidence in the environment and is beginning to be more independent. This emerging self-knowledge is increased by the acquisition of category labels including gender categories (e.g., boy, girl) and age categories (e.g., child, grown-up) (Harter, 1988).

The two-year old can play by independently imitating his/her own play and imitating adult behaviors in play. S/he will respond to simple commands by adults, but may become quite angry if their activities are interrupted. However, the two-year-old is beginning to realize that s/he cannot always have his/her own way. The social relationships of the two-year-old with other children are still quite awkward and may degenerate into fighting or other aggressive behavior. The child's mother continues to be the most important single person in his life. Generally, the development of social and emotional behavioral patterns follow a similar sequence for most children.

## Interactions with Adults

A child's initial social and emotional growth is facilitated through his/her interactions and attachments to parents and other familiar adults. These early attachments form the basis of bonding with other primary adults throughout the child's lifetime. The young child's personality characteristics or behavioral patterns affect how mother, and later other adults, react to and interact with him/her. Caregivers respond differently to children of different temperaments, and these responses may lead to different social developmental outcomes (Lerner et.al., 1987). Therefore, an important factor in the development of the child's social and affective behaviors with adults is the child's contribution to the relationship via his/her temperament.

Attachment is critical to the child's growth and development in emotional and social skills, in cognitive and communicative abilities, in sensory development, and in the development of a self-identity or self-concept. Attachment provides the child his/her first social relationships (Lerner et.al. 1987). Bonding appears to be a critical component in the rate of cognitive development and in the acquisition of perceptual-conceptual skills. Through the attachment process, mother encourages **visual development** (e.g. fixation, following, spatial relationships), **auditory development** (e.g., localization—mother's voice, discrimination—mother's voice from others), **tactile development** (e.g., touching, caressing, bathing, drying, smoothing on lotion/powder), **vestibular development** (e.g., carries baby upright, rocks baby in rocking chair).

Bonding is also important to the development of communication as the child learns intonation, body language, joint-attending and linguistic labeling, and patterning of communication exchanges as mother talks to and cares for the child. Mother provides a secure base from which to explore as the child crawls out, toddles out, or darts out to explore and investigate the environment, running back for safety if startled or fearful. Attachment assists the child in developing a clear concept of self-identity (Fallen & Umansky, 1985). It provides the security to grow and develop in an accepting environment.

Adult interactions, then, provide the basis for the infant's future learning. Interactions with adults determine the rate of growth and development of the child, not only in communication, cognitive, perceptual, social, and emotional skills, but also stimulate curiosity and exploration which, in turn, enable the infant to gain some control over body movements and to refine actions (Barraga, 1983).

The interactions developed with adults during the sensorimotor stage serve as patterns to establish relationships with other primary adults throughout life. The early interactions children have with adults are primarily responsive in nature. The child smiles responsively and cooperates passively. Gradually, the child is able to discriminate familiar adults visually, auditorally, and tactilely and to react differently to strangers than to familiar people. S/he stops an activity in response to "No" paired with intonation, and responds to two sequential adult interactions.

As the child matures, s/he begins to initiate interactions with adults by attracting their attention (e.g., kicking, cooing, or laughing). The sensorimotor stage child begins to participate in adult manipulation through action songs, to imitate simple actions of adults, and to play games with adults. The child becomes more dependent upon social interactions with adults and actively seeks to maintain interactions as the adult prepares to leave.

## Interactions with Children

A child expresses social and emotional skills at play and in interactions with other children (Fallen & Umansky, 1985). The socialization skills of the sensorimotor stage child are at the initial stage of development as the child continues to be egocentric and focused on his/her own rapid growth and development. Initial interactions with other children are reactive in nature. The infant's first interactions with other children are generally with siblings or children of significant adults. Gradually, the infant responds to familiar children by smiling and vocalizing, and later responds to another child's attempts to play.

As the young child grows and develops, especially in motor and communication skills, s/he begins taking the initiative in social situations by vocalizing to face or touch, and by showing interest in the same object as another child, even attempting to take it away. The sensorimotor stage child may attempt to play with another child by offering or showing a toy, by playing games with another child such as rolling a ball, and by showing preference for another child. At a more sophisticated level, the sensorimotor stage child may seek the help of another child and may reverse play roles with another child.

By kindergarten, some three or four years hence, the child will be expected to be a friendly socialized child, demonstrating his/her awareness of other people as separate persons (Fallen & Umansky, 1985). However,

> Until a child is able to view a situation from another's perspective, it is impossible for her to exhibit the qualities that comprise prosocial behavior. Sharing, cooperation, turn-taking, empathy, and helpfulness require an understanding of another person's needs and feelings (Fallen & Umansky, 1985, 336).

## Interactions with the Environment

During the sensorimotor stage of development, the young child's social and emotional behavior is extremely variable, depending upon environmental and situational conditions, including the regularity of the child's schedule, presence of familiar persons or strangers, the location of the interaction (e.g., familiar or unfamiliar place, quiet place or shopping mall), and the number of persons present. The young child is easily over-stimulated by changes in schedule and activities, changes in diet, changes in location, changes in the number of people present, and the amount of activity within the environment. In secure, familiar settings with familiar persons, the young child's behavioral responses may begin to establish a fairly predictable pattern.

Initially, the infant's interactions with his/her environment are responsive in nature. The infant shows awareness to presence of light, sound, tactile stimulation; shows an eating pattern or preferred feeding schedule; responds to different temperatures (e.g., warm bath); shows awareness to body movements (e.g., sucks fingers). Gradually, the child learns to differentiate familiar and unfamiliar environments, and responds to noticeable changes in his/her familiar environment. The child may respond to frustrating situations in a number of ways (e.g., withdrawal, temper tantrums, self-stimulation). The young sensorimotor stage child learns to anticipate familiar events from environmental cues.

The infant begins to interact with the environment soon after birth. As the child's abilities in gross and fine motor skills and communication skills begin to be more proficient, s/he has more skills with which to interact with the environment. The infant's initial interactions with the environment may involve attempts to move or change positions, engaging in self-stimulation (e.g., thumb sucking), vocalizing to show discomfort. Gradually, the child learns to differentiate emotions and sources of discomfort and makes different vocalizations for different situations and circumstances.

The child exerts some control over the environment as s/he expresses preferences for particular foods. Developing fine motor skills allows the child to explore the environment by reaching out to touch toys, mobiles, and later to manipulate new toys. Development of gross motor skills allows the child to use locomotion to explore the environment and locate objects in the room. Toward the end of the sensorimotor stage, the child may tease adults by threatening unacceptable behavior, but demonstrates social knowledge about table manners and not being aggressive to others.

The two-year-old at the end of the sensorimotor stage has some control over his/her environment in using objects for their specific function, in ability to indicate wants and needs, in ability to move within the environment to gain items, and has some degree of skill in self-help areas (e.g., self-feeding). The child's view of the environment and of his place in that environment determines his reactions and behaviors (Yamamoto, 1972).

## Self-Awareness Development

The self-concept begins to develop in infancy and continues throughout one's lifetime, constantly undergoing modification in response to the environment (Lerner & Shea, 1982). By the time the child is six months old, he has begun to give evidence of having formed some definite concepts about himself. These early self-concepts or awareness of self characteristics involve understanding of body awareness, recognition of attention, and body image.

The process of developing an accurate body image begins with body awareness which initially is manifested as total body responses to sensory stimulation and movement. Gradually, the child becomes aware of his/her body through visual exploration of self; sensory exploration with hands and mouth; and studying himself/herself in the mirror. The concepts of body awareness and body image develop concurrently with cognitive and fine and gross motor skills.

During the sensorimotor stage, as the child develops an understanding of object concept, s/he is able to discriminate himself/herself from objects and others. Body image continues to develop as the child uses locomotion to move through space and become aware of directionality. Body image as related to concepts of maleness and femaleness begin to develop as the young child identifies with the same sex parent and imitates them and their sex role during play activities.

The child's initial recognition of attention to himself/herself by others is related to the development of negative or positive concepts of self. The baby is an egocentric being and thrives on attention. The young child soon learns to differentiate positive and negative attention and may cry when scolded and laugh when praised. Since preschoolers are quite egocentric in their thinking, they are partially insulated from subtle negative responses from others (Helms & Turner, 1976). The negative or positive attention from others is not always interpreted by young children, so these responses do not have the significant effect upon him/her that may occur with the older child.

A number of factors are involved in the development of the child's concept of his/her own capabilities including the following: athletic skill, leadership qualities, moral code, temperament, peer acceptance, academic success, physical attractiveness, intelligence, and special aptitudes. These factors are not of significant importance to the sensorimotor stage child, but are crucial to the self-concepts of elementary school-aged children and adolescents. The athletic skill differences in play among preschoolers is not significant as they generally are involved in free play or noncompetitive activities of short duration (Biehler & Hudson, 1986). Among young children, leadership qualities are not of tremendous concern as children rapidly switch or reverse roles (e.g., runner becomes chaser). Biehler & Hudson (1986) indicate that preschool children develop only a rudimentary understanding of moral codes, and if they break the rules or behave in immoral ways, their behavior is excused due to immaturity. Temperament, generally reflected as social attractiveness, begins to be important during preschool years, as adults and children alike prefer to interact with a pleasant, easy going child. Young children are seldom involved in peer selection for play as adults are involved and present during activities, encouraging participation by all. Academic success, physical attractiveness, intelligence, and special aptitudes are not relevant to self-conception at the sensorimotor stage. These qualities, however, take on importance relevant to the importance prescribed them by significant others, especially parents.

## Play Skills Development

Play is the work of a child. It is a natural activity that serves an essential role in the young child's development (Lerner et. al., 1987). "The spontaneous and creative activities of play make invaluable contributions toward the child's learning of cognitive, language, motor, and social skills" (Lerner et. al., 1987, 252). Through play, the child gives expression to his impulses and to behavior that is social in nature. He displays his kind and degree of imagination, his ability to cooperate, and his sense of fair play.

Numerous theories exist regarding the functions, stages, purposes, and developmental sequences of play. Biehler and Hudson (1986) indicate the major functions of play as follows:

1. Play permits children to explore and experiment without risk.
2. Play permits children to practice roles.

3. Play permits practice without pressure to accomplish some specific task.
4. Play fosters imaginative and creative abilities.
5. Play permits release of emotional tension (333–334).

Fallen and Umansky (1985) discuss Piaget's three levels of play complexity: (1) practice play, (2) symbolic play, and (3) games with rules. Practice play emerges in the normal child between birth and four months of age as the infant plays by repeating satisfying bodily activities and simple repetitive movements with an object such as shaking a rattle. The infant engages in exploratory play (e.g., self and environment) and manipulates objects. The seven-to-nine-month-old child learns that actions affect objects as s/he makes mobiles swing, bangs toys, shakes toys to make different sounds, grasps dangling objects, and uncovers hidden toys.

The 10-to-12-month-old child begins to apply learned movements to new situations and is concerned with the pleasure of the activity rather than the end result (Fallen & Umansky, 1985). S/he engages in numerous fine motor activities such as squeezing a doll to make it squeak, holding a crayon and imitating scribbling, stacking rings on a peg, putting small objects in and out of a container with intention; and gross motor activities such as learning to roll balls. The play of the 13-to-18-month-old child is characterized by experimentation and ritualized play in activities such as dropping objects from his/her highchair and throwing objects from the play pen (Fallen & Umansky, 1985). S/he engages in solitary or on-looker play, initiates their own play, scribbles spontaneously with a crayon, uses pull toys, carries or hugs a doll, puts pegs in a pegboard.

"The emergence of symbolic play is evident in the last stage of the sensorimotor period (stage 6, 18-to-24 months). In this stage, the child uses familiar actions with new objects" (Fallen & Umansky, 1985, 410). Symbolic play at this level is usually solitary in nature and is the child's attempt to understand reality in ways that are meaningful. The 18-to-24-month-old child uses concrete objects to substitute for objects not there (e.g., rides broom for horse) as s/he begins to pretend. The child becomes more adept at fine and gross motor skills and plays refining those skills. The 18-to-24-month-old child moves to music, throws a small ball overhand, imitates adult behaviors in play, transports blocks or other toys in a wagon, strings beads, plays with clay or playdough, builds a block tower, puts rings on a stick, paints with a large brush. Throughout the remaining preschool years, the child continues to refine symbolic skills; about three years of age, s/he begins social, interactive pretense play; and by about seven years begins Piaget's third stage of play—games with rules (Biehler & Hudson, 1986).

## PRESCHOOL-AGE SOCIAL/EMOTIONAL DEVELOPMENT

Physical, mental, social, and emotional interactive developmental behaviors continue to play an important role in the socialization of preschool children, ages 2–5 years. During this period of rapid growth and development, verbal communication takes on an increasingly important role in the child's interactions with adults and other children. For preschool-aged children, the major areas of social/emotional developmental concerns include normal social/emotional developmental sequences, social interactions, and the development of the self-concept.

### Normal Preschool-Age Social/Emotional Development

"The development of the emotional behavior in the growing infant and child from early infancy on reveals that ages of emotional equilibrium tend to alternate with ages of disequilibrium" (Ames & Ilg, 1976a, 15). Ages of developmental equilibrium appear to be characterized by emotional calmness, acceptance of self, and enhanced abilities in motor, verbal, and cognitive abilities (Ames & Ilg, 1976a). "The good, solid equilibrium of any earlier age seems to break up into disequilibrium before the child can reach a higher or more mature stage of equilibrium, which again will be followed by disequilibrium" (Ames & Ilg, 1976a, 4–5).

Brazelton (1990, 76) refers to these periods of disintegration as "touch-points" that can be used to predict a growth spurt or an approaching period of rapid learning. These periods of behavior disintegration in which children revert to a less mature behavior (i.e., whine and temper tantrum; regress in language, physical, and/or cognitive skills) are predictable occurrences prior to a growth spurt and result primarily from changes within the child rather than environmental changes.

### Two-Year-Old Child's Social/Emotional Development

The typical two-year-old tends to be gentle, friendly, affectionate, and happy much of the time. S/he enjoys the security of daily routines and seems emotionally comfortable and secure. The typical two-year-old is emotionally calm, sure, balanced, lovable, engaging, enthusiastic, and appreciative, and expresses affection warmly. The age of Two usually provides a brief and welcome breathing space for parents and nursery school teachers, coming as it does between the difficult, demanding time of Eighteen to Twenty-One months and the even more difficult and demanding age of Two-and-a-Half that is so soon to follow (Ames & Ilg, 1976a).

Socially the 2-3 year-old knows gender identity, participates in simple group activities involving singing and dancing, begins to share automatically, asks for things they want, and will defend their own possessions. Though Mother continues to be a very important person in the child's life and while social interactions are still very limited, it is not uncommon to make a special friend by age three.

Play of the two-to-three-year-old mostly involves parallel play in which a child plays near other children, and/or on-looker play in which the child primarily watches other children but may join them briefly. Most two-to-three-year-olds begin imaginative play with domestic make-believe (e.g., playing house), and they enjoy imitating mother and working side-by-side with her using miniature equipment. They begin to be able to symbolically use self and objects in play (e.g., "I am a cowboy and this broom is my horse"). They are beginning cooperative play and participation in simple group games.

The two-and-a-half-year-old is in the "the terrible twos," and is almost the complete opposite of the calm, affectionate, easy-going two-year-old child. Though the two-and-a-half-year-old can be delightful, s/he seems to be on an emotional roller coaster—frequently tense, rigid, and explosive (Ames & Ilg, 1976a, 4). A striking characteristic of the two-and-a-half-year-old is their demand for sameness, for ritualism and routine, everything in the house has its place, tasks or activities should always be carried out in the same way, in the same order, and at the same time (Ames & Ilg, 1976a).

The two-and-a-half-year-old child seems to be easily frustrated by such things as their lack of skill in making something with their hands, and interruptions to their play (Ames & Ilg, 1976a). They will scream and temper tantrum for little apparent reason. However, temper tantrums of the two-and-a-half-year-old serve the important function of teaching the child about negativism, and occur as the child tries to face the decision of taking over his/her own choice-making (Brazelton, 1990).

> Sometime between their second and third birthdays, children complete the period of development called infancy. Like all major stage transitions, the end of infancy is marked by biological processes and physical and mental abilities, and by the appearance of a new relationship to the social world (Cole & Cole, 1989, 240).

### Three-Year-Old-Child's Social/Emotional Development

" . . . by three, many children seem to be developing a rather good self-concept, seem to have a solid set of feelings about themselves" (Ames & Ilg, 1976b, 2). Again, the child moves into a period of equilibrium characterized by smoothness, integration, self-control, and desire to please the significant others in his/her life.

Socially the three-to-four-year-old child finds friends more interesting than adults, shares his/her toys, takes turns with assistance, shows affection for younger siblings, begins to take responsibility, and interprets the emotions of others from facial expressions and vocal intonation. The three-to-four-year-old child continues to enjoy mother, but finds father becoming increasingly important in his/her life.

Play usually involves the three-year-old engaged in associative play in which children engage in disorganized play with other children, but gradually they move to cooperative play which is organized and children work together for some aim (Biehler & Snowman, 1986). The three-to-four-year-old child begins dramatic play-acting, uses imaginative play with dolls, and enjoys imaginary companions. Emotionally, the three-year-old is sensitive to praise; enjoys friendly humor; conforms easily; is eager to please, is calm, collected; and emotionally in control having developed some ability to tolerate frustration (Ames & Ilg, 1976b).

As the pendulum swings, the three-and-a-half-year-old child moves into another period of disequilibrium becoming emotionally and physically insecure as evidenced by stuttering, stumbling, thumb sucking, and nail biting. The three-and-a-half-year-old is characterized by refusing to obey; and rebelling at dressing, eating, toileting, getting up and going to bed, etc. (Ames & Ilg, 1976b). The child's behavior is marked by inconsistency and emotional extremes ranging from shy withdrawn behavior one minute to overbold behavior the next (Ames & Ilg, 1976b).

## Four-Year-Old Child's Social/Emotional Development

The typical Four-Year-Old loves adventure, loves excursions, loves excitement, loves anything new. He adores new people, new places, new games, new play things, new books, new activities. No one is more responsive to the adult effort to entertain. He will accept what you have to offer with delightfully uncritical enthusiasm (Ames & Ilg, 1976c, 2–3).

Socially, the four-to-five-year-old is still home and mother oriented, but plays and interacts cooperatively with other children in small groups of two to five children, and can be spurred on by rivalry in an activity. The four-year-old is developing a sense of responsibility and can play outdoors with little supervision, enjoys doing things for him/her self, likes to be trusted, and is beginning to learn to take care of his/her own property. The four-year-old's dramatic play is closer to reality than before, and s/he loves to dress-up. Their play is very imaginative and they have developed the ability to engage in imaginative play with other children. The four-year-old understands social problem-solving.

The attention-span of the four-year-old child is very short, thus, they move quickly from one activity to another. The four-year-old is not interested in perfection in school or play tasks, only in getting finished to go onto the next activity (Ames & Ilg, 1976c). Emotionally, the four-year-old exhibits a definite personality, and shows concern and empathy for others.

The secure behavior of the four-year-old disintegrates as the child moves toward four-and-a-half-years-old in which his/her behavior becomes exaggerated by extremes—extreme loves and extreme hates.

A normally vigorous and well-endowed child of this age may seem out-of-bounds in almost every area of living. Motor-wise, he not only hits and kicks and spits (if aroused) but may even go so far as to run away from home if things don't please him. He races up and down stairs, dashes here and there on his trusty tricycle. Emotionally, too, he tends to be extremely out-of-bounds. He laughs almost too hilariously when things please him, howls and cries more than too loudly when things go wrong.... But it is his verbally out-of-bounds expressions that are most conspicuous (Ames & Ilg, 1976c, 7).

The four-and-a-half-year-old exaggerates and boasts, prevaricates and uses profanity, persistently makes demands, and displays unpredictable behavior (Ames & Ilg, 1976c).

## Five-Year-Old Child's Social/Emotional Development

Typical Five-Year-Old's live in the present and care very much about their own possessions — their room, their home, their street, their neighborhood, and their kindergarten room. "He is not particularly interested in the new and strange and usually does not seek adventure for its own sake" (Ames & Ilg, 1976d, 4).

Kindergarteners are quite skillful with language and like to talk in front of a group (Biehler & Snowman, 1986) in such activities as "Show 'N Tell." They enjoy being read to, being talked to, learning new facts, and practicing their intellectual abilities.

Socially, mother is still the center of the five-year-old's world. The typical Five-Year-Old wants to do what is expected, respects reasonable authority, shows willingness to play with most children in their class, engages with other children in cooperative and fair play, chooses his/her own friends, and frequently has one or two best friends of the same sex. At the kindergarten age an awareness of sex roles begins, and the child is willing to play with other children in a role assignment.

Five is considered a "golden age" (Ames & Ilg, 1976d, 5). "Perhaps the most delightful of all his characteristics is that he enjoys life so much and looks so consistently on its sunny side" (Ames & Ilg, 1976d, 1). Five is an age of emotional equilibrium in which the child is secure, protects himself/herself from overstimulation, reduces frustration by being self-limiting, likes life the way it is and is satisfied with himself/herself.

By age Five-and-a-Half-Years-Old the emotional smoothness has been replaced by a child who quarrels frequently, expresses emotions freely and openly, engages frequently in anger outbursts, shows jealousy of classmates, and appears ready to disobey. The "Five-and-a-Half is characteristically hesitant, dawdling, indecisive, or at the opposite extreme, overdemanding and explosive" (Ames & Ilg, 1976b, 6). The child vacillates from one emotional extreme to another (e.g., shy & bold, affectionate & antagonistic).

Many Fives play reasonably well with older siblings and tend to be extremely kind and protective to those who are younger (Ames & Ilg, 1976d, 14). Cognitively, the five-year-old has progressed to a stage where s/he can play games with rules, competitive games, and simple table games; though in free play, due to short attention span, they play in small loosely organized groups and change play frequently.

## Preschool Social Interactions

Social interactions among preschoolers are very immature. Preschoolers tend to be quite flexible socially. They are willing to play with most other children as requested, and many friendships develop between boys and girls (Biehler & Snowman, 1986). Social cognition begins to develop during the preschool years as the child learns to take the perspective of another person or to empathize. "Social cognition refers to the child's knowledge of various social phenomena and includes an understanding of selfhood, an awareness of others and their social roles, and an understanding of social institutions" (Daehler & Bukato, 1985, 357).

The outstanding characteristic of social life at age two-years is parallel play. Frequently among two-year-olds, two or three children may all be doing more or less the same thing, playing with similar materials in close proximity, but without much interaction (Ames & Ilg, 1976a, 20). Though typical two-year-olds have limited verbal skills and talk mostly to themselves, their social conversations are usually with adults and are limited to showing something or making a request; there is very little conversation with other children (Ames & Ilg, 1976a).

Two-and-one-half-year-olds are involved in considerable interaction, but very little cooperation. Social interactions at this age are primarily aggressive and may be quite violent. "It is by no means unusual for a child to grab an object from another child, to chase and shout for an object, to push a child out of the way and then grab something, or to hit another child on the head and climb onto him and grab his toy" (Ames & Ilg, 1976a, 20). However, two-year-olds do enjoy the company of other children.

Though three-year-olds continue to be socially immature and more comfortable with adults than with other children, they tend to be extremely enthusiastic about other children (Ames & Ilg, 1976b). Cooperative play begins as some children use turn-taking or sharing spontaneously. Much conversation is social and friendly concerning real or imaginary play activity. Three-year-olds are beginning to be interested in other children's feelings and are beginning to empathize. They may talk, act, smile, cooperate, tantalize, flirt; and among boys there is considerable silly clowning and many foolish antics (Ames & Ilg, 1976c, 20).

Four-year-old children enjoy the company of each other so much that play time goes smoothly without too much adult interference. Cooperation, sharing, taking turns now tend to come quite easily to most children

(Ames & Ilg, 1976c). Four-year-olds display considerable social maturity in their use of social problem-solving, for example, if two children want the same toy they may suggest turn-taking (Ames & Ilg, 1976c).

Social problem-solving is the process of achieving personal goals in social interactions and involves sensitivity to social problems and social consequences (Rose-Krasnor, 1988). The child is thought to learn appropriate patterns of behavior and social problem-solving within the family setting through interactions with siblings, parents, and other caregivers (Christopherson, 1988).

Four-year-olds want friends to like and approve of them. They spend considerable time in their play group involved in imaginative cooperative play (e.g., playing house, tea parties, etc.) Frequently, they can even organize a cooperative play activity by themselves without adult help or suggestions; however, four-year-olds may get along with friends much better than with siblings. Due to high energy levels, Four-year-olds usually enjoy attending a lively nonacademic nursery school for interactions with other children, and because of the wide variety of toys and activities provided (Ames & Ilg, 1976c).

Many five-year-old children are enrolled in kindergarten, so a large portion of their day is composed of organized activities. The teacher frequently chooses play-partners or teams for various activities.

> The Five-Year-Old is not an exceptionally social individual. Often if given a free choice he keeps pretty much to himself, especially in a strange situation. He may rely a good deal on a best friend, but just the notion of making friends for its own sake may have lost the charm it held a few months earlier (Ames & Ilg, 1976d, 68).

Five-year-olds frequently socialize better with children outside their immediate family, especially if the children are his/her own age. They tend to play better in a team of two rather than a group of three or more children.

## Preschool Peer Relationships

The area of peer relationships has at its core the socialization of the child. The heart of socialization efforts take place within the family constellation. Parents and/or primary caregivers utilize deliberate socialization techniques (intentional efforts to teach and influence the child regarding desired behavior) and nondeliberate socialization techniques (modeling through daily informal interactions) in their effort to socialize children (Christopherson, 1988, 132).

"The learning of gender roles and sex-role orientation reflects one of the earliest and most profound focuses in the family socialization process" (Christopherson, 1988, 129). Research strongly suggests that in our contemporary culture we socialize children differently based on the child's sex (Honig, 1983). The tendency for children to identify with the same sex parent also contributes in a major way to sex-role orientation (Christopherson, 1988, 130). The process of identifying oneself as a "girl" or "boy" begins about age 2 years, when children are gaining a distinctive sense of themselves and beginning to form complex concepts (Cole & Cole, 1989, 361). By the time they enter kindergarten, most children have developed awareness of sex differences, and of masculine and feminine roles (Biehler & Snowman, 1986).

The formation and maintenance of friendships and interpersonal peer relationships requires a higher level of cognitive and social functioning than is possessed by preschoolers. In the early stages of friendship, young children are aware of the physical properties of peers, the momentary aspects of play, and they expect merely that their peers please them. Among preschool children, shared role-play and fantasy play appear important in developing friendship.

Preschool children spend much of their day involved in play activities. Free-Play kinds of activities are very important to the development of young children in many ways besides the enhancement of motor skills. Play fosters social development and peer relationships as children learn to cooperate, share, and take turns. Interactions with other children during play sessions promotes flexibility by increasing the child's behavior options. Imaginative play enables preschoolers to practice recently acquired skills, to practice new language patterns and words, to comprehend and create meaning through recreation of roles and sequences of behavior as they "play house," "play cowboys" etc. Sociodramatic play, a form of social pretense, helps children to understand and integrate the sequence of events in their every day lives such as going to the grocery store or the doctor's office, by seeing the different character's points of view on the same event, and by practicing appropriate new vocabulary (Smilansky, 1968).

### Self-Concept of the Young Child

During infancy (the sensorimotor stage) the child becomes aware of his/her body; begins to recognize the ramifications of social attention; begins to develop a concept of body image, and begins to be aware of sex roles or sex typing characteristics. This awareness stage is the beginning of the development of the self-concept.

Beginning about age two years, the child matures in social, physical, emotional, cognitive, and language skills and moves into the stage of Early Childhood. "Consciousness of self is among the many characteristics said to distinguish human beings from other species and two-year-olds from younger children" (Cole & Cole, 1989, 238). This new sense of self consciousness is manifested in the following: "1) A growing sensitivity to adult standards, 2) Concern about living up to those standards, 3) A new ability to set one's own goals and standards, 4) Self-reference in language, 5) Immediate recognition of one's image in a mirror" (Cole & Cole, 1989, 241).

Consciousness of self or the self-concept or the development of the personality begins, then, in infancy with the social attention paid to the child by the significant others in their lives. In early childhood the child becomes conscious of adult standards for his/her behavior and modifies his behavior based on the negative or positive social reactions to the behavior. Thus, "Personality development is closely intertwined with socialization. Crucial to one's sense of self is all of the feedback that one receives from the social environment" (Cole & Cole, 1989, 345).

The preschooler's portrait of the self reflects cognitive limitations in his/her ability to understand logical relations and to make generalizations. "The child can only make reference to a variety of very specific behaviors or characteristics rather than higher order concepts about the self" (Harter, 1988, 48). For example, the child could state that s/he can bounce a ball, run very fast, climb on the jungle gym, etc. but not be able to organize these skills and arrive at a generalization that s/he is good in sports or physical activities.

The preschool-aged child is beginning to be able to evaluate the behavior of other children, but is unable to critically observe and evaluate himself/herself (Harter, 1988). The young "child cannot differentiate one's real from one's ideal self-image" as s/he does not have the cognitive ability to test or logically determine if the judgments are realistic (Harter, 1988, 48). Research findings demonstrate that the young child is very inaccurate in judging his or her abilities, if one compares the child's self-perceptions to more objective standards such as teachers' ratings (Harter & Pike, 1984). The child typically evaluates the self as more skillful than does the teacher because he is unable to evaluate his competence. In general, the preschool-aged child usually inflates his/her ability and is very positive about the things that s/he can do.

## SUMMARY

Social and emotional growth and development are closely linked with all aspects of child development. Most children within the Infancy and Early Childhood Stages follow "normal" range social/emotional developmental patterns in their interactions with adults, interactions with children, interactions with the environment, play skill development, and self-concept development.

Though the newborn has few ways of expressing feelings and emotions, by the time the average child has reached two years of age and the end of the sensorimotor stage of development, s/he has an almost complete store of emotional expressions including fear, anger, teasing, enjoyment, persuasion, protest, guilt, anxiety, and affection. The two-year-old child is still very dependent on mother, however, s/he is beginning to show some independence in play as well as self-care skills. Attachment is central to the child's social and emotional development, as well as to cognitive and communicative abilities, to sensory development, and to the development of a self-identity or self-concept. The young child's attachment or bonding with caregivers provides his/her first social interactions and provides the child with a mediator to interpret the environment. The earliest interactions with adults are responsive in nature, but well before the end of the sensorimotor stage the child has begun to initiate interactions with adults.

The sensorimotor stage child's interactions with other children are very awkward and at the initial stage of development. By the end of the sensorimotor stage, the child may attempt to initiate interactions with other children by showing a toy, play a very simple game such as rolling a ball, or seeking an older child for assistance. Young children do not have the ability to sustain social interactions.

The sensorimotor stage child's greatest success involves gaining control within his/her environment to achieve wants/needs. Play allows the child to practice new motor, cognitive and communicative skills as the child interacts with adults and children in the environment. By the end of the sensorimotor stage, the development of symbolic play allows the child to imagine, pretend, and use representational imitation.

The development of the self-concept begins with self-awareness and developing a body image. By the end of the sensorimotor stage the child's evolving understanding of sex roles and sex typing characteristics contributes to the development of the self-image.

Sometime between the ages of two and three years, children complete the period of infancy and move into Early Childhood. During the preschool years, ages two through five, the child is involved in a period of rapid growth and development in all areas especially in verbal communication.

The emotional development of children from infancy through adolescence appears to be characterized by alternating periods of equilibrium (friendly, affectionate, happy periods) and disequilibrium (periods of emotional turmoil). The early months of any age often are marked by equilibrium and calmness, while the later months of an age reflect explosive behavior marked by insecurity and low frustration tolerance.

Social interactions among young preschoolers continues to be very immature, but by age five-years children are able to cooperate, share, and take turns; use social problem-solving; and display sensitivity to social problems and social consequences. It is through play that these social interactions and skills are practiced. Through social interactions the preschool-aged child continues to develop his/her self-concept. At this age, however, the child tends to inflate his/her abilities and is very positive about what s/he can do.

# Chapter Three

# MIDDLE CHILDHOOD
## SOCIAL/EMOTIONAL DEVELOPMENT

*Concepts of the self potentially affect every thought, feeling, word, and behavior that we have* (McDonald, 1980, 51).

---

66 In the United States and most industrialized societies, the onset of middle childhood is marked by the beginning of formal schooling in literacy and arithmetic" (Cole & Cole, 1989, 406). Middle childhood is that period of time in the life of a child that spans the elementary school years including the primary grade years—grades 1–3, and the intermediate grade years—grades 4–6. During this period, ages 6 to 12, the child makes significant changes and/or growth in cognitive, physical, communicative, and social/emotional abilities.

## PRIMARY AGE/GRADE
## SOCIAL/EMOTIONAL DEVELOPMENT

Physical, mental, social and emotional interactive developmental behaviors continue to play an important role in the socialization of primary grade children. Significant physical development during this period provides the child the ability to complete tasks independently. Mental development is demonstrated through increased problem-solving abilities, perspective-taking, and the use of mental strategies to increase memory ability. Social and emotional gains are evident in increased responsibility for self-control, the development of social relationships, and moral understandings. For primary grade children, the major areas of social/emotional development concern normal social/emotional developmental sequences, social interactions, and the development of the self-concept.

## Normal Primary Social/Emotional Development

Adult expectations for children entering middle childhood increase dramatically from those expectations held during early childhood. Primary grade children, ages 6 to 8, have excellent control of their bodies and develop considerable confidence in their skills (Biehler & Hudson, 1986). Increased physical capacities enable primary grade children to perform expected tasks independently (Cole & Cole, 1989).

During middle childhood, children are expected to participate in their own socialization. Primary grade children are expected to assume responsibility for behaving themselves in a variety of situations. They are expected to demonstrate appropriate behavior in (1) solitary situations—where children are expected to complete tasks/chores independently, (2) instructional situations—where children are controlled by one or few adults, and (3) peer situations—where children are controlled by others of their own age (Cole & Cole, 1989). The ability to assume increased responsibility stems from cognitive advances that result in "a greatly increased ability to think more deeply and logically, to follow through on a problem once it is undertaken, and to keep track of more than one aspect of a situation at a time" (Cole & Cole, 1989, 407).

> The major theorists of child development, despite their differences, also agree that there is an important shift in mental functioning around this time (ages 5–7 years). For Piaget, this age marks a major turning point in cognitive development: the shift from intuitive to operational thought. For the Russian developmental theorists Vygotsky and Luria, this age is characterized by a critical shift in mental processes: the internalization of language (Skolnick, 1986, 354).

### Six-Year-Old Child

The "typical six-year-old is a paradoxical little person, and bipolarity is the name of his game. Whatever he does, he does the opposite just as readily" (Ames & Ilg, 1979, 1). Emotionally, the six-year-old is very trying for himself/herself and for others. S/he wants both of any two opposites; finds it difficult to make-up his/her mind, but once made up it is very difficult to change. The six-year-old is demanding and difficult, the center of his/her own universe, and wants to be first and best in everything, so tantrums, argues, and is oppositional to get his/her way. The six-year-old is insecure, sensitive to criticism or ridicule, and finds adjusting to failure very difficult. However, the six-year-old is extremely enthusiastic for adventure, new games, new ideas; and can be extremely warm and affectionate with parents. "When happy, he not only smiles and laughs, he fairly dances with joy. His enthusiasm is contagious" (Ames & Ilg, 1979, 8).

Socially the six-year-old is at his/her best and worst with the primary caregivers. The relationship with mother is one of the greatest problems of the six-year old as s/he tries to separate and become more independent. S/he experiences difficulty with siblings due to his/her competitive, combative nature. S/he quarrels frequently with older siblings and is very bossy with younger siblings.

The six-year-old child mellows as s/he approaches six-and-a-half years of age and becomes delightful. S/he is amusing and has a wonderful sense of humor, is lively intellectually and loves to play guessing games. The six-and-a-half- year old shows "boundless enthusiasm for any prospect or proposal"; "loves exploration, physical and intellectual"; "loves new places, new ideas, new bits of information, and his own new accomplishments" (Ames & Ilg, 1979, 10).

## Seven-Year-Old Child

Seven is an age of emotional withdrawal in which the child is often moody morose, and melancholy. The child feels that people do not like him/her and are mean, especially the teachers. Sevens have no sense of humor. Fairness is very important to the seven-year old who feels that his "parents like his brothers and sisters better than they like him and that they do more for others in the family than they do for him" (Ames & Haber, 1985, 5). Seven is extremely self-absorbed, easily disappointed, and in addition to having many worries and fears, feels that s/he has "all the bad luck."

The seven-year-old child is making emotional strides in gaining control of his/her temper, in becoming sensitive to friends' attitudes, and increasing reasonableness and willingness to listen to someone else's side of the story. The typical seven-year-old is developing ethical standards and wants to do things right.

Socially, the seven-year-old usually gets along well with mother, but sometimes engages in a battle of wills with her. Seven is anxious to be accepted by the peer group, plays more harmoniously than at age 6, and usually prefers to withdraw rather than to fight (Ames & Haber, 1985). The seven-year-old is better with much older and much younger siblings, than those nearer his/her own age; and at this age boys generally begin to discriminate against girls. The seven-year-old, however, is highly sociable and makes little trouble in social situations.

### Eight-Year-Old Child

Eight is an age of equilibrium—emotional calmness, acceptance of self, gentle, affectionate, and happy much of the time. Socially eight-year-olds are somewhat more selective in their choice of friends; and may have a permanent best friend and a semipermanent enemy (Biehler & Hudson, 1986).

Primary grade children like organized games in small groups, but may become overly concerned with the rules of the game or get carried away with team spirit. The eight-year-old's literal interpretation of rules may cause him/her to be a tattletale in an effort to get others to follow the rules. Eight-year-olds view rules as edicts handed down by authority; thus, they focus on physical consequences rather than obeying rules for their own benefit (Biehler & Hudson, 1986).

Eight-year-olds use language as their medium of social interaction (Kegan, 1985). They gradually gain more facility in speech and in writing and gradually acquire the ability to solve problems by generalizing from concrete experiences (Biehler & Hudson, 1986). Quarrels are still frequent, but words are used more often than physical aggression (Biehler & Hudson, 1986).

Emotionally, the eight year old is very sensitive to criticism and ridicule, and may have difficulty adjusting to failure. Most primary grade children are eager to please their teacher; and are becoming sensitive to the feelings of others. About age eight, children have developed the idea that each person has a private, subjective self that is not always easily read from behavior (Cole & Cole, 1989, 506).

Primary grade children are extremely physically active and often under estimate the danger involved in their risk-taking activities. Thus, the accident rate among children is at a peak in the third grade (Biehler &

Hudson, 1986, 106). Since primary grade students are frequently forced to participate in sedentary pursuits, energy is often released in the form of nervous habits (e.g., pencil chewing, fingernail biting, hair twirling, and general fidgeting) (Biehler & Hudson, 1986).

## Primary Age/Grade Social Interactions

"School-age children live in at least three separate worlds, each with its own rules and styles of behavior: the family, the school, and the peer group" (Skolnick, 1986, 414). Socialization of the child is of primary importance to the family as the child learns to interact with adults of all ages (e.g., parents, grandparents, aunts, and uncles), and children of all ages (e.g., older and younger siblings, cousins, teen-aged baby-sitters, etc.). Education is "a form of socialization in which adults engage in deliberate teaching of the young to ensure the acquisition of specialized knowledge and skills" (Cole & Cole, 1989, 428).

### Family Interactions

During middle childhood, children "are moving out into the world and parents must share their influence with the child's friends, the school, and the mass media" (Skolnick, 1986, 401). This movement away from total reliance on the parents is the first step "toward the independent identity and separate sense of self that are required of adults in our culture" (Skolnick, 1986, 415). Parents, however, continue to be a significant influence on their elementary school-aged children particularly in the areas of authority and affection.

During the middle childhood years, children learn about their parents' social position in the community. They learn about social system hierarchies and the types of occupations, levels of income, styles of dress and speech, and acceptable behaviors of each hierarchial level. They learn about the social system level in which they are expected to function.

Children's new, more independent, status during middle childhood influences the quality of their relationships with their parents. Parents rely on their children' use of higher level cognitive skills and their "greater understanding of the consequences of their actions and on their desire to comply with adult standards" (Cole & Cole, 1989, 478). As children's level of logical reasoning increases parents use indirect socialization techniques such as discussion and explanation rather than using physical force such as spanking and physical restraint to influence their children's behavior (Cole & Cole, 1989).

## Peer Interactions

Friendship and peer relations make valuable contributions to a child's social and emotional development. "Unlike adult-child relationships, peers relate to one another on a reciprocal, egalitarian basis. This kind of interaction helps to lay the groundwork for adult relationships" (Skolnick, 1986, 423).

> One of the most important social accomplishments of the school years is becoming a valued member of one's peer group, an achievement that requires much more than simply being of the same age as one's peers. Among the skills required are an understanding of self and others and an increasing independence from adults (Berger, 1986, 420).

The formation and maintenance of peer relationships involves facility with a number of high level abilities including—(1) self-knowledge, (2) perspective-taking ability, (3) friendship expectations, (4) knowledge of appropriate behavior in various social situations, (5) social evaluation— ability to evaluate one's own and others' behaviors, (6) knowledge of peer group norms, and (7) social problem-solving (Oden, 1988). These factors in turn facilitate the development of the self-concept.

## Friendship Expectations

As children grow older they spend increasing amounts of time in the company of peers without adult supervision. Peer interactions are important opportunities for exploring social relationships and moral feelings, and for the development of personal identities (Cole & Cole, 1989). For most children, by the time they are 1st graders, they are socially well accepted by peers of similar interests and have some preferred activity partners or friendships.

During the primary grades friendships become increasingly important and children's understanding of friendship becomes increasingly complex (Berger, 1986). Research has indicated that primary school-aged children value kindness, sharing, and helping as characteristics of their best friends (Youniss, 1978). As children grow older friendships become more intense and more intimate, older children demand more of their friends, change friends less often, find it harder to make new friends, and are more upset when a friendship breaks up (Berger, 1986).

Children become increasingly choosy about selecting best friends and usually select friends who are from the same sex, race, and economic background (Hartup, 1983). Friendship groups then become smaller as children grow older and more selective in their friendships. "Thus, as children grow older, friendship patterns become more rigidly set, so that by the age of 9 years or so, everyone knows who hangs out with whom, and few dare to break into an established group or pair of friends" (Berger, 1986, 432).

## Self-Concept of the Primary Age/Grade Student

### Self-Knowledge

During middle childhood when "children spend more time among their peers, the sense of self they acquired in their families no longer suffices and they must learn to reconcile their old identities with the new ones they begin to form in the new contexts they inhabit" (Cole & Cole, 1989, 478). Self-descriptions begin to include "trait labels such as popular, helpful, smart, and references to athletic ability and physical attractiveness. The child at this age combines a number of specific behaviors into a more generalized concept about the self" (Harter, 1988, 48).

"Regardless of the theory used to explain it, a good deal of evidence suggests that by the time children are about 6 or 7 years old, they have formed a stable concept of their own identity as male or female" (Cole & Cole, 1989, 353).

Others' opinions, especially those of peers and close friends, begin to have an effect on the child's self-evaluation as s/he becomes concerned about what others think about their attractiveness, sociability, intelligence, etc. The child incorporates the opinions of valued others into his/her own self-description (Harter, 1988).

"Another feature of self-description at this stage is the use of social comparison as a means of determining the competence or adequacy of the self" (Harter, 1988, 52). For example, a third grader's judgment about his/her academic competence is based on a comparison of performance with that of classmates. The student assigned to Group II in reading may conclude that his/her reading abilities are average by knowing that Group I is reading a 4th grade basal reader, and Group III is reading the same reader that s/he read last year. This same process of social comparison occurs in all important, relevant areas including physical attractiveness and athletic ability.

## Perspective-Taking Ability

Children's perspective-taking ability increases significantly during the middle childhood years. "As children's perspective-taking ability develops, they become more aware of their own intentions and feelings and later develop greater awareness of their own and others' internal processes and their own individual personality" (Christopherson, 1988, 149).

During middle childhood children develop social cognition which involves role-taking, the ability to see things from another person's point of view; personality perception, the child's conceptions of other people; and moral judgment, the understanding of rules and conventions (Skolnick, 1986, 388). During middle childhood, children become increasingly skilled at metacognitive aspects of social cognition—the ability to think about what another person is thinking, and anticipate his or her behavior (Skolnick, 1986, 389). Thus, there appears to be a reciprocal relationship between the development of perspective-taking ability, and social and cognitive development. "In many ways as Piaget originally pointed out, the ability to see a situation from the other person's point-of-view with some accuracy seems central to social and cognitive development" (Christopherson, 1988, 156).

## Social Evaluation

Social evaluation, "the ability to observe, evaluate, and criticize the self" is developmental in nature, progressing through a series of stages that ultimately enables children to compare their "self" to their peer group (Harter, 1985, 61). The first stage leading to self-evaluation begins at age 5 years when the child can observe other children and evaluate their behavior, but is unable to recognize that other children are also observing and evaluating him (Harter, 1985). During the second stage, Harter (1985) suggests the child begins to understand that other children are evaluating him, but he cannot determine the accuracy of their perceptions because he cannot yet critically observe himself. Primary grade children (1st and 2nd graders) become concerned about what others might think of them, worry about making mistakes, and are careful not to expose themselves to criticism (Harter, 1985). "At this point children have developed the idea that each person has a private, subjective self that is not always easy to read from behavior" (Cole & Cole, 1989, 506).

Harter's (1985) third stage in the development of social evaluation emerges around the age of 8 years, when children begin to incorporate the observations of others into their own self-perceptions, and directly evaluate themselves. As children become interested in evaluating their own performance based on the standards others have for them, they internalize these expectations into self-standards and develop the capacity for self-criticism (Harter, 1985, 61). Once the child is able to evaluate himself he can also compare himself to others. "The child can now simultaneously observe both self and other, and this ability to engage in social comparison in cognitive competence, social competence, and physical competence provides a major index of the self's adequacy" (Harter, 1988, 61). Prior to age 8 years, children are not capable of constructing a global concept of themselves as a person that can be evaluated in terms of overall worth (Harter, 1985), thus, a major achievement during the primary grade years is to begin to develop a global self-worth or global self-concept.

## INTERMEDIATE AGE/GRADE SOCIAL/EMOTIONAL DEVELOPMENT

Later Middle Childhood occurs at about ages 9–12 years, during the intermediate grades (4th-6th) in most American schools (Biehler & Snowman, 1986). During the intermediate grades children make significant developmental/maturational strides. Many cognitive, language, and fine and gross motor skills are at an automatic level by the intermediate grades. Social/emotional developmental gains are evident in increased self-knowledge, perspective-taking abilities, social evaluation and comparison, and social problem-solving abilities.

### Normal Intermediate Age/Grade Social/Emotional Development

Adult expectations for children during later middle childhood increase dramatically from those expectations held during early childhood. Enhanced abilities in memory capacity, use of mediation strategies and metacognitive abilities are evident in their higher level academic functioning. Intermediate grade students have mastered the basics of learning to read, write, and calculate. Utilizing these basic skills with some degree of automaticity, they now read, write, and calculate to learn. Automaticity in using fine and gross motor skills changes the educational focus from mastering basic motor skills to using the motor skills to compete in sports, to play musical instruments, and to create art works. Facility in oral and written language changes the educational focus from concern with form (sentence structure, grammar, and articulation) to concern with content (creative writing, oral reports, pragmatics or social conversation).

In the school setting itself, intermediate grade students are expected to take more responsibility for completing assignments, staying on task, using various study methods, monitoring errors and progress, and remembering to turn in homework. Intermediate grade students are expected to show self-motivation and initiative in designing projects, and take on an active role in their own education. Intermediate grade students spend increased out-of-school time with peers in unsupervised situations, and are expected to behave in a socially appropriate manner.

During later middle childhood, as the child's abilities in cognitive integration expand, it becomes increasingly difficult to discuss and/or analyze social, emotional, and self-concept development as separate entities. The social/emotional/self-concept development of intermediate grade students is concerned with acquiring new levels of self-knowledge, increased abilities in perspective-taking, understanding social evaluation and comparison especially in relationship to peer group norms, utilizing social problem-solving, and a growing awareness of one's own moral beliefs.

## Self-Knowledge/Self-Evaluation

Late Middle Childhood is characterized by an increased understanding of the self and development of a self-theory or self-definition. This new self-understanding occurs in part because "a major cognitive advance in middle childhood results in new found abilities at conceptual integration" (Harter, 1985, 53). These new cognitive advances enhance the child's ability to classify, organize, and place concepts in a hierarchial sequence. Using these abilities, s/he can organize the observable behaviors of the self into trait labels (Harter, 1985).

During late middle childhood, children begin to think about trait stability and consistency of the attributes that define the self. For example, a 5th grade student may indicate that she's been good at reading since first grade and has always had problems in math, and anticipates this pattern to continue in the future. Thus, the child is able to compare herself in the present with herself in the past and observe the continuity of the self. The intermediate grade child organizes trait labels around particular themes that represent different domains relevant to the child's self-portrait or self-definition (Harter, 1988). In determining relevant themes, the child uses self-evaluation to analyze areas of competence and feelings of self-worth.

By later middle childhood, children have evaluated their competence in at least three areas—social competence, cognitive competence, and physical competence (Harter, 1988). Feelings of competence appear to be closely related to the child's sense of control and personal initiative. Research has consistently indicated that students who understand what factors control their successes as opposed to failures perceive their competence to be higher than that of students who say they do not understand what controls successes and failures. Personal initiative and a sense of responsibility for one's successes also appears to be positively related to feelings of competence within a domain.

Competence is viewed as one of several dimensions that feed into our sense of self-worth (Harter, 1985). The critical factor in gaining a positive self-worth seems to be feeling that one is competent at varying tasks. The child with the highest sense of overall worth as a person feels competent in areas of importance to significant others. Low self-worth individuals are not competent in areas where they wish to be successful (Harter, 1988). Perceived positive regard from significant others is strongly related to self-worth, suggesting that children (ages 10-13) adopt the attitudes and opinions that they feel others hold toward the self (Harter, 1988). Thus, during the intermediate grades, children use higher level cognitive skills in self-evaluation to determine competence and create/generate global evaluations of self worth.

During the intermediate grades, children make strides in understanding their personal emotional characteristics which leads naturally to an increased ability to control one's emotions and related behaviors. The increased ability to control one's emotions and related behaviors, particularly anger, is an important dimension of self-evaluation to the intermediate grade child. The emergence of self-control as an evaluation criteria indicates higher level cognitive functioning. While young children may experience a full range of emotional expression, they are unable to consistently control their responses and they do not see self-control as a characteristic of the self (Harter, 1985). The ability to express emotions directed toward the self, for example, in terms of self-shame for not controlling ones' behaviors or self-pride for performance at a band concert emerge during middle childhood.

## Social Perspective-Taking

During later Middle Childhood, children develop increasingly sophisticated social-cognitive and metacognitive skills which allow them to infer personality characteristics of others and to anticipate how these characteristics will affect the person's behavior. This ability to make social inferences about others and their reactions enables the child to make modifications in their own behavior.

The intermediate grade child becomes increasingly able to simultaneously observe his/her self and others and engage in social comparison. This ability to engage in social comparison provides awareness that others have preferences and characteristics that are different from their own; while at the same time becoming better able to adjust their behavior to interact appropriately with others (Berger, 1986). Social comparison and interpersonal skill development enable the child to check on his or her beliefs or assumptions about another's perspective through behavioral or conversational strategies (Cole & Cole, 1989). This increased ability of an intermediate grade child to evaluate the self and to evaluate one's relationships, then, appears to increase his/her ability to understand other persons through social perspective-taking.

The process of making social inferences and social comparisons contributes to the child's understanding about the reciprocal nature of social interactions. Primary grade youngsters experience difficulty in understanding reciprocity in a relationship; and experience difficulty seeing a relationship between their treatment of peers and the resultant reactions of peers. Thus, through social inferences, social comparison, social evaluation, and interpersonal development, intermediate grade children develop a greater awareness of the many social roles that an individual may play.

By the end of middle childhood most children will develop a more complex sense of themselves as a consequence of social comparison (Cole & Cole, 1989). Social comparison incorporates the acts of self-evaluation and self-competence as the child makes numerous specific comparisons in different settings to numerous peers in redefining his/her self-portrait. Social comparison, then, is intrinsic to social perspective-taking.

## Moral Development/Social Regulation

The intermediate grade child understands society's expectations to conform to several sets of rules simultaneously regarding moral codes and behaviors. The most basic level of rules are "moral rules, obligatory social regulations based on principles of justice and welfare—such as the prohibition against killing another human being or the obligation to take care of one's children. Such moral rules define obligations necessary to the maintenance of the social group" (Cole & Cole, 1989, 482). Moral rules include society's regulations against doing physical or psychological harm to others, rules of fairness and rights of others, and the expectancy to engage in prosocial behaviors (Turiel, Killen, & Helwig, 1987). "Moral behavior is affected by reasoning ability, and also by culture, family influences, and the particular situation. Prosocial behavior, such as cooperation, can be encouraged or discouraged depending on the child's social world" (Berger, 1986, 424).

In addition to basic moral rules of society, the intermediate grade child is becoming increasingly more capable of regulating his/her own behavior according to agreed-upon social rules and/or rule governed play. It is felt that "...rule-based games help children to coordinate extended interactions with their peers, enabling them to get along with others in the absence of adult authority" (Cole & Cole, 1989, 480). Social rules, social norms, or "social conventions coordinate the behavior of individuals within a social system, but differ from society to society" (Cole & Cole, 1989, 482). These rules may include school rules, forms of address, appropriate behavior for males and females, dress codes, etiquette (Turiel, et. al., 1987).

The intermediate grade child with a basic understanding of moral rules and social rules learns social regulation through indirect socialization techniques such as discussion and explanation, and becomes increasingly aware of the nuances of written and unwritten rules and codes of conduct. This growing understanding of him/her self and others in social interactions results in an increased ability to get along with people, and to understand that appropriate behavior differs in various social settings. The maturing child is increasingly sensitive to negative reactions by others. S/he realizes that self-shame is an emotional reaction to society's determination that s/he participated in antisocial conduct or displayed a lack of appropriate moral behavior.

## Social Problem-Solving

The intermediate grade child continues to develop more sophistication in using social problem-solving skills. Social problem-solving is the process of achieving personal goals in social interactions (Krasnor &

Rubin, 1983) and involves sensitivity to social problems and social consequences. The child initially learns appropriate patterns of behavior and social problem-solving skills within the family setting through interactions with siblings, parents, and other caregivers. The intermediate grade child, however, continues to enhance these skills through interactions with peers within various social settings.

Continued development in the area of social problem-solving skills during later middle childhood requires, not only, knowledge of basic social and moral rules of society, and perspective-taking abilities to note changes in others' reactions that signal a breach in social behavior, but also, requires higher level cognitive thinking abilities. The use of higher level cognitive processes involving analysis and evaluation, cause-effect reasoning, metacognition, and logical reasoning which emerge during later middle childhood facilitate social problem-solving abilities.

Additionally, to engage in complex social problem-solving, the child must have knowledge of his/her social self through social comparison and knowledge of the social self of others. Upper intermediate grade children must, then, become sensitive not only to social problems, but also, to social consequences usually gained through social comparison and perspective-taking. Throughout life individuals must engage in social problem-solving as they interact with others in increasingly more complex social situations.

Metacognitive skills enable an individual to monitor and analyze their social problem-solving situations and determine a course of action. Initially an individual must be sensitive to the existence of a social problem situation. Using higher level cognitive processes, the child can analyze the social problem, determine his/her outcome goal in solving the problem, pose possible solutions based on knowledge of cause-effect relationships in social problems, evaluate the possible solutions decide which one would result in the most desired situation, then decide which social strategy to implement for problem-solving. Younger intermediate grade children may need to work through this strategy with their teacher in solving their peer-relationship problems. Older Middle Childhood youth become increasingly sophisticated in the social-problem solving process and practice it in their peer/adult relationships.

## Intermediate Age/Grade Social Interactions

### Peer Relationships

Important tasks during later Middle Childhood involve re-establishing the self-concept in relation to peers rather than families, and an emerging emotional independence from parents and growing dependence on peers. The accomplishment of this task is possible due to their cognitive, social, and emotional advances that enable them to understand society's moral and social rules; to use social skills such as social perspective-taking, social comparison and evaluation, and social problem-solving skills.

During the intermediate grades, friendships become increasingly important, more intense, and fewer in number. Friends are no longer just anyone you play with, but are people you know well, who have common interests, similarities in abilities, and compatible personalities (Cole & Cole, 1989, 493). The development of friendships is closely associated with the acquisition of social perspective-taking and social problem-solving enabling the child to personally understand the friend's feelings, thoughts and emotions, and to repair misunderstandings when they occur.

For many children, emerging independence from parents during middle childhood is linked to growing dependence on peers. "A universal social contribution to the changes that occur in middle childhood is the rise of the peer group as a major context for development" (Cole & Cole, 1989, 510). The peer group typically specifies codes of behavior which frequently demand independence from adults, a special vocabulary, dress code, appropriate things to do and places to go, "in" clubs and organizations. From a developmental perspective, peer clubs or gangs serve many functions including building self-esteem, sharpening social skills, and teaching social cooperation (Berger, 1986). In addition to learning the arts of social interaction and making friends, there is evidence that children learn from their peers how to cope with aggression and sex (Skolnick, 1986, 416). The peer group is important because, for the first time, children are in the position of achieving their status within a group of those with relatively equal power and status without the intervention of adults (Cole & Cole, 1989).

"During middle childhood, children in all cultures tend to be segregated sexually" (Cole & Cole, 1989, 494). Children are learning sex-role parameters through socialization in sexually segregated clubs and activities.

"Boys appear to be socialized for competition with one another in activities bound by rule systems, while girls are socialized for cooperation and interpersonal sensitivity in circumstances with only implicit rules" (Cole & Cole, 1989, 496).

Intermediate grade years are significant ages in terms of membership in organized groups and clubs. Girl and Boy Scouts, Little League, and other sexually segregated organized clubs consume large portions of "free" time after school and on week-ends. When not involved in organized activities, intermediate grade children tend to organize neighborhood ball games, birthday parties, and other activities that involve peer groups.

## Family Relationships

Parental standards for their children's behavior continues to increase throughout Middle Childhood. Parents expect children to show increased ability to function according to moral and society's rules, and family rules and regulations without constant adult monitoring. They expect children to become dependable and reliable, to show initiative in problem-solving by viewing different aspects of a problem or weighing different points of view simultaneously, and in general to display skills valuable in citizenship and adulthood.

Assuming a minimum amount of responsibility outside the home becomes important by the end of latter Middle Childhood. Many girls are involved in babysitting and assuming greater responsibility regarding chores in the home. Boys frequently are involved in outdoor chores such as mowing the lawn and may mow lawns for several neighbors as a part-time job.

Parents use coregulation (Maccoby, 1984) techniques to share the responsibility for controlling their children with the children themselves.

> Coregulation is built on parent-child cooperation. It requires parents to work out methods of monitoring, guiding, and supporting their children when adults are not present, using the time they are together to reinforce their children's understandings of right and wrong, what is safe and unsafe, and when they need to come to adults for help. For coregulation to succeed, children must be willing to inform their parents of their whereabouts, their activities, and their problems (Cole & Cole, 1989, 505).

During Middle Childhood boys and girls, even when both parents work outside the home, begin turning to father more than mother when they need information about things outside the home. Mother continues to maintain importance in the home, in their social and club activities, and in children's school and church activities, especially as a sponsor and provider of "refreshments". For the most part, relationships with grandparents continue to be reciprocally warm and admiring. Grandparents provide noncontingent positive regard which is extremely important in self-concept development. Many intermediate grade children spend increasing amounts of time with grandparents and in doing part-time jobs for them.

Sibling relationships tend to be better with siblings much older or younger than near the same age. Disagreements tend to be settled verbally rather than physically, and often without parental intervention.

## Self-Concept of the Intermediate Age/Grade Student

The importance of the self-image as a major determinant of human behavior has long been recognized. The development of children's conceptions of themselves parallels the development of the ways they conceive of other people (Skolnick, 1986). Children develop complex theories about themselves and their behavior based on their past experiences, the opinions of others, and untested assumptions about themselves. One's relationship to others, particularly peers and close friends, are internalized and become salient dimensions of the self (Rosenberg, 1979). Thus, social perspective-taking and social comparison/social evaluation play an important role in redefining and reconstructing the self-theory in late Middle Childhood. As children grow older, the self is increasingly described as a private, unique world of thought and experience (Skolnick, 1986, 392).

Numerous researchers (e.g. Havighurst, 1952; Harter, 1983) have indicated that the self-concept of the intermediate grade child includes the following competence domains: (1) intellectual or cognitive skills, (2) achievement (3) physical or athletic competence, (4) social competence in peer relationships, (5) moral beliefs and interpersonal social skills. The child's self-concept or overall feelings of self-worth emerge as the child uses social perspective-taking and social comparison to determine his or her adequacy in each area in comparison to others and in comparison to performance in each of the other domains. Generally, we conceive that the child may concurrently hold both negative and positive conceptions of self in various domains or areas. The degree of importance of the domain or activity to the child will determine the degree to which success or failure affects one's overall self-evaluation.

By late Middle Childhood, the self-concept of the child has changed significantly from that evidenced in Early Childhood when the child could not differentiate the "real" from the "ideal" self-image. During early Middle Childhood (primary grades), the child began to use trait labels in self-descriptions and began to incorporate the opinions of valued others. Early Middle Childhood saw the emergence of sophisticated cognitive and metacognitive skills which allowed him/her to begin using complex cognitive tasks such as social perspective-taking and social comparison or evaluation, and to simultaneously observe both self and others. During late Middle Childhood, the child has become efficient in using social perspective-taking, social competence, self-comparison or self-evaluation, self-regulation, and problem-solving strategies. S/he has organized various trait labels into categories of competence internalizing the values of significant others and emerging with a much better defined self-concept.

## SUMMARY

Middle Childhood is that period of time in the life of a child that spans the elementary school years including the primary grades, 1st-3rd grade, and the intermediate grades, 4th-6th grade. During the primary grades children make significant growth and development in cognitive skills, in fine and gross motor skills, in language skills, and in academics. The major educational focus of the primary grades is acquisition of basic skills—learning how to read, write, calculate; learning to play games requiring fine and gross motor skills; learning to use language to express thoughts and ideas both orally and in written form. Enhanced cognitive development provides the primary grade child new insights in terms of perspective-taking, memory capacity, and self-control.

Socially the primary grade child learns to function in three separate worlds—the family, the school, and the peer group—each with its own rules and styles of behavior. Important social developments during the primary grade years involve emerging understandings of social relationships and moral feelings, and the development of a new personal identity incorporating the opinions of valued others. Social comparison or social evaluation is an emerging skill which allows the child to determine the competence or adequacy of "his/her" self.

The intermediate grade child is significantly more mature than the primary grade child. Many cognitive, language, fine and gross motor skills, and social skills are at an automatic functioning level. The academic focus in the intermediate grades is on using basic skills automatically in search of information. Automaticity in fine and gross motor skills allows the intermediate grade child to participate in competitive sports. Facility in oral and written language, changes the focus from acquisition of form and mechanics to focus on content.

Social and emotional development during later Middle Childhood enables the child to have evaluated their competence in at least several areas—social, cognitive, and physical—and to understand what factors control their successes. A major task during the intermediate grades is to create a global concept of self-worth. Increasingly sophisticated social-cognitive and metacognitive skills allow the intermediate grade child to make social inferences about the personality characteristics of others and to understand others through social perspective-taking. Intermediate grade children understand society's moral rules, social conventions, and various peer group norms. Advances in cognitive processes facilitate understanding and using social problem-solving techniques.

# Chapter Four

# ADOLESCENT SOCIAL/
# EMOTIONAL DEVELOPMENT

*Adolescence is probably the stage of life when uncertainty about the self-concept is at its peak* (Rosenberg, 1985, 223).

Major Adolescent Developmental Tasks
    Increase Quantitative Academic Level
    Develop Adult Cognitive Survival Skills
    Mature Socially and Physically
    Develop Realistic Self-Concept and Function in Peer Group
    Desatellization from Home
    Function as a Responsible Citizen
    Make Career/Vocational Choice
Adolescent Social Interactions
Self-Concept of the Adolescent
Summary

---

The transition from middle childhood to adolescence is marked by a number of significant changes in the child. Biological maturity results in physical changes, not only, in body size and shape, but also, in sexual development that ultimately results in the ability to reproduce. Another major difference between the child and the adolescent occurs in the area of cognition in which the adolescent acquires abstract thought processes, reasoning, hypothesizing, metacognitive thinking skills. These higher level cognitive abilities provide the adolescent the ability to engage in complex perspective-taking in fundamental issues such as social relations, morality, politics, and religion. The final task of adolescence is to complete the integration of the developmental changes— biological, psychological, cognitive, social—into a well adjusted young adult.

# MAJOR ADOLESCENT DEVELOPMENTAL TASKS

The educational establishment plays a significant role in the life of an adolescent. The school provides a realm of operation in which to earn status, to experiment with adult ideas and behaviors, and to test environmental constraints. The school provides the laboratory setting necessary for successful performance and adaptation in adult life. The Junior High and Senior High School are responsible for facilitating the developmental tasks of adolescents. The major tasks of adolescents in high school include the following: (1) Increasing their quantitative and qualitative academic levels, (2) Developing intellectual and cognitive adult survival skills, (3) Maturing socially and physically, (4) Developing realistic self-concepts and functioning in a peer group, (5) Desatellizing from home, (6) Learning to function as a responsible citizen, and (7) Making realistic career and vocational choices (McCandless & Coop, 1979).

The majority of high school students are able to accomplish at least an average degree of success in each of the developmental task areas and to emerge from high school with a realistic self-concept and the ability to function as an adult citizen secure in social areas. Most students have been adequately successful in increasing their quantitative achievement level, in developing adult cognitive and intellectual survival skills, in desatellizing from home, and are eager to begin working at an occupation or to pursue higher education.

## Increase Quantitative Academic Level

One obvious function of the High School is to increase the quantitative academic level of the students. The high school curriculum must be designed in order to fulfill the following main functions: (1) provide traditional academic schooling, (2) provide vocational training in job skills, and (3) provide programs for handicapped and disadvantaged students (McCandless & Coop, 1979). These functions are achieved basically through utilization of three curriculums: A core or general education curriculum, specialized curriculums, and an action-learning curriculum.

Traditional academic schooling is provided primarily by the core curriculum subjects, which are continuations of the academic subject spirals begun in elementary school. Basic core subjects are required by law to guarantee a literate populace. Traditional core curriculum courses include sciences, math, English and literature, reading, history, civics, physical education, and fine arts. The advanced core curriculum courses provide academic preparation for college bound students. Nationwide many state legislatures have mandated acquisition of minimum basic academic and functional standards, not only, for high school graduation, but also, for passage from grade to grade and/or to determine who must attend summer school. The original goals of the testing programs were to determine if students were achieving at least minimum core curriculum skills. In many cases, there is a fourth curriculum, a hidden curriculum—the minimum competency test itself.

Vocational/prevocational training in job skills is obtainable through specialized curriculums, and action learning programs. Specialized curriculums usually introduced at the Junior High or Middle School level include home economics, vocational education, automobile mechanics, business education, industrial arts, and work study programs. Students frequently diversify their required core curriculum by incorporating selected courses from the specialized curriculums. Vocational and prevocational training in the secondary school is an integral part of the curriculum of disadvantaged and handicapped students, students who prefer to attend vocational technical schools rather than college, and for students who plan to work immediately after high school.

Action Learning Skills (Coleman, et. al., 1974) are frequently integrated into both the core curriculum and the specialized curriculum. The action learning program includes the development of verbal communication skills, decision-making skills, survival skills, emergency skills, bureaucratic skills, occupational skills, and mechanical skills. The facilitation of these skills has often been the responsibility of special education programs and remedial programs for handicapped and disadvantaged students.

Currently, new curricular designs for handicapped, disadvantaged, and lowacademic functioning students focusing on acquisition of basic learning strategies, functional competencies, prosocial skills, and transitioning from school to work, attempt to integrate the major developmental tasks of adolescents into an organized curriculum. Numerous special education professionals stress a program of prosocial skills which includes classroom survival skills, friend-ship making skills, stress prevention or stress-relieving skills, and alternatives to aggression (McGinnis & Goldstein, 1984).

As a result of the 1983 Amendment to Public Law 94-142, Education for All Handicapped Children Act, adolescent transition programs are being designed and implemented to assist handicapped, disadvantaged, and potential drop-outs to learn skills and abilities necessary for successfully assuming adult status. "Transition planning can be broken down into two general domains (life and support)" (Polloway, et. al, 1989, 420). Life areas often include community citizenship, vocation/education, home and family, recreation/leisure; whereas, support areas include emotional/ physical health and financial support (Hawaii Transition Project, 1987).

A functional curriculum generally integrates learning basic academic competencies with functional life skills. For example, curricular materials on the topics of consumer economics, occupational knowledge, health, community resources, and government and law are used in teaching reading, writing, mathematics, communication skills (speaking, listening, viewing), problem-solving, and interpersonal relations (APL Model of Functional Competency, 1981). Thus, the specialized curriculums have been expanded in concept and implementation strategies to serve as adolescent transition programs for those students who are handicapped, disadvantaged, or who for other reasons are not functioning at "near" grade level expectancy.

### Develop Adult Cognitive Survival Skills

"There is broad agreement among theorists of development, dating back at least to Rousseau, that the transition from middle childhood to adulthood requires the development of a new quality of mind" (Cole & Cole, 1989, 560). This new quality of mind involves developing cognitive and intellectual skills appropriate for meeting the demands and requirements for adult life. Such intellectual abilities include abstract thinking, logical reasoning, cause-effect reasoning, thinking about alternatives, metacognitive thinking, and re-evaluating the fundamental issues of social relations, morality, and politics and religion (Keating, 1980). Impairment in the development of these skills is manifested as incompetencies in the ability to think abstractly.

"Adolescent thought processes differ in many ways from those of younger children. Adolescents think about the past and future, become absorbed in philosophical speculations about life and death and the meaning of things" (Skolnick, 1986, 488). The thought processes of young people exhibit a new level of systematicity and logic as they begin to make the transition to adulthood (Cole & Cole, 1989). According to Piaget, most adolescents progress gradually from the concrete thinking stage to the formal operational thinking stage which involves abstract reasoning (Biehler & Snowman, 1986). Piaget describes cognitive development as the gradual acquiring of the ability to think logically (Copeland, 1988). Elkind (1970) revealed that all adolescents do not attain formal operational ability at the same age in all problem-solving areas, and some never attain this ability.

Logical thinking involves analyzing, reasoning, and making sound judgments through generating all possible solutions to a problem and systematically eliminating the irrelevant. "Adolescents' new ability to search for inconsistencies among longheld beliefs comes with the ability to think logically which also increases their interest in ideal systems of thought" (Cole & Cole, 1989, 575). During adolescence students begin to utilize the logical processes of inductive and deductive reasoning. The ability to abstractly derive new information from something known or assumed emerges. Adolescents learn to draw conclusions from observations and/or experiences. Utilizing abstract symbolism involves conceiving thoughts not related to concrete realities, but that exist only as ideas. Adolescents begin a greater understanding of their present and imagine their future.

Flavell (1985) indicates that adolescents acquire metacognition skills or metathinking, the ability to think about the thinking process, rather than just thinking about the content of their thoughts. They become aware of the systematic strategies that are needed for learning (Lerner, 1989, 188). They experiment with the whole new realm of abstracting. "Adolescents also acquire the ability to engage in second-order thinking; that is, they can develop rules about rules, holding two disparate rule systems in mind while mulling them over" (Cole & Cole, 1989, 561).

An extremely valuable cognitive skill emerging in adolescence is the ability to comprehend cause-effect relationships. This noting of the relationship between actions and events is of primary importance in adult interpersonal relationships as well as in business and professional dealings. The ability to perceive the cause which starts a chain of events into motion allows one to predict or alter outcomes.

Structure and organization skills are crucial in all aspects of life. Adolescents must learn to recognize the structure or the interrelated parts of a system. Organizational skills are essential in accomplishing tasks, in planning time schedules for short and long term assignments, in budgeting time, in correlating the subparts of a task with the time allotted for completion. Without good organizational skills adolescents will not be able to complete assignments and work demands on time.

Higher level cognition and metacognition acquired during adolescence facilitate planning and organization, and monitoring one's progress.

One manifestation of an adolescent's "new mode of thinking is the special sensitivity toward adult opinions and toward the proprieties of adult behavior that adolescents express. They become critical of received wisdom and even more critical of the differences between adult ideals and adult behavior" (Cole & Cole, 1989, 560). Parents often find this an extremely difficult period in their child's life as the child criticizes and analyzes parental lifestyle, parental accomplishments, parental beliefs, and parental recommendations and suggestions, and finds parents not 'measuring up to their expectations'.

## Mature Socially and Physically

The facilitation of the social maturation of adolescents as a responsibility of the school is a fairly recent concept. In addition to social development through vicarious sports and social activities sponsored by the school, many high school curriculums include classes such as human sexuality, and family living to assist in the social maturation of students.

A primary adolescent developmental task is to understand and to accept the biological changes playing havoc with their bodies forcing the development of a new self-image. " . . . Adolescence is a critical period for the achievement of sexual identity and conceptions of self. During this period young people must come to terms with sexual maturation of their bodies, develop relationships with the opposite sex in general and with sexual partners in particular, and define their future goals in regard to work, marriage, and parenthood" (Skolnick, 1986, 467).

Adolescents must become comfortable with their adult bodies, understand the parameters of maleness and femaleness, and become cognizant of adult responsibilities associated with their sexuality. They must learn to cope with social problems regarding sex differences, to learn socially acceptable and unacceptable behaviors, and to deal with the interpersonal dynamics of sex differences. "For many adolescents, defining themselves with regard to sexuality and sex roles is the most difficult, confusing, and anxious aspect of growing up, as well as one of the most pleasurable and exciting" (Skolnick, 1986, 469). The resolution of these sex difference confusions should enable the adolescent to be comfortable and successful in dating situations.

The focus of psychosocial development in adolescence is identity vs. identity confusion (Erikson, 1968). Adolescents must establish their identity through reconciling their biological and self-image changes with social expectations of adults and other adolescents, and with their own individual preferences and developmental patterns. "During adolescence, the individual is evaluating his/her own adequacy as a person in terms of the gender schema—trying to match inner preferences and attitudes, personal attributes, and social skills with the model provided by the larger society" (Skolnick, 1986, 468–469). Thus, the adolescent must resolve identity and identity confusion and define himself/herself.

### Develop Realistic Self-Concept and Function in Peer Group

School is the major arena in which adolescents earn status. School provides the setting in which adolescents practice casual social interactions and complex social interrelationships. Resolving identity confusions and emerging with a realistic self-concept, and the ability to function successfully and comfortably within a peer group are major developmental tasks during adolescence.

Numerous factors involved in the development and enhancement of the self-concept during adolescence include the following: (1) Realistically evaluating one's intellectual competence, (2) Developing competitive physical and athletic skills, (3) Accepting and enhancing one's level of physical attractiveness, (4) Learning skills involved in becoming socially attractive, (5) Understanding and adhering to socially appropriate sex-typing characteristics, (6) Developing leadership qualities, (7) Developing a personal moral belief system, (8) Developing a sense of humor.

The self-concept "emerges over time and is far more multifaceted in adolescence than during the primary years" (Pullis, 1988, 78). The self-concept is developed through internalizing the negative and positive reactions of others to the actions, behaviors, verbal expressions, and accomplishments of the individual. The self-concept is influenced by one's intellectual competence and the way significant others view ones' intellectual abilities. Students who are in advanced placement/college placement classes and who are successful in those academic placements, frequently are involved in Student Council, debate, competitive academic teams, and other activities important to the enhancement of the respect of the school as a producer of intellectual youth. Therefore, adolescents may gain status through demonstrating superior intellectual competence.

The self-concept is influenced by one's physical skills and abilities in school and community sponsored competitive sports activities including football, basketball, and soccer. One only has to look at the salaries of major sports figures and college coaches to see the importance of sports in our daily lives. Youth who are successful on the field or at the hoops are held in very high esteem by other high school students and community adults. Sports competitions are used to build school spirit, rally the alumni around the school, and to encourage the alumni to donate funds to the support of the school. Youth who demonstrate outstanding abilities in popular team competitive sports such as football and basketball are held in high esteem by peers and adults whether they possess intellectual competence or not.

The self-concept is influenced by one's physical attractiveness. In our society physical attractiveness is very highly sought after by young and old alike. Physical attractiveness includes not only, physical beauty, but also involves good grooming and posture, attractive and stylish dressing, acceptable hair styles and make-up, and a good feeling about one's own looks. Millions of dollars are spent annually on various creams and beauty aids, on hair care and styling, on clothing to "make the man or woman," and on exercise parlors which "guarantee" a slender desirable figure. Students who possess physical attractiveness are held in high esteem and become trend setters for clothes styles, hair styles, and behaviors. Physically attractive students frequently become the cheerleaders, the Homecoming King and Queen, and the students' that others emulate.

Social attractiveness is another factor that influences self-concept development. Social attractiveness involves using appropriate manners in various social situations, the ability to empathize and feel true concern for others, feeling an enjoyment of life, and being liked by members of ones own and opposite sex. Social attractiveness is a very desirable quality and when paired with other self-concept factors such as physical attractiveness and/or physical competence, and/or intellectual attractiveness enhances a student's acceptance by peers and adults alike.

The self-concept is influenced by sex-typing characteristics, which include the qualities that differentiate men from women including clothes and hair styles, mannerisms, vocabulary usage, and topics of interest, and behaviors. Students who do not adhere to the "accepted norms" of one adolescent group or another are considered very strange and unacceptable. Adolescence is a period of uncertainty as youth move from middle childhood toward adulthood. They must learn new roles and new ways of interacting with peers and others. Adolescents are especially concerned, during this transition period, that there be no doubt about their sexual orientation.

The development of leadership qualities is important in self-concept enhancement. Leadership qualities include demonstrating confidence in one's ability to make decisions and talk before groups, showing expertise in logical thinking and verbal convincing skills, proving one's reliability and hard work in accomplishing group tasks, and showing concern for the group's interest. Leaders emerge in areas of intellectual competence, athletic skills, physical attractiveness, social attractiveness, morality, and humor. The adolescent who excels in one or more than one area enhances his/her position in the school system's hierarchy while at the same time enhancing his/her own self-confidence and feelings of acceptance.

The self-concept is influenced by personal moral beliefs and behaviors, the internalization of society's ethical and legal codes of behavior, fair and honest interactions with adults and peers. Adolescents are beginning to take responsibility for themselves and their actions. Many adolescents have internalized the standards of their parents' religion and of society, and have developed their own personal interpretation of "morality," so they are self-monitoring. They can regulate their own behaviors in the absence of adult supervisors. These internalized standards help them judge the "rightness" or "wrongness" of various behaviors.

The self-concept is influenced by one's sense of humor. A sense of humor involves alertness to amusing incidents of life, ability to laugh with others and even at oneself, ability to enjoy life, being "fun" to be around, and being optimistic. A great sense of humor can "make a person" attractive and popular with peers inspite of lacking physical attractiveness and competitive sports ability. A highly developed sense of humor is a great equalizer.

Thus, the development of the self-concept during adolescence is dependent to a great extent on the qualities that one possesses that are held in esteem by peers. An adolescent must learn to function within his/her peer group. In the adolescent culture, youth evaluate each other according to valued characteristics to create a hierarchy of acceptance standards. Students excelling in physical skills, physical attractiveness, leadership qualities, and intellectual competence who bring glory to their schools as well as themselves possess the greatest amount of earned status. They are in the highest hierarchy level and receive the most esteem from peers.

In order to function in a peer group, adolescents must adopt that subculture's standards and moral values. They must assume the group's common mode of behavior and become proficient in speaking the common language. Their dress, make-up, and hair style must follow group dictates. Adolescents must listen to and know the music sanctioned by their chosen peer group. They must frequent the accepted social hangouts. In these ways adolescents create a "we" status of group membership and an identity for themselves in a very unsure period of their lives.

**Desatellization from Home**

A major task of adolescence is desatellization from home. Desatellizing from home includes the following: (1) Becoming less physically, psychologically, and emotionally dependent on parents, (2) Developing responsibility, independence, and self-confidence, (3) Participating in achievement and independence training (transitioning), and (4) Understanding and accepting noncontingent positive regard.

Desatellization is the process in which adolescents are gradually weaned from physical, psychological, and emotional dependence on parents to emerge relatively independent. Adolescents must learn to provide their own physical needs by learning to cook, clean house, launder their clothes, as well as financially providing their needs of food, shelter, and transportation. Psychologically, adolescents begin to rely on their peers for support regarding personal and career decisions. Emotional stability, also, becomes more focused on the peer group than on the family for support and approval. However, "adolescents do not simply move away from parental influence into a decision-making world all their own. As adolescents move toward becoming more autonomous individuals, it is healthy for them to be attached to their parents" (Santrock, 1990, 227).

For many adolescents the desatellization process is facilitated by "going off to college." The adolescent still relies primarily on parents to pay tuition and major living expenses, but gains experience in organizing and monitoring completion of school tasks as well as self-care responsibilities such as laundering and ironing their own clothes, caring for their possessions, frequently cooking meals and cleaning an apartment, while holding a part-time job.

Elder (1962) contends that the democratic parenting style provides training in responsibility, independence, and confidence to allow for a more successful desatellization from home and transition to adulthood. Characteristic of the democratic parenting style is parental explanation of rules and expectations, realistic goal setting, developing skills in independence planning, developing a frustration tolerance, and a capacity for realistic self-criticism. A more democratic teaching style provides the same advantages in schools.

Desatellization from home is much more successful for adolescents who have been provided achievement and independence training. Training for achievement involves learning strategies of approaching a task, regrouping for secondary attempts, courage to attempt difficult tasks, viewing nonachievement as a further opportunity rather than as a failure, and problem-solving techniques. Independence training primarily involves decision-making and critical evaluation skills, and predicting outcomes of behaviors. Independence skills are predicated upon a good self-concept, confidence in ability to perform required tasks and acceptance of responsibility.

An important prerequisite to desatellization from home is an adolescent's knowledge that s/he possesses noncontingent positive regard (Johnson, 1963) or the acceptance of one as valued regardless of behavior, attitudes, and appearance, from teachers and parents contributes to the development of a positive self-concept, confidence in one's ability to achieve, and in one's ability to be independent. It is crucial to the development of positive personal regard of the individual self. "When final desatellization is reached, individuals have secure feelings about themselves and do not demonstrate the need to prove themselves" (Santrock, 1990, 225).

## Function as a Responsible Citizen

The sixth major adolescent developmental task is to function as a responsible citizen. Requirements essential to the development of the ability to function as a responsible citizen include the following: (1) Developing moral standards, (2) Simultaneously fulfilling duties to one's conscience and to society's demands, (3) Assuming responsibility for one's own beliefs, commitments, and attitudes, (4) Learning adult autonomy and responsibility, and (5) Getting a job and/or doing volunteer work.

Most people reach the conventional level of moral development during adolescence (Kohlberg, 1976). The conventional level is characterized by the ability to internalize or identify with the rules prescribed by social groups and with the expectations of others especially authorities. At the conventional level individuals can see problems from the viewpoints of others and can identify with society at large. It is during this stage of moral development that adolescents evaluate, discriminate, and refine their beliefs and incorporate some of the expectations of society into their own moral code.

The seeds of the values and ethical system that one will eventually adopt are presented through all the influences that act on individuals in a society. Parents' values, peer and community values, and the values and ethical system of one's church are most readily available to the developing person. The conclusions one makes about his or her own values include a strong element of self (Manaster, 1989, 18).

Adolescence is the period in which youth must for the first time take responsibility for their own commitments, life style, beliefs, and attitudes. Fowler (1976) identifies this as a period of developing an "individuating and reflexive faith." Characteristic decisions during this phase of development involve dealing with the polar issues of individuality vs. community centeredness, self-fulfillment vs. service to others, relative vs. absolute, and objectivity vs. subjectivity. However, the primary developmental achievement is that of assuming individual responsibility.

Adolescents must learn skills and develop abilities which will enable them to become autonomous and responsible adults. They must accept the responsibility for themselves socially, politically, and economically. Social autonomy refers to being able to conduct oneself in socially prescribed ways, able to vary conduct as to be acceptable in the various settings in which they wish to participate. Political autonomy requires a knowledge of our political system, keeping currently informed on issues, and ability to make decisions regarding the common good when voting in elections.

Many adolescents begin the development toward autonomy in adulthood through part-time employment and/or volunteer work. Of primary importance in attaining independence from parents is securing employment which will allow one to economically provide for all major needs and to eventually support a family.

### Make Career/Vocational Choices

Another major task of adolescents in high school is to make reasonable career/vocational choices. Many social factors influencing career/vocational choices are interwoven into the child's environment including the socio-economic status of the family, the education level of the parents, the adolescent's own personal aptitude and achievement, the school-community environment, the adolescent's status seeking among peers, and the adolescent's desire for economic independence.

The socio-economic status of the family affects career/vocational choices by influencing which career choices are socially acceptable to the family.

The amount of money the family has to spend or is willing to spend on higher education, the jobs/occupations of parents and the socio-economic level of the family's neighborhood affect career/vocational choices. Occupational selections are also influenced by the career/vocational choices of siblings and the grants, student loans or scholarships available based on socio-economic conditions.

Another social factor influencing career/vocational choice is the educational level attained by the parents. The parents' attitudes toward education, their own school experiences, and their educational aspirations for their children influence the educational level to which the children strive. Parental aptitude and the richness of background experiences they provide, as well as the example they set with their personal reading habits and selections, influence the value the children place on learning. The parental hobbies, the hobbies the children are encouraged to pursue, and the breadth of career exposure affect career/vocational choices.

The individual's personal aptitude and academic achievement level greatly influence the career options available for choice. Aptitude particularly average and low serves to eliminate many occupational choices from consideration due to inability to attain the academic requirements. The student's attitude toward school affects the educational level to which s/he is willing to strive. The student's personal achievement level in terms of grades and skills mastered, courses taken, study habits, organizational skills, willingness to study, concern for grades, acceptance of delayed gratification, personal hobbies and extra curricular activities all actively influence the career or vocational selection.

Career/vocational choice is also influenced by the school environment and the community for which the curriculum was designed. The curriculum of rural high schools tends to be more vocational oriented to meet the needs of farming communities. Rural schools frequently have less financial assets and fewer students, restricting the number and types of classes that can be offered. Rural schools tend to emphasize specialized curriculums including vocational education, home economics, business education, and industrial arts. Educational programs in metropolitan areas are designed to meet the needs of students from a much wider variety of backgrounds and reflecting a wide variety of needs. The larger number of students and greater financial resources enables the school system to offer a widely varied and diverse curriculum. Students residing in a metropolitan area are exposed to a large variety of occupations from which to choose.

An individual's occupational choice is also affected by the choices deemed desirable and acceptable by his/her peer group. The degree to which the choice is affected by peers is determined in part by the amount of status the individual seeks within the peer group.

The desire for economic independence is a further consideration of high school students in occupational selection. If the student wishes to be an autonomous adult immediately or within a year after high school they greatly narrow their career selection possibilities. Students who are willing to delay adult autonomy and economic independence usually pursue careers which require more formal education.

## ADOLESCENT SOCIAL INTERACTIONS (PEERS)

Primary social interactions during adolescence center around the peer group, and the more intimate friendship group. "Society expects, and certainly middle-class parents expect, social development and social successes. Middle-class parents and subculture present adolescents with more formal, organized, social group opportunities" (Manaster, 1989, 15). Good peer relationships appear to be necessary for normal social development in adolescence.

During adolescence the peer group becomes the general source of rules of appropriate behavior. The pressure to conform to a certain peer group (i.e. jocks, nerds, druggies, etc.) becomes very strong during adolescent years. Conformity involves agreeing with the expressed group opinion; concurring with the rules and social practices of a specific culture including the use of slang or jargon, dress code, and behavioral mannerisms that reflect conformity (Santrock, 1990, 249). "Developing a code of behavior is a move toward adult independence" (Biehler & Snowman, 1986, 124) through assisting the adolescent in establishing "a sense of individual identity, to find a way to be one of the gang and yet stand out from the crowd" (Berger, 1986, 516).

The peer group functions as a source of information about the world outside the family providing the adolescent feedback about their abilities in comparison to other adolescents (Santrock, 1990). Peer groups are comprised of voluntary memberships. "The element of choice in peer group membership reflects the increased control adolescents have in choosing the settings in which they find themselves, the people they associate with, and the things they do" (Cole & Cole, 1989, 536).

Friendships become increasingly important during adolescence as friends help each other confront and make sense of uncertain and often anxiety-provoking situations—parental expectations, dating, etc. Friendships serve a number of important functions including the companionship of a familiar partner; stimulation and source of interesting information; physical support and assistance; ego support in terms of encouragement; social comparison; and an intimate trusting relationship (Santrock, 1990). "Loyalty is an outgrowth of both the mutual understanding and the intimacy that friends share" (Cole & Cole, 1989, 533).

Adolescents tend to form friendships with others from the same socioeconomic background (Hollingshead, 1975). Friends and dates are likely to share similar intelligence, attitudes, behaviors, life-style, and values. "Adolescents are motivated to form close relationships with others who are similar to them because similarity provides consensual validation of the adolescent's own attitudes and behaviors" (Santrock, 1990, 275).

In the long run, the adolescent's success in social development, in peer group social situations, and in friendship-making influence mate selection, occupational choice, sense of self, and the quality of adult social life (Manaster, 1989). For a large number of adolescents in industrialized societies who continue their education beyond high school, the period of adolescence is extended another four or five years before the individual reaches adult status and autonomy.

## SELF-CONCEPT OF THE ADOLESCENT

Numerous researchers have indicated that the self-concept changes between early childhood and early adulthood. Leahy & Shirk (1985, 145–146) indicate the self-concept appears to develop in a series of stages or levels including the following: (1) OBJECTIVE SELF—The young child describes the self in terms of physical qualities; (2) SUBJECTIVE SELF—The middle childhood-aged child develops the ability to use social comparison and perspective-taking to judge the self's performance (e.g., compare real and ideal self-image); (3) SUBJECTIVE PROCESS— The adolescent develops the ability to use the perspective of a "universal person" or nonparticipating observer, to recognize that the self is known in different ways by different people, to view the self as varying across situations and time, and attempts to integrate conflicting qualities in the

self; (4) PROCESS OF THE SELF'S CONSTRUCTION OR CHANGE—
The young adult or adult facing major life changes (e.g., leaving college,
starting or losing a job) may reflect on the process of the self's construction or change.

For the adolescent, self-concept development involves integration of
one's social, sexual, familial, ideological, and occupational roles (Harter,
1985). The enormity of the task of constructing an entire self portrait in
which the different characteristics of the self are integrated explains why
the adolescent appears to be preoccupied with his or her own personality
(Harter, 1985). During this period of intense preoccupation with the self,
the adolescent turns to friends for support, self-clarification, and self-
validation. Due to the role experimentation, physiological changes, new
social demands, and mood swings, the adolescent's self-expression is
often inconsistent. The adolescent functioning cognitively at the formal
operational level possesses the ability to detect inconsistencies as they
subject themselves and their behavior to scrutiny and analysis, attempting
to construct a general self-concept (Harter, 1985).

Elkind (1970) has termed this period of self-consciousness and self-
preoccupation as adolescent egocentrism. Adolescents' tend to create a
personal fable (Elkind, 1970) in which the adolescent feels "that one's
own experiences are so unique and novel that no one else could possibly
appreciate them, particularly one's parents and those outside one's clos-
est circle of friends" (Harter, 1985).

The self-concept develops and changes with experiences and new
cognitive abilities (Manaster, 1989, 116). "The self-concept of the adolescent incorporates a view of self as an intimate, sensitive, and spontaneous
being. Such aspects of the self do not appear to be part of the self-concept
of the preadolescent" (Smollar & Youniss, 1985, 254). "Compared to
younger children, early adolescents are highly self-conscious and have
uncertain, shaky images of themselves. They have lower overall self-
esteem, and lesser opinions of themselves with regard to certain qualities
they value" (Skolnick, 1986, 463).

"Although the self-concept is important at all life stages, it is probably
most problematic during adolescence" (Rosenberg, 1985, 206). The tendency for contradictions within the self to be observed and to cause
conflict is in large part based on new cognitive abilities now possessed in
middle adolescence (Harter, 1986). Adolescents realize that they possess
different selves depending on the particular role or context. The adoles-

cent is now capable of constructing a theory of the self, which involves the integration of the multiple concepts of the self (Fischer, 1980).

For the adolescent, the self-concept now functions as a standard for evaluating and predicting performance socially, objectively, personally; and functions to limit performance for the purpose of maintaining and enhancing itself (Manaster, 1986, 116). Adolescents are able to maintain a reasonably positive self-image by identifying positive attributes as core constructs in their self-portrait and considering negative attributes or behaviors as foreign to their true self (Harter, 1986).

## SUMMARY

Adolescence is that period in life marked by a number of significant changes—biological, physical, psychological, cognitive, social—that must be accepted and integrated to produce a well-adjusted, autonomous young adult. Major developmental tasks during the period of adolescence include increasing their quantitative academic level, developing adult survival skills, maturing socially and physically, developing a realistic self-concept and functioning in a peer group, desatellizing from home, functioning as a responsible citizen, and making a career or vocational choice.

During high school adolescents increase their quantitative academic level through three primary curriculums—core curriculum or general education courses; specialized curriculums such as vocational training in job skills, college preparation courses, functional curriculums; and an action-learning curriculum. Adolescents develop adult cognitive survival skills including abstract thinking, cause-effect reasoning, problem-solving, and metacognitive thinking.

The school has accepted the responsibility of assisting adolescents in understanding the biological changes that result in sexual maturation and cause the development of a new self-image. Adolescents must learn to cope with social problems regarding sex differences, and with socially acceptable and unacceptable behaviors, and establish their identity. Developing a realistic self-concept involves realistically evaluating one's character or personality traits including intellectual competence, physical and athletic skills, physical attractiveness, social attractiveness, sex-typing characteristics, leadership qualities, moral belief system, and sense of humor. Self-concept development involves enhancing one's strengths and weaknesses, and accepting what cannot be changed. Adolescents must select an appropriate peer group and learn to function within it by adopting its culture.

By the end of the high school years, the adolescent should be in the process of desatellizing from home by becoming less dependent on parents physically, psychologically, and emotionally. For adolescents who continue their education this process may not be complete for another four or five years, however, they must develop a positive self-concept, confidence in their ability to achieve and to be independent. Adolescents should accept responsibility for their own beliefs and behaviors.

Primary social interactions during adolescence center around peers and friends. Peer groups serve as a socializing agent and friends provide the support needed during this difficult period of self-concept building. Adolescents tend to form friendships with others from the same socioeconomic backgrounds. During adolescence one's self-concept matures to serve as a standard for evaluating and predicting performance socially, objectively, personally in the various roles that s/he must play.

## Chapter Five

# IMPACT OF SELF-CONCEPT
# ON ACADEMIC ACHIEVEMENT

*Academic success or failure appears to be as deeply rooted in concepts of the self as it is in measured mental ability, if not deeper* (Purkey, 1970, 14).

---

Analyses of research studies in psychiatry and psychology indicate essentially that the student's ability to utilize the power to learn is determined by one's self-concept, one's perception of their world including personal goals, purposes, and values. Succinctly, the learner's awareness, thoughts, and feelings are what primarily guides, controls, and regulates his/her performance (Arieti, 1970).

## SELF-CONCEPTS OF ACADEMIC ABILITY/ACHIEVEMENT

A student's perceptions of the evaluations of his academic ability by his significant others results in a self-concept of academic ability (Brookover & Erickson, 1962). An individual's self-concept of academic ability is an important variable in the decisions he makes to carry out the role of student. A student's concept of his role as a student indicates to him the personal value of certain learnings, the probability of accomplishing the required tasks, and the time and place to apply himself to learn the tasks (Brookover & Erickson, 1962).

Educators have discussed the high positive correlation between enhancing concepts of self and high academic achievement levels in school. They have, also, noted that "a negative self-concept is a significant factor contributing to low academic achievement" (Battle, 1982, 61). Successful students usually have a positive and healthy self-concept, while it is likely that those who are achieving poorly in school have a negative self-concept (Hansen & Maynard, 1973). Farls (1967) studied intermediate grade students and found the high achieving boys and girls reported significantly higher self-concepts in general and self-concepts as students than low achieving boys and girls. "Studies which support the notion that underachievers tend to have negative self-concepts are numerous" (Purkey, 1970, 20).

Research evidence clearly indicates a persistent and significant relationship between the self-concept and academic achievement (Purkey, 1970, 17). Self-concept of academic ability seems to be associated with academic achievement at each grade level. Self-esteem, is not something separate from performance, but rather integral to it (Covington & Beery, 1976).

To facilitate understanding the academic self-concept, Song and Hattie (1984, 1270) have proposed a model of the hierarchial structures of the self-concept. Their model suggests that the general self-concept is composed of three major self-concepts: (1) academic self-concept, (2) social self-concept, and (3) presentation of self. The academic self-concept is influenced by three major factors or self-concepts: (1) classroom self-concept, (2) ability self-concept, and (3) achievement self-concept which are based on success in various academic subject areas.

Results of their study indicate that the "academic self-concept has the most effect on academic achievement" directly, and the effects of social self-concept (peers and family) and presentation of self (self-confidence) primarily have effects on achievement indirectly via the general self-concept (Song & Hattie, 1984, 1279). In order to gain a more comprehensive understanding of the academic self-concept, one must analyze in more detail the self-concept factors of students' perceptions of his/her classroom standing, cognitive ability, and achievement in terms of the nature of the child's own sense of control over his/her learning. Some factors involved in producing a sense of control over academic performance include metacognition, motivation, attributions, and learning styles.

## Sense of Personal Control

In examining the self-concept factors of academic ability and academic achievement, it is necessary to consider the sense of personal control the child feels over his/her learning. "A considerable body of research indicates that those children who possess an awareness that they must be responsible for their own learning by taking an active role in that process are the most successful students" (Reid, 1988, 41).

Purkey, (1970, 394) suggests that four student self-control factors are likely to lead to school success: (1) asserting: experiencing a sense of self-control, (2) relating to others, (3) investing: encouraging students to get involved with learning and with classmates, and (4) coping: how well students meet most school expectations. All of the factors actually consider the student's sense of personal self-control as s/he takes an active role in learning.

"Learning is not considered adequate until children can construct and control information for themselves, that is, until they can draw relationships among the concepts learned and use that information to make inferences about yet other relationships" (Reid, 1988, 41). Thus, the learner gains a sense of personal control during the learning process which involves the interaction of learner characteristics (social, emotional, cognitive, motivational factors), the task, and the nature of the materials to be learned.

### Metacognition

The interrelationships among cognitive development and other developmental factors, especially social, emotional, self-concept development has been consistently recognized. "Most elementary school children have only limited knowledge of how their cognitive processes work and when to use them" (Biehler & Snowman, 1986, 438). However, adolescents make great strides in abstract cognitive processing. Adolescents functioning at the formal operational level can ponder simultaneously several different approaches to solve a problem, then consciously evaluate each approach or solution and select the best. Adolescents study other people's thought processes and are interested in speculation such as considering several different hypotheses (Levine, 1987). In other words, adolescents develop the ability to use metacognition or metacognitive thinking.

Metacognition refers to both the knowledge about cognition and the regulation of cognition (Reid, 1988). It concerns what we know about our own thought processes and how that knowledge or lack of it affects learning. Metacognition is the ability to reflect on one's own thinking (Levine, 1987). The first aspect of "metacognition refers to the awareness of one's systematic thinking strategies that are needed for learning" (Lerner, 1989, 188). This ability to reflect on one's cognition or to possess knowledge about cognition, develops during adolescence at a time in which the adolescent can step back and think about their cognitive processes (Reid, 1988). "In school situations, metacognitive awareness refers to a pupil's knowledge of tasks assigned, the solutions to be achieved, the ways to achieve it, and the cognitive strengths and weaknesses" (Mann & Sabatino, 1985, 222).

"The second type of metacognition, regulation of learning, is generally acquired quite early" (Reid, 1988, 14). "Metacognitive self-regulation, i.e., the control of one's own cognitive processes, directly affects a pupil's school performance" (Mann & Sabatino, 1985, 222). Metacognition involves one's self-regulation higher-order conceptualization skills including the following: (1) Self-Planning: predicting outcomes, scheduling strategies, (2) Self-Monitoring: testing, revising, and rescheduling the strategies, (3) Self-Checking: determining if one's actions are effective and efficient, (4) Self-Correction: monitoring and correcting errors, and (5) Self-Direction: decision-making (Mann & Sabatino, 1985).

Metacognitive planning involves predicting outcomes, scheduling strategies, and imagining forms of trial and error (Reid, 1988). Some common examples of metacognitive planning include "developing lists of things to do to help organize and complete tasks, outlining difficult reading material to facilitate comprehension, highlighting important information in reading material, and verbally repeating information to help remember" (Mercer, 1987, 235).

Another important metacognitive regulating function involves activating cognitive rules and strategies (Mussen et. al., 1990). "Cognitive strategies are planned ways of using one's cognitive abilities to achieve specific goals or results" (Mann & Sabatino, 1985, 211). Cognitive strategies include "information processing strategies, information storage strategies, and knowledge and competence expression strategies" (Mercer, 1987, 237). Specific cognitive strategies include self-questioning, verbal rehearsal, organization, memory, predicting, monitoring (Mercer, 1987).

Monitoring one's learning activities, another aspect of metacognition, involves testing, revising, and rescheduling the strategies that were planned (Reid, 1988). Regulating one's cognitive processes also involves controlling attention, memory, distraction, and anxiety (Mussen, 1990). This ability to reflect on one's own thinking allows students to "devise consciously the most effective strategies for figuring things out" (Levine, 1987, 187). "As children grow older, they not only monitor the learning process but become more likely to determine when they have reached a solution or learned what they set out to learn; that is, they evaluate the product" (Mussen, 1990, 325). "Effective metacognition skills require that one possesses cognitive strategies and use them to regulate independent learning successfully" (Robinson & Deshler, 1988, 125).

Thus, adolescents who are developing metacognitive skills gain a much greater sense of personal control over what they are learning, than do children during the early and middle childhood years. The "powers" of metacognition provide the adolescent with numerous ways of simultaneously organizing and analyzing the information to be learned; and in social situations allows them to assume another's perspective and by so doing infers correct behavior through situational observation.

## Motivation

"There is no point at which motivation ends and cognition begins" (Sorrentino & Higgins, 1986, vii). "The relationship between self-concept, motivation, and achievement has long been an integral part of humanistic and open education programs" (Biehler & Snowman, 1986, 519).

"Motivation cannot be fully understood without reference to the self-concept" (Cantor, et. al., 1986, 97) as "motivation does not reside outside the self-concept but, instead, derives from enduring self-knowledge that represents the individual's potentials, desires, and values" (Sorrentino & Higgins, 1986, 100). Motivation concerns people's goals and motives, their life tasks, and the roles or selves involved in achieving these goals.

"Motivation is the inner force that moves a person to take action toward a specific end" (Levine, 1989, 210). "Ideas about what the individual hopes to accomplish or notions about what is possible for him or her to be, to think, to feel, or to experience thus provide a specific impetus and direction for action" (Sorrentino & Higgins, 1986, 100).

Motivation concerns itself with changes in behavior and with the factors that direct the change. In the classroom the changes in behavior involve "getting students to move towards instructional goals, move into academic learning, and move forward in the acquisition of skills and values" (McDaniel, 1985, 19). Additionally, teachers are concerned with motivating students to increase time on task, to improve task completion and accuracy, to use prosocial skills in interactions with other students and adults, and to develop self-discipline and confidence. Social learning theory, however, emphasizes that regardless of the level of need, behavior is not undertaken unless there is some likelihood that the action will result in goal attainment (Brown & Weiner, 1984).

For nonhandicapped students the self-knowledge aspect of motivation serves as a "significant regulator of on-going behavior. Self-knowledge provides a set of interpretative frameworks for making sense of past behavior but it also provides the means-end patterns for new behavior" (Cantor, et. al., 1986). Motivation and metacognition interact to assist the student in evaluating their own behavior in numerous situations through perspective-taking, in determining accuracy of the behavior through social comparisons, and in providing patterns of behavior to allow them to function in socially appropriate ways.

> Motivation is a function of teaching values and character development. Students learn about the value of positive action and gain an understanding of the consequences of inaction or negative action. The key principle in motivation toward positive behavior patterns is whether the end result or goal, is considered desirable and worth the effort (Levine, 1989, 210).

## Attributions

"An outstanding characteristic of man is his capacity to sense the value in the quality of his experience. This experience value attribute is a pervasive and inseparable aspect of every experience" (Cantril, 1988, 42–43). It involves an individual's "cognitive representations of their environment: Their perceptions, inferences, and interpretations of social experience" (Graham, 1986, 39). Individuals apply their experience value attribute to all aspects of their life assessing their abilities and performances.

In school settings attributions are children's explanations and/or inferences about the causes of their academic, behavioral, or social performances and their evaluations (Forsyth, 1986). "Attributions are formed over time and result from experiences within learning contexts. They represent students' ideas about their control over learning as well as achievement" (Reid, 1988, 89).

In achievement contexts, students will usually describe their reasons for success or failure as due to some ability factor that includes both aptitude and acquired skills, a motivation factor such as temporary or sustained effort, the difficulty of the task, luck, personality, and help or hindrance from others (Cooper & Burger, 1980). The causal ascriptions used by students usually include (1) effort, (2) ability, (3) luck, or (4) task difficulty (Reid, 1988). The most dominant perceived causes of success and failure appear to be ability and effort (Graham, 1986).

The Attribution Model suggests there are three major causal dimensions or underlying properties of a cause which help to describe or explain the reasons students' ascribe certain causes to their successes and failures (Weiner, 1984). These three properties include the following: (1) Locus: the location of the cause as internal or external to the individual, (2) Stability: the stability of the cause as constant or varying over time, and (3) Controllability: the perceived personal responsibility or whether a cause is subject to ones' volitional influences (Weiner, 1984).

**Locus.** The Locus or location of the cause may be internal or external. "Internal responses reflect factors residing within children" (Reid, 1988, 89). Ability and effort are internal attributions because they reflect characteristics of the individual (Graham, 1986, 41). "External responses represent factors over which children perceive that they have little control" (Reid, 1988, 89). Task difficulty and luck are external or environmental determinants of outcomes since the student has no direct control over these factors.

Research findings show that students who typically respond with internal attributions are more confident about achieving, actually achieve at higher levels, persist on tasks because they feel that they can score well, and feel like they have control over achievement outcomes (Weiner, 1979). When students succeed they increase their confidence and sense of personal worth by attributing their performance to internal, personal factors (Forsyth, 1986). "In contrast, when students fail, they can avoid the esteem damaging consequences of their performance by denying responsibility for their performance, blaming their grades on such factors as the teacher, their home life, or the difficulty of the material" (Forsyth, 1986, 20). In other words after failures, students generally focus on external attributions such as bad luck and difficulty of the test.

Research (Dweck & Licht, 1980) indicates that students who display learned helplessness and mastery-oriented students behave similarly after successes, but when failure occurs they display significantly different reactions. After failure, mastery-oriented students show escalated effort, intensified concentration, increased persistence, more sophisticated strategy use, and enhanced performance; while helpless children show reduced efforts, deterioration of use of strategies, and disrupted performance (Dweck & Licht, 1980). Additionally, helpless students underestimate their successes, overestimate their failures, and avoid attributing their performance to ability (Diener & Dweck, 1978).

**Stability.** "The stability dimension designates causes as constant or varying across time" (Graham, 1986, 42). Ability or aptitude for certain tasks is relatively stable, while effort, mood, and task difficulty are unstable because they may show situational variance (Graham, 1986).

In attribution theory the causal dimension of stability is more closely linked to expectancy for success than locus or controllability. "Attributions for outcomes to stable causes lead to smaller changes in future expectations than do inferences to unstable causes" (Graham, 1986, 42). In other words, if the causes of events, both successes and failures, are likely to remain unchanged or stable, then one has greater confidence that these events (successes or failures) will be repeated in the future than if the causes are subject to change. Thus, when success is attributed to high aptitude or ability, a stable cause, a student is more certain of future success than if his/her success is attributed to a temporary, unstable cause such as luck.

**Controllability.** The controllability dimension of attributions refers to personal responsibility in the outcome of a learning experience or task. "Effort is controllable because individuals are believed to be responsible for how hard they try" (Graham, 1986, 42). Effort is a cause that is internal, unstable, and controllable, thus, failure due to lack of effort suggests a situation that is modifiable by one's own volitional behavior (Graham, 1986). In contrast, aptitude and luck are generally perceived to be beyond one's personal control.

"Ability is an internal, stable, and uncontrollable cause. This means that failure due to low ability is perceived as a characteristic of the failing individual, enduring over time, and beyond one's personal control" (Graham, 1986, 42).

In school settings, a great deal of evidence exists to support that high effort is rewarded by teachers more than high ability following success, and that lack of effort is punished more than lack of ability following failure (Harari & Covington, 1981). In fact, the most rewarded student is the individual who tries hard but has low ability, and the least rewarded or most punished student is the individual who has high ability but does not try (Graham, 1986).

In summary, attributions are the causes students give for their successes and failures. These causes can be divided into three separate but interacting categories including internal or external locus, stability, and controllability. Success due to internal causes such as ability and effort produces pride and positive self-esteem. Failure due to low ability results in humiliation and embarrassment (Brown & Weiner, 1984), and failure due to lack of effort produces guilt. Success due to external causes such as help from others results in gratitude, while failure due to others' hindrance results in anger. Success or failure attributed to luck result in surprise (Reid, 1988).

The stability dimension of attributions is related to expectancy for success, controllability is linked to interpersonal evaluation, and all of the dimensions are uniquely related to a prevalent set of achievement-related affects that includes pride, guilt, gratitude, shame, anger, sympathy, and hopelessness (Graham, 1986). These psychological processes then influence a variety of motivational factors including persistence, choice, and quality of performance (Graham, 1986).

"The attributions that children develop through their school history become powerful influences on their achievement strivings. Attributions are, in effect, predictions about (1) the degree of children's control over their learning, and (2) the feelings they develop about their performance" (Reid, 1988, 89). "Attributions also influence a range of academic behaviors, including examination performances, persistence at difficult intellectual tasks, and even attendance at study lessons" (Forsyth, 1986, 29).

## Academic Self-Concept of Achievers

The self-concept "which includes one's beliefs, convictions, values, and aspirations" (Battle, 1982, 30) plays an important role in the lives of all human beings. Human beings want to know that they are valued by others. They want to "experience a sense of self-worth and self-respect" (Cantril, 1988, 98). "One's successes, in addition to impressions received from significant others, are a major force in shaping one's perception of personal worth" (Battle, 1982, 29). The self-concept is generally thought to influence the way one behaves, and ones' actions, in turn, are thought to influence the way one perceives himself/herself (Battle, 1982).

There is a tendency in our society to equate achievement with human worth. "School offers the first major opportunity outside the home for a child to test his abilities and to gain admiration and respect" (Covington & Beery, 1976, 7). "Achievement is a primary means by which a child validates himself. Achievement and self-worth are inextricably linked" (Greene, 1986, 289). However, "achievement is rarely accidental" (Greene, 1986, 284). "Achieving children tend to be competitive. Through competing they seek to test themselves, their resources, and the barriers which limit their potential achievement" (Greene, 1986, 287).

"The achieving child is typically the one who pushes himself to the limits of his abilities. He not only accepts the challenges inherent in the educational system, but he also intentionally creates his own challenges" (Greene, 1986, 23). Challenges offer an opportunity for a child to learn how to use frustration constructively, to develop a sense of power and appreciation for his/her own capabilities (Greene, 1986). The achieving child receives repeated affirmations of his/her ability which results in high degrees of desire to continue achieving. This achievement motivation is the desire of a child or youth "to satisfy his or her needs, to satisfy drives to know and understand, to acquire feelings of personal adequacy, to receive approval from others, and to master the environment" (Thomas, 1980, 67).

Success and failure in school depend on a person's performance relative to personal goals and to classroom standards. "The nature of a person's goals can offer a profound insight into that person's *sense of self*" (Greene, 1986, 24). A person's goals establish a system of priorities, and serve to focus and direct intellectual, emotional and physical energies (Greene, 1986). The child who creates goals, establishes standards of performance, and prevails over challenges acquires faith in himself and a respect for the value of effort. "Accomplishing our goals enables us to exert a degree of power and control over our destiny. The attainment of our goals is a requisite to the development of self-esteem" (Greene, 1986, 25).

"In research on self-evaluation, it is widely assumed that people set themselves certain performance standards and react to their own behavior in accordance with these self-imposed demands" (Hannover, 1988, 2). When an individual's performance falls below these standards, s/he experiences a sense of failure and tends to judge himself/herself in critical ways. Successful individuals have learned to interpret success as evidence of their ability. When the individual meets or surpasses the accepted standards, s/he experiences feelings of success and well-being and judges himself/herself in self-appraising ways (Covington & Beery, 1976). When successful people fail they are more likely than unsuccessful people to blame the failure on their lack of effort rather than their lack of ability (Thomas, 1980).

Little is known, however, about how people acquire the standards that serve as goals for self-evaluation of their performance. It is probable that these standards consist of numerous items including the following: (1) prior self-produced performance results; (2) task-inherent properties, such as probability of success; and (3) performances of social comparison persons (Hannover, 1988, 6).

Research on the relationship between success in school and the self-concept has consistently shown a positive relationship between self-concept variables and academic achievement (e.g., Coopersmith, 1959; Purkey, 1970; etc.). In a series of extensive research projects carried out over the years 1962–68, Brookover and his associates reported self-concept of scholastic ability and school achievement was significantly related for both boys and girls. Self-concept accounts for a significant portion of achievement independent of measured intelligence, socioeconomic status, educational aspirations, and the expectations of family, friends, and teachers (Brookover et. al., 1964).

The academic self-concept of achievers, then, is actually three self-concepts including the student's classroom self-concept, their ability self-concept, and their achievement self-concept. The classroom self-concept of achievers suggests they are popular with peers, aware of their status in the classroom, choose to associate with others who are academically successful, and successfully meets classroom and school expectations. The ability self-concept of achievers indicates positive expectations for success, feelings of self-respect and self worth, possesses desire to succeed, understands their own cognitive processes, and attributes success to ability and effort. The achievement self-concept of achievers reveals they establish their own goals, demonstrate academic proficiency, possess a high degree of achievement motivation, demonstrate the ability to learn and use organizational skills and memory techniques (learning strategies), shows a high degree of academic success, and a sense of personal control during the learning process.

Greene (1986) suggests the primary characteristics that distinguish achievement-oriented students with a high ZQ (zest for learning) from other children include the following: (1) orientation toward goals, (2) positive expectations, (3) confidence, (4) resiliency, (5) self-discipline, (6) pride in accomplishment, (7) academic proficiency, (8) endurance, (9) courage. "Although intelligence, aptitude, potential, developed ability, and a positive self-concept are requisite to achievement, these factors alone are not enough. Desire is the fuel which transforms potential into developed ability and achievement" (Greene, 1986, 74).

## Academic Self-Concept of Underachievers

Lecky (1945) was one of the first investigators to demonstrate that academic achievement was often due to a child's definition of himself as a nonlearner. "The underachiever is in the unenviable position of lacking the ability to meet the demands of school, so that he must, unless the school makes special arrangements for him, face repeated failure" (Purkey, 1970, 22).

Much of the research conducted with underachievers to determine their motivations, attributions, and self-concept characteristics occurred prior to 1975 and the passage of P.L. 94-142, Education for All Handicapped Children Act. Much of the research since the mid-70's has involved categorically labeled handicapped children receiving educational services in various settings such as resource room or self-contained classroom.

### Classroom Self-Concept

**Interrelationships with Others.** The child's concept of himself/herself as a student, as a participant in a classroom involves many areas including his/her interrelationships with others, his/her emotional behavior at school, and his/her behaviors in the classroom as a student. Underachievers and/or "children experiencing learning problems tend to esteem themselves lower than their counterparts who do not have learning problems" (Battle, 1979, 70).

The negativeness seen in underachievers is often related to their entire life situation. Their interactions with peers and adults at home, at school, and in the community may be very unrewarding. Underachievers are often overly critical of others and exhibit asocial behavior (Gowan, 1957), either withdrawn or aggressive. Underachievers may, due to a lack of perspective-taking abilities and a lack of metacognitive skills, experience difficulty forming friendships and interacting appropriately with peers. Underachievers frequently demonstrate poor social skills, low consideration for others' feelings and property, lack dependability in interpersonal relationships, and lack feelings of belonging.

In the classroom underachievers may physically or verbally demand excessive attention and interfere with the learning of others. Underachievers may experience difficulty making judgments especially in social situations. Underachievers may be resistant to or react inappropriately to authority figures; they cannot seem to comply with the controls and expectations of parents, teachers, or peers.

Some underachieving children resist their parents in ways designed to avoid direct confrontation; they may resist passively (Greene, 1986). Passive resistance includes such behaviors as "procrastination, irresponsibility, indifference, poor work habits, deceit, and avoidance. Because the passively resistant child is often out of touch with his emotions, he may deny that he is angry, resentful, or hostile" (Greene, 1986, 261).

"Underachievers typically gravitate toward other underachievers" (Greene, 1986, 97). Associating with other underachievers may be a powerful motivation to continue the poor school and social achievement in order to belong to a peer group. Peer relationships, though important for all preadolescents and adolescents, appear to be of particular importance to underachievers (Battle, 1982). Thus, an underachiever's "fear that success would trigger resentment and jealousy in his friends may be quite justified. Fear of social rejection can traumatize a child and can be a powerful deterrent to achievement" (Greene, 1986, 97).

**Emotional Behavior at School.** There is a cyclical interaction of stress, negative self-esteem, underachievement, and emotional problems (Greene, 1986). The interactive relationship of these factors is often referred to as a *vicious cycle.* The underachieving child may be highly emotional, restless, changeable, impulsive, and unhappy (Walsh, 1956). S/he may fear social rejection, however, the stress and related emotional problems may "incapacitate a child academically and socially. They interfere with a child's ability to focus and direct his emotional, intellectual, and physical energies" (Greene, 1986, 247).

Numerous studies indicate that underachievers experience more emotional trauma, and more variable emotional feelings than average achieving peers. Underachievers demonstrate less mature behavior than peers tending to be more withdrawing, to lack self-reliance, to lack a sense of personal self-worth, and to lack a feeling of belonging (Durr & Schmatz, 1964).

Behaviors and attitudes resulting from poor school performance are generally referred to by educators as an *emotional overlay.* Problems of emotional overlay include poor self-esteem, irresponsibility, frustration, counterproductive behavior, poor self-confidence, avoidance behaviors. Children experiencing an emotional overlay and chronic school failure and frustration often develop emotional problems involving either aggression or withdrawal.

Chronic underachieving children may exhibit so much anger and frustration at inabilities that they engage in chronic misbehavior involving explosive anger, profanity, and physical attack. On the other hand, the underachieving child may be overwhelmed by frustration and hopelessness and withdraw because s/he feels incapable of meeting parents or teachers expectations. A severely withdrawn child may be subject to sadness and depression, may use emotional defenses to protect his/her self, and/or exhibit psychosomatic symptoms. "Children who fail at everything are at risk emotionally because they have no alternative sources for emotional reinforcement" (Greene, 1986, 90).

**Student Behaviors in the Classroom.** Underachievers demonstrate poor academic performance in the classroom; experience learning problems such as problems in organization, metacognition, perception, attention and memory; and possess poor academic skills and poor study skills. In learning situations frustration, anxiety, stress, and fear of failure often interfere with task focus and task completion. The student may engage in off-task behaviors such as playing with pencils or toys brought to school, staring out the window or door, hanging over the side of his chair, dropping his supplies, sharpening his pencil, hunting for paper. The purpose of the off-task behaviors is to cover-up for not working on assignments.

Underachievers in comparison to achievers tend to be more unable to delay gratification, possess greater impulsivity and less inhibition, and low academic orientation; however, they possess high social pleasure-seeking orientation, and either unrealistic long-term goals or none at all (Santrock, 1990, 223). These behaviors result in a student who is unable to derive much benefit from school.

Underachievers tend to be passive learners who do not take command of their own learning or understand their responsibility in the learning process, thus, seem irresponsible. Students who fail to progress appropriately in school usually feel negative towards themselves and emit self-defeating and self-derogatory responses.

### Ability Self-Concept

Song and Hattie (1984) indicate that ability self-concept is one of the components of the academic self-concept. "One aspect of the self that necessarily has a strong personal influence on achievement is intelligence"

(Santrock, 1990, 218). Underachievers frequently feel enormous anxiety about their intelligence and their ability to achieve academically. Without consistent reinforcement that they possess average range intelligence, and with consistent failure in academics, the underachievers may doubt that s/he has the ability to be successful in the classroom.

Underachievers frequently feel that they are "stupid" and publicly berate themselves displaying self-derogatory remarks and self-hatred. The negative self-concept indicates to the child that he is inadequate, inferior, and unworthy, thus reducing the child's feelings of self-reliance, self-confidence, and self-acceptance, and reducing or eliminating motivation to complete academic tasks.

The child who perceives that s/he does not possess the ability to meet demands of parents and teachers consistently feels distress. "Without positive reinforcement, there is a real danger that the struggling child may conclude that he is incapable of success and unworthy of appreciation" (Greene, 1986, 38). Underachievers are, therefore, pessimistic about the future.

Insecure children tend to resist change and reject the unknown. Failure and lack of appropriate performance, however, provide the underachiever with a semblance of security and control because his/her performance is predictable (Greene, 1986, 99).

> Because underachieving children seldom experience significant success at anything they undertake, they lack tangible proof of their ability. Although they may have only subtle problems, they may nevertheless conclude that they are incapable of success. This negative self-image can become a permanent part of their personalities (Greene, 1986, 101).

## Achievement Self-Concept

"Adequate functioning in our society, and the individual's conception of his own worth, depend on his ability to cope with problems, and on his self-evaluation of his achievement" (Mischel, 1971, 239). The school is the major determining variable at the 5th–6th grade level in the development of the academic self-concept, taking over the earlier role of relative achievement and home concern. The academic self-concept continues to be primarily controlled by the relative achievement standing (Burns, 1982).

The underachiever tends to have a poor perception of his scholastic performance (Borislow, 1962). "Although many compulsive underachievers actually have the ability to succeed, they are driven by unconscious psychological forces to reject success" (Greene, 1986, 24).

> ...children do not fail because they lack potential to succeed, but rather because they refuse to learn. These children are experiencing what is called *failure to learn syndrome* — a pathological condition characterized by self-defeating patterns which include underachievement, deviant behavior, and apathy and negativism which are accompanied by low self-esteem (Battle, 1982, 76).

Underachievers perform at a low academic achievement level, lack interest in academic areas, and have no stated academic goals. Low-achieving students function differently during learning activities demonstrating involvement only about forty percent of the time, while high-achieving students may spend eighty percent of their time effectively (Evertson, 1980). Additionally, high achieving students finished their academic tasks then went off-task; low-achieving students went off-task while they were working on academic tasks (Evertson, 1980). A frequent area of underachievement is in the area of reading. Achievement in reading "appears to be highly related to healthy personality adjustment. Failure in reading thus impedes a child's personal development and lowers his self-esteem, as it relates to himself and to others as well" (Battle, 1982, 76).

After a period of elective underachievement or nonachievement, the child may discover that by missing the instructional learning opportunities s/he may be seriously deficit in academic skills, study skills, and thinking skills. Careful examination of underachieving, ego-damaged children reveals several common denominators: (1) skills deficits, (2) attitudinal deficits, (3) diminished self-quotient (self-concept), (4) diminished level of expectations, (5) feelings of unworthiness (Greene, 1986, 93).

Underachieving children may experience a fear of success. Underachievers who have performed irresponsibly by refusing to study and learn, may fear success because they would be expected to be successful on a consistent basis. Underachievers are frequently given shorter assignments in less difficult books that require lower levels of performance (e.g., circling an answer rather than writing a sentence or paragraph). They may fear that they are incapable of consistent success which would require that they change not only their behaviors but also their self-perceptions.

Learned helplessness or acquired helplessness is a condition frequently seen among children functioning in the bottom groups in a classroom.

Research on children's perceptions of grouping in reading indicate that children are very aware of the status of their group even in the first grade (Greene, 1986), and are aware of the differences in teaching style and expectations. The teacher does not encourage the lower group of children to attempt assignments independently, but expects them to wait until she finishes the other groups, so that she can "spoon-feed" the assignments. As a result, these children are unlikely to attempt school tasks they perceive as difficult and lose a great deal of instructional time waiting for the teacher. Thus, teacher has taught the students to be totally dependent on her, and since this does not require the student to be invested in his own learning, responsible, independent, task-focused, or competitive, the child readily learns to be helpless.

Studies which support the notion that underachievers tend to have negative self-concepts are numerous (Purkey, 1970). There is evidence to indicate that students with negative self-concept show less accuracy and speed in problem-solving tasks and more physiological indicators of anxiety; and when the task induced failure or threat of failure, made comments about their selves rather than about the task at hand (Stennett, 1966).

Underachievers tend to have a general self-depreciation and a high degree of anxiety which demoralizes personal and academic activity (Mitchell, 1959). The degree to which a student is able to handle his anxiety is directly related to his level of achievement (Taylor, 1964).

## IMPACT OF SCHOOL ENVIRONMENT
## ON SELF-CONCEPT DEVELOPMENT

The child most likely to succeed at school is one who is both productive and happy. His behavior reflects confidence, organization, initiative, persistence, self-control, and pride in accomplishment. The successful child relates well to others. Among his peers, he is usually outgoing, friendly, popular, and able to take a leadership role. His relationship to adults and authority figures is characterized by confidence, respect, and cooperation (Wallace & Kauffman, 1978, 5).

"The goal of education from society's viewpoint is the production of adequate personalities, people who can be counted upon to behave effectively and efficiently and to contribute to the welfare of all" (Combs & Snygg, 1959, 365). However, the acceptance by the schools for the social, emotional, and affective development of children is relatively recent.

For many young children the school is second only to the home as an institution which determines the growing child's concept of himself and his attitudes toward self acceptance or self-rejection (Jersild, 1952). "Probably no other agency in our society outside the family has a more profound effect on the development of the individual's concept of self" (Combs & Snygg, 1959, 377).

"Self development is an important aim of education for several reasons. It is an important quality of the existential situation of the person, and it may be an important predictor of behavior and achievement" (Stangvik, 1979, 158). Numerous research studies have indicated that individual self-concept, particularly self-concept in academic roles, is positively related to achievement. "Because self-esteem and achievement are so closely interrelated, it is essential that educators develop procedures designed to enhance self-esteem (Battle, 1982, 101). Important variables influencing the impact of the school climate on a child's self-concept development include the teacher, the classroom climate, and their interactions.

## Teacher Influences on Self-Concept Development

"There is little question that teachers have a profound influence on students' behavior, achievement, and feelings of self-worth. The way in which the teacher interacts with a student can either seriously impede or greatly facilitate the student's success in school" (Gearheart et. al., 1988, 99). "The teacher is the most significant other affecting the self-esteem of children after they enter school" (Battle, 1982, 100). "Thus, if a child interacts with a teacher who establishes a positive teacher-pupil interactive process, the child will learn more; and this experience will have a positive effect on his self-esteem" (Battle, 1982, 117).

"Teachers cannot be truly effective if they ignore affective considerations. The relationship between the affective domain and learning is inextricable" (Kauchak & Eggen, 1989, 370). Teachers' "beliefs about the role of schools and what children should learn, their own capacity to help students, and their general philosophical approach to living all affect the decisions they make" (Kauchak & Eggen, 1989, 199). Teachers with philosophical commitments to excellence take more personal responsibility for student failures and increase their efforts to help underachieving students (Ames, 1984b). Less committed teachers are more likely to attribute lack of achievement to student shortcomings (Ames, 1984b).

"Teachers communicate many affective messages every day through the words they use, the tone of their voice, and their nonverbal cues. The topics and student behaviors the teacher emphasizes all reflect the importance he or she places on them" (Kauchak & Eggen, 1989, 370). "The relationship between the teacher and the children does not have to be informal, but it must be one in which the children feel psychologically and emotionally comfortable" (Jarolimek, 1989, 281). Teachers who are caring but firm, versus critical and harsh, not only create more pleasant classroom environments but also produce more learning (Good and Brophy, 1984).

"The nature and quality of the interaction between the teacher and student can be strongly influenced by the teacher's expectations" (Gearheart et. al., 1988, 99). "Teachers spend less effort in working with perceived low achievers" (Kauchak & Eggen, 1989, 44). Teachers are less likely to use time-consuming methods with low achievers even when the methods have been demonstrated as effective (Swan & Snyder, 1980). Teachers who work with low achievers are often less enthusiastic, teach at a lower conceptual level, and presentations are more fragmented, lacking in conceptual themes, and more vague than lessons prepared for average achievers (Good and Brophy, 1984). Teachers often give low ability students tasks that are beyond their abilities, and, consequently, too difficult to complete causing frustration and inattention (Anderson et. al., 1985).

"Teachers tend to react negatively to students in whom they perceive a negative attitude, and, as a result, the students are treated less well than those judged to have more positive attitudes" (Kauchak & Eggen, 1989, 373). "There is overwhelming evidence that those children who have poor images of themselves are not only likely to be low achievers, but they show other evidence of maladaptive behavior" (Jarolimek, 1989, 244). Thus, the vicious cycle of teacher and student negative attitudes and behaviors reinforce each other.

## Classroom Climate Influences on Self-Concept Development

"It is imperative that the teacher establish a good social climate and a classroom environment where children learn to feel good about themselves. It should be a place in which people are more valued than things" (Jarolimek, 1989). In a risk-free classroom children are not afraid to take learning risks because they do not fear failure.

## Classroom Management

It is the teacher who sets the good emotional climate of the classroom—the climate that facilitates social interaction based on trust, respect, and integrity (Jarolimek, 1989, 245). Classroom climate is concerned with the emotional tone and quality of the human relations that prevail in the classroom (Jarolimek, 1989). In order to establish an emotionally positive learning environment, the teacher must be an effective classroom manager who is well organized and focused on students' academic performance. "It is virtually impossible to manage a classroom without simultaneous effective instruction" (Kauchak & Eggen, 1989, 149).

The teacher who is "an effective manager establishes a climate with high expectations for all students; the teacher models appropriate behaviors; he or she is warm, enthusiastic, and dynamic within the boundaries of his or her natural personality; and he or she consistently communicates all these factors both verbally and nonverbally" (Kauchak & Eggen, 1989, 149). The teacher who is an effective manager is well organized. They come to class prepared and on time; they have materials, demonstrations, and activities planned in advance and ready to go. Their daily routines allow instructional time to be maximized. They interact effectively with their students both on a personal level and through skilled questioning. They communicate clearly, and their assignments are consistent with their classwork (Kauchak & Eggen, 1989).

Perhaps the most powerful force affecting classroom climate is statements made by the teacher. If the teacher uses a preponderance of negative and directive statements, the level of tension and hostility in the classroom will be elevated (Jarolimek, 1989). However, one of the most effective ways to reduce hostility and aggression in groups is to increase the number of positive, constructive statements made by the teacher, and to eliminate those that are negative, directive, and critical (Jarolimek, 1989).

## Success

Virtually all the research on abilities and personality lead one to believe that the key factor in educational attainment is that students must repeatedly experience success in school. It is through achievement that academic self-confidence grows, and increased confidence in turn promotes achievement through inspiring further learning (Thomas, 1980). In general, younger students, low achievers, and students from low socioeconomic backgrounds, need higher rates of success than their older, higher achieving, more advantaged counterparts (Kauchak & Eggen, 1989). "High success rates are one way to increase student perseverance" (Kauchak & Eggen, 1989, 71). For students of all ages, "success experiences are positive and predictable in their effect on the individual, whereas individuals are more variable in their response to failure" (Jarolimek, 1989, 228).

## Attitudes and Values

"Effective motivational and classroom management strategies also depend heavily on the teacher's ability to understand and accommodate student attitudes and values" (Kauchak & Eggen, 1989, 372). Values are standards that the human personality uses to determine what an individual perceives as important and unimportant, what s/he thinks is worth striving for, what is believed to be right and wrong (Jarolimek, 1989). "Attitudes are important because they endure unless some specific experience intervenes" (Kauchak & Eggen, 1989, 372). "Positive attitudes toward school can lead to continued and lifelong learning, while negative attitudes can result in an aversion to any kind of intellectual growth. In school, negative attitudes also result in disruptive behavior, student absences, and dropping out" (Kauchak & Eggen, 1989, 372).

Research on effective teaching has shown consistently that positive attitudes are found in classrooms where students achieve the most (Brophy & Good, 1986). We make inferences about others' attitudes based on our observations of people's verbal and nonverbal behavior (Kauchak & Eggen, 1989, 372). Generally speaking, positive feedback is more productive in maintaining a high level of motivation and promoting successful performance than is negative feedback (Jarolimek, 1989).

"Helping children build good self-images is probably the single most important thing a teacher can do in terms of the total development of a young human being. Healthy self-images develop in caring environments that help children build backlogs of success experiences. Self-images are destroyed in environments in which children get the impression that no one really cares" (Jarolimek, 1989, 244).

# SUMMARY

The child's self-concept plays an important role in the level of academic achievement attained in the classroom. Teachers have long noted that children with a positive self-concept achieve better and perform the role of student better than a child with a negative self-concept. Students with negative self-concepts frequently become underachievers in school, and may even become so frustrated and depressed that they completely drop-out of school cognitively and emotionally even if they physically attend school.

Among the self-concepts it appears that the academic self-concept composed of a classroom self-concept, an ability self-concept, and an achievement self-concept have the greatest impact on a child's academic achievement in the classroom.

Children who feel a sense of personal control over their learning and who feel responsible by taking an active role in the learning process are the most successful students. A number of self-control factors found in successful students includes possession of metacognitive skills or the ability to self-plan, self-organize, and self-monitor during the learning process. Successful students are highly motivated and spend large amounts of time on task with high rates of task completion and high rates of accuracy; use prosocial skills in interactions with other students and adults, and develop self-discipline and confidence.

In school settings children tend to attribute their successes or failures to a number of circumstances. Successful students usually attribute success to their effort and ability, while underachieving students attribute success to luck. Successful students attribute their failures to lack of effort and renew their efforts to master the assignment, while underachievers generally attribute their failure to bad luck or task difficulty. Success due to internal causes such as ability and effort produces pride and positive self-esteem. Failure due to low ability results in humiliation, and failure due to lack of effort produces guilt.

Since school achievement is a primary means by which a child validates himself, a child who is achieving successfully tends to have a positive self-concept and achievement motivation. Successful students have learned to interpret success as evidence of ability. In the classroom achievers establish their own goals, use good study and organizational skills, show a sense of personal control, possess a desire to achieve, and understand their own learning style.

Underachievers appear to not only have a negative academic self-concept but this is validated by a negative classroom self-concept, negative ability self-concept, and a negative achievement self-concept. The underachiever appears to be threatened on all sides, experiencing difficulty in adult and peer relationships, lacking the academic and social skills for success in the classroom, and constant negative reinforcement to his already negative self-concept. Underachievers experience enormous anxiety and frustration within the classroom and about the tasks required. These emotional feelings coupled with academic failure reinforce that he is inadequate and inferior, and may result in self-hatred.

For the successful child with a positive self-concept, the continued success in the school setting and the encouragement of teachers continues to reinforce positive feelings toward the self and spur the child on to continued successes. For the underachieving unsuccessful child, the teacher's behavior often serves to reinforce that s/he is unworthy of her attention and time, and the school setting and teacher's behavior continue to reinforce the negative self-concept.

# Unit Two
# CATEGORICAL PERSPECTIVES

# Chapter Six

# LEARNING DISABLED STUDENTS

*Learning disabled students tend to report significantly lower academic self-concepts than do normally achieving peers (Chapman, 1987).*

Definition of Learning Disabilities
Characteristics of Learning Disabled Students
    Academic Learning Problems
    Cognitive Learning Problems
    Social-Emotional Problems
Sense of Personal Control
    Metacognitive Deficits
    Motivation Deficits
    Attribution Deficits
Self-Concepts of Learning Disabled Students
    General Self-Concept
    Self-Concept of Academic Achievement
*Summary

---

"More than 4 million students in the nation have been identified in all categories of handicap, which is about 11 percent of the school population" (Lerner, 1989, 18). Learning disabilities is the largest category of exceptionality, comprising almost 5 percent of the total school population; speech impaired enrollment, almost 3 percent; mental retardation enrollment, almost 2 percent; and emotionally disturbed enrollment, almost 1 percent of the total school enrollment (U.S. Department of Education, 1988). These four categories of handicapped students comprise the high incidence handicap categories, and are frequently referred to as mildly handicapped categories. During the 1989–90 academic year 1,941,731 learning disabled students (an increase of 37,384 students) ages 6–21 or 47% of the total special education population were provided special education services (U.S. Office of Education, 1989).

## DEFINITION OF LEARNING DISABLED STUDENTS

"The term *learning disabilities* emerged from a need to identify and serve students who continually fail in school, yet elude the traditional categories of exceptionality" (Mercer, 1987, 29). The concern regarding functioning of learning disabled students, and interventions to prevent, remediate, or compensate for deficiencies now spans ages preschool through adulthood with current emphases for new programming at the preschool and adolescent transition levels.

Probably the most widely used definition is the one incorporated in Public Law 94-142, the Education for All Handicapped Children Act (1975). This definition, as follows, is also the basis for most state definitions:

> "Specific learning disability" means a disorder in one or more of the basic psychological processes involved in understanding or in using language, spoken or written, which may manifest itself in an imperfect ability to listen, think, speak, read, write, spell, or to do mathematical calculations. The term includes such conditions as perceptual handicaps, brain injury, minimal brain dysfunction, dyslexia, and developmental aphasia. The term does not include children who have learning problems which are primarily the result of visual, hearing, or motor handicaps, of mental retardation, or emotional disturbance, or of environmental, cultural, or economic disadvantage (USOE, 1977, p. 65083).

The operational portion of the definition of learning disabilities appears in the Federal Register (USOE, Dec. 29, 1977). "It states that a student has a specific learning disability if (1) the student does not achieve at the proper age and ability levels in one or more of several specific areas when provided with appropriate learning experiences, and (2) the student has a severe discrepancy between achievement and intellectual ability in one or more of these seven areas: (a) oral expression, (b) listening comprehension, (c) written expression, (d) basic reading skill, (e) reading comprehension, (f) mathematics calculation, and (g) mathematics reasoning" (Lerner, 1989, 7).

In summary, the federal definition of learning disabilities in P.L. 94-142 contains the following major concepts: (1) *Psychological Processing Component:* The individual has a disorder in one or more of the basic psychological processes including perceptual processing, attention, and memory. (2) *Academic Component:* The individual has difficulty in learning, specifically in speaking, listening, writing, reading and mathematics. (3) *Exclusionary Component:* The problem is not primarily due to other handicaps, such as visual or hearing impairments, motor handicaps, mental retardation, emotional disturbance, or economic, environmental, or cultural disadvantage. (4) *Severe Discrepancy Component:* A severe discrepancy exists between the student's apparent potential for learning and low level of academic achievement. (5) *Language Component:* There is an underlying language processing problem in which the child may have difficulty "in understanding or in using language, spoken or written, which may manifest itself in an imperfect ability to listen, think, speak . . . write, spell" (Lerner, 1989; Mercer, 1987; USOE, 1977).

## CHARACTERISTICS OF LEARNING DISABLED STUDENTS

A variety of characteristics have been attributed to learning disabled children. "The identification criteria presented in the 1977 *Federal Register* provide an initial framework for examining LD characteristics, with the focus on academic and language difficulties" (Haring & McCormick, 1990, 119). However, in order to be diagnosed LD the child must meet the potential-achievement discrepancy in one or more of the specified academic areas. Mercer (1987, 47) categorized the major characteristics of learning disabled students into three categories: (1) *Academic Discrepancy:* basic reading skills, reading comprehension, math calculation, math reasoning, written expression, oral expression, listening comprehension; (2) *Cognitive Problems:* short attention, perceptual, motor, memory, problem-solving, metacognition; (3) *Social-Emotional Problems:* hyperactivity, self-concept, learned helplessness, social-imperception, distractability, motivation.

### Academic Learning Problems

Academic problems are the most widely accepted characteristics of learning disabled individuals. The academic areas specified previously are indicated in the operational definition of learning disabilities. Academically, "LD children bring a configuration of skills and abilities to instructional negotiations that is more like that of younger normally achieving children than that of their peers" (Reid, 1988, 16).

#### Preschool "At-Risk" Students

It is difficult to identify young children as learning disabled because they have not as yet failed academically. P.L. 99-457 does not require that preschool children be labeled a categorical label, but that they be labeled "developmentally delayed." However, when potential learning problems can be identified early, learning failures can be reduced or prevented through enrichment, developmental, and/or remedial programs. Early screening identifies children who are likely to experience significant difficulty in school, thus, they are labeled "at-risk" for educational problems.

"Among the characteristics seen in learning disabled preschool children are inadequate motor development, language delays, speech disorders, and poor cognitive and concept development" (Lerner, 1989, 15). Preschool children are assessed in the various developmental areas to determine amount of delay in developmental milestones. These developmental areas include the following: (1) sensory acuity and perception: auditory and visual; (2) motor development: fine, gross, and perceptual-motor integration; (3) concept and cognitive development, and attention; (4) language skills: expressive, receptive, and speech; (5) social and affective development: interactions with adults, children, and the environment; (6) adaptive skills: eating, dressing, toileting. A child is frequently diagnosed "at-risk" if two or more areas are significantly delayed.

### Kindergarten and First Grade

During kindergarten and first grade, "at-risk" students frequently experience difficulty in the following areas: (1) Academic Readiness Skills: alphabet knowledge, quantitative concepts, directional concepts; (2) Language Skills: receptive and expressive; (3) Perception: visual and auditory; (4) Gross and fine motor: (5) Attention; (6) Hyperactivity; (7) Social skills (Mercer, 1987, 44).

Young children frequently experience difficulty in math due to lack of acquisition of math cognitive prerequisite skills. Lerner (1989) indicates:

The ability to count, match, sort, compare, and understand one-to-one correspondence hinges on the child's experiences in manipulating objects. The student with a short attention span, disturbed perceptual skills, or inadequate motor development may not have sufficient or appropriate experiences with activities of manipulation that would prepare for understandings of space, form, order, time, distance, and quantity (432).

Lack of understanding of cognitive concepts and language terminology such as up-down, over-under, top-bottom, more-less, larger-smaller, add-take away, minus-plus will hinder progress in mathematics processes (addition, subtraction, multiplication, and division). Children with math disabilities have been observed to have difficulty with activities that require motor and visual-perception association (Lerner, 1989).

Young children frequently experience difficulty in skills prerequisites for reading. The kindergarten–1st grade child who does not begin to discriminate some letters especially those in his/her name, who lacks left-to-right orientation, who has an inadequate conceptual background and lacks age-appropriate language development skills will probably experience difficulty in learning to read without remediation. A lack of adequate auditory skill development in phonological awareness of letter sounds, auditory attending, discrimination, sound counting, and memory will probably result in difficulty in learning to read. Additionally, the kindergarten child who experiences difficulty in reading letters and numbers, in copying geometric patterns, and in matching printed letters and words will often experience difficulty in learning to read.

## Elementary Grades

Learning disabilities first become apparent when children enter school and fail to acquire academic skills. Learning disabled children in the elementary schools experience difficulty in reading skills (word recognition and word attack), reading comprehension, arithmetic calculation and reasoning (word problems), written expression (handwriting, spelling, composition skills and written composition), verbal expression, receptive language, attention and memory, and social/emotional skills for coping in the classroom and interacting with others.

Poor fine motor skills as evidenced in the awkward handling of a pencil and in poor handwriting may result in deficits in written language production and paper-pencil tasks. Poor receptive language, poor auditory perception skills, and poor visual perception skills hamper the acquisition of adequate sight vocabulary and the development of decoding skills such as phonics. "A reader who must exert a great deal of effort to recognize words has little processing capacity remaining for comprehension" (Lerner, 1989, 353). Reading comprehension can also be hindered if the child lacks an adequate conceptual background, if the child does not get actively involved and thinking during the reading process.

Language problems of one form or another are the underlying basis for many learning disabilities. Oral language disorders include poor phonological awareness, delayed speech, disorders of grammar or syntax, deficiencies in vocabulary acquisition, and poor understanding of oral language (Lerner, 1989). Research shows that many learning disabled students do not do well in situations requiring extensive language interactions and conversations and that they are less skillful than their non-learning disabled peers in maintaining a conversation (Pearl, et. al., 1986). A majority of LD students experience problems in spelling due to poor auditory and visual perception, poor memory skills, poor phonics skills, difficulty with visualization, and poor handwriting. A combination of deficits including poor handwriting, deficient vocabulary, poor memory, and deficit concepts make creative and functional composition very difficult and nearly impossible for many learning disabled students.

Problems in math are frequently noted if the child lacks math cognitive prerequisite skills including classification, ordering and seriation, one-to-one correspondence, and conservation. "A disturbance in spatial relationships can interfere with the visualization of the entire number system" (Lerner, 1989, 433). A student with an auditory and/or visual memory deficit may be unable to recall number facts automatically, and may experience difficulty remembering the steps in computing the basic arithmetic processes (addition, subtraction, multiplication, division). Additionally, students who have difficulties with spatial relationships, and visual and auditory perception often experience difficulty with sense of direction and time. Intermediate grade LD students frequently experience difficulty understanding place value, regrouping, fractions, multiplication, and especially division because it requires the integrated use of several math processes, decimals, percent, estimating, and reasoning problems (Mercer, 1987).

> In the later elementary years, as the curriculum becomes more difficult, problems may emerge in other areas, such as social studies or science. Emotional problems also become more of an impediment after several years of repeated failure, and students become more conscious of their poor achievement in comparison with peers. For some students, social problems and the ability to make and keep friends increase in importance at this age level (Lerner, 1989, 16).

### Secondary Level: 7th to 12th Grades

"There is a radical change in schooling at the secondary level, and adolescents find that learning disabilities begin to take a greater toll. The tougher demands of the junior and senior high school curriculum and teachers, the turmoil of adolescence, and the continued academic failure all sometimes combine to intensify the learning disability" (Lerner,

1989, 16). Learning disabled adolescents frequently experience problems in reading skills, arithmetic skills, written and verbal expression, listening skills, study skills, metacognition, social/emotional skills, attention and motivation.

Research (Deshler et. al., 1980) indicates many learning disabled adolescents reach a plateau at 4th or 5th grade academic achievement during 10th grade and fail to progress. The most common academic disability of LD students is a pervasive reading disability which adversely affects performance in all subject areas. Problems in learning phonics and word analysis skills adversely effect acquiring an adequate, fluent reading vocabulary. Difficulty in understanding sequence, predicting outcomes, analyzing cause-effect, and finding the main idea adversely effect comprehension. The lack of higher level content vocabulary impedes progress in content area subjects.

Research indicates that learning disabled adolescents have poorer language and communication skills than their counterparts who are achieving normally (Johnson & Blalock, 1987). Deficits in reading and written expression are often due to underlying problems in processing oral language.

## Cognitive Learning Problems

Children and youth must develop intellectual and cognitive skills appropriate for meeting the demands of school and eventually for adult life. Major cognitive problems of learning disabled students include (1) attention problems, (2) perceptual problems, (3) memory problems, (4) problem-solving, and (5) metacognition (Mercer & Mercer, 1989).

### Attention Problems

"To succeed in school, a student must recognize and maintain thought on relevant classroom tasks and must be able to shift attention to new tasks" (Haring & McCormick, 1990, 124). "Often we find that although learning disabled students are attending, they are attending to the wrong stimuli. This problem is known as selective attention, that is, the ability to attend to relevant (central) information in the face of irrelevant (incidental) information" (Lerner, 1989, 211). "Students with attention problems cannot screen out extraneous stimuli, and irrelevant stimuli attract them" (Haring & McCormick, 1990, 124). "Dysfunctions of selective attention and selective intention are probably the most common sources of underachievement and school related maladaptation" (Levine, 1987, 15). Children with selective attention problems, may also, show reduced response to feedback and deficient self-monitoring skills. "Failure to monitor themselves causes these children to commit profuse errors; they may be resistant to checking their work, proofreading, or revising" (Levine, 1987, 25).

Many children who have deficits in attention, also, exhibit deficits in intention. These children may experience difficulty with (1) verbal disinhibition: fail to monitor what they say; (2) impulsive behavior: poorly planned, inappropriate action; (3) impulsive performance: sacrifice accuracy for rapid completion; (4) inconsistent performance: erratic academic performance and unpredictable test scores; (5) impersistence: seldom completes projects or assignments, experiences difficulty with transitions; (6) reduced response to feedback: little if any quality control, numerous errors, fail to learn from experience (Levine, 1987).

### Perceptual and Motor Disabilities

"Perception can be defined as the detection, recognition, and interpretation of sensory stimuli" (Mussen, et. al., 1990, 311). The major areas of concern include auditory perception, visual perception, tactile and kinesthetic perception, and perceptual-motor integration. "Specialists in learning disabilities have traditionally given much attention to perceptual problems that affect learning, especially to visual and auditory disabilities" (Haring & McCormick, 1990, 122). "Visual perception plays a significant role in school learning, particularly in reading" (Lerner, 1989, 286). Learning disabled children frequently experience difficulty with all areas of auditory perception, the ability to recognize or interpret what is heard.

"LD students manifest disorders in coordinating visual or auditory behaviors with motor responses" (Cheek et. al., 1989, 408). "Visual-motor integration involves the ability to integrate perceived visual stimuli with movements of body parts. Young children with visual-motor deficits may have difficulty in buttoning, cutting, copying from the chalkboard, and handwriting" (Mercer, 1987, 230). With older children one of the most significant visual-motor integration deficits involves lack of automaticity in handwriting which interferes with progress in all academic areas requiring paper-pencil responses, especially writing an essay, a term paper, answering essay questions on a test. Any activity involving eye-hand coordination and eye-foot coordination require good visual-motor integration skills.

"It has been observed clinically that learning disabled children often have difficulty in physical activities involving the use of motor skills. They may have difficulty balancing, walking, running, jumping, skipping, throwing, and catching" (Hallahan & Kauffman, 1988, 409). Learning disabled children are often observed to have "awkward motor functions, unstable balance causing frequent falls, or a lack of manual dexterity. Parents may report a delay in acquiring motor skills, such as riding a bicycle, buttoning a coat, catching a ball, or using eating utensils" (Lerner, 1989, 273). "A general description frequently used to describe the coordination of LD students is 'clumsy' " (Cheek et. al., 1989, 409). "For many learning disabled students, motor incoordination is a serious impediment. They may exhibit motor behaviors that are typical of much younger children" (Lerner, 1989, 274).

### Disorders of Memory

There are at least three stages of memory in which the child with learning disabilities could have difficulty: (1) reception, (2) storage or consolidation of data, and (3) retrieval (Levine, 1987).

**Reception Difficulties.** "LD students may have problems remembering or recalling auditory, visual, and kinesthetic information. When told or shown how to do a task, they may forget the instructions before the teacher turns around. Elementary LD students may not even be able to repeat a two-step command immediately after hearing it" (Cheek et. al., 1989, 408). Deficits in attention frequently interfere with the acquisition of sensory information.

**Short-Term Memory.** Learning disabled children and youth may experience difficulty with short-term memory and/or working memory. They may experience difficulty holding onto information while they are attempting to solve problems or read words. "Children with active working memory dysfunction may become seriously frustrated. They may study hard for examinations but find when they take tests that the material fails to cohere. They appear to do particularly poorly under timed conditions" (Levine, 1987, 115). Deficits in sustained attention, language, and high levels of anxiety often make it difficult to hold information in short-term memory long enough to process it to long-term memory.

**Long-Term Memory.** Many learning disabled students experience "difficulty consolidating data in long-term memory. Consolidation weaknesses are often seen in students who over rely on rote learning and fail to engage in elaboration. They are less prone to relate new information to their prior knowledge, nor are they apt to extrapolate, reason, or speculate upon their new knowledge" (Levine, 1987, 116). "Learning disabled children often have trouble integrating what they learn. There is some interference that prevents them from pulling information together to draw conclusions, to make associations or simply to use building blocks of information to learn material adequately" (Bley & Thornton, 1981, 13).

**Retrieval Problems.** "Retrieval dysfunctions become particularly problematic in late elementary and junior high school, when there is an enormous stress on retrieval abilities. Much of what has been learned during the earlier grades must be recalled with speed, ease, and precision" (Levine, 1987, 118). "When asked a question, an affected child's response time may be prolonged due either to slowness of retrieval of the information sought or difficulty finding the right words with which to encode a response" (Levine, 1987, 117).

**Language Processing Problems.** Learning disabled students may have difficulty remembering due to language processing problems and "poor language skills, which make verbal material particularly difficult for them to remember" (Hallahan & Kauffman, 1988, 120). They may experience specific language deficits such as recalling phoneme sequences, retrieving words within selected categories, and understanding and remembering semantic relations such as verbal analogies, cause-effect relationships, and linguistic concepts (Wiig & Semel, 1984). "Many LD children have difficulty encoding linguistic information. Their poor language skills may interfere with their remembering verbal information. Thus, many LD youth perform poorly on memory tasks in which information is remembered best through language associations" (Robinson & Deshler, 1988, 125).

**Strategy Deficits.** Learning disabled students do not spontaneously use strategies that nondisabled students readily use (Mercer, 1987). "Many learning disabled children do not use task appropriate strategies to help themselves remember in situations in which nondisabled peers typically do. For example, verbal rehearsal and clustering are strategies that efficient learners automatically use to help themselves remember information" (Robinson & Deshler, 1988, 125). It is "especially difficult for some children to use strategic maneuvers to aid registration, consolidation, and retrieval. Subvocalizing, imaging, verbal mediation, and other such techniques may feel alien to certain children, who consequently exhibit deficient memory (Levine, 1987, 121). Some students develop very little insight into the workings of their own memories, thus, fail to develop good memory strategies (Levine, 1989).

**Lack of Automatization.** For efficient learning, an individual's memory in many areas of performance must become an automatic, habitual response to stimuli. "The concept of automatization is related to retrieval memory. Automatization is rapid and unconscious (or nearly unconscious) retrieval memory" (Levine, 1987, 119). For learning disabled children, the flow of information is hampered because they have difficulty acquiring the automatization needed for successful learning (Stanovich, 1986). "Learning-disabled children are slower and more gradual in their acquisition of automatization abilities than normal learners. They must exert too much effort on tasks that should be automatic, having little left with which to attack other areas of the learning process (Lerner, 1989, 185).

## Social-Emotional Problems

"Social success with peers is of paramount importance to most school children. The avoidance of humiliation at all costs is a relentless campaign, as is the quest for friendship and popularity" (Levine, 1987, 240). "Since a deficit in social skills implies a lack of sensitivity to people and a poor perception of social situations, the deficit affects almost every aspect of the student's life and is probably one of the most crippling disabilities a student can have" (Lerner, 1989, 468–469).

Research shows that when learning disabled students are compared to their nonhandicapped peers, their social behaviors are less acceptable in the following ways: (1) Less ability to predict the consequences for their behaviors, (2) Greater misinterpretation of social cues, (3) More difficulty adapting their behaviors to the characteristics of their listeners, and (4) More frequent performance of inappropriate social behaviors (Schumaker & Hazel, 1984). Interactions with peers, teachers, parents and other adults, and siblings are frequently marred by the inappropriate behavior of the learning disabled student. Social interactions rely heavily on numerous abilities of youngsters including communication abilities: their higher-order cognitive abilities (memory, logical thinking, cause-effect reasoning, automatic generalization, social problem-solving, imitation, selective attention); metacognitive abilities (planning, self-monitoring of communication and behavior, self-assessing); motivation; attribution; and self-concepts.

## Communication/Language Deficits

"Linguistic proficiency has been shown frequently to relate to social-ization" (Levine, 1987, 263). "The learning-disabled child's tendency to have trouble communicating with others, both as a listener and as a speaker, put that child at risk to have social difficulties" (Hallahan & Kauffman, 1988, 124). They experience difficulty with syntax, semantics, the intonation system, pragmatics, transformations, tenses, pronouns, and complex or unusual wording in sentences.

**Syntax.** Many learning disabled youngsters experience problems in understanding past tense and future tense. They often live in the here and now. This factor causes enormous difficulties because they cannot monitor their behavior prior to it occurring. They are sometimes shocked at the results of their behavior. They can not predict that if they say thus and so, that Mom will get really angry or that teacher will send him to the office or that he will insult a friend.

**Semantics.** "Semantics deals with the meanings of words (including multiple meanings) and word combinations" (Oyer et. al., 1987, 60). Data on the semantic skills of LD youngsters support the notion that they have less well developed meaning systems and poorer comprehension of language than their nondisabled peers (Robinson & Deshler, 1988). "Children with language disabilities have smaller vocabularies and, thus, use fewer words to express themselves in comparison to their peers. This may mean that they communicate fewer concepts, and what they do communicate, they may communicate less effectively. Learning disabled students experience difficulty in understanding humor. Research indicates that learning disabled students did not exhibit the increase in understanding humor at the intermediate or middle school age levels that non-LD students showed (Bruno et. al., 1987).

"One of the highest levels for comprehending language involves the ability to discern information that was implied, but not provided. That ability reflects an awareness of possible causes and is yet another area in which many learning disabled youngsters have problems" (Lovitt, 1989, 154). "Understanding figurative language in the form of idioms, proverbs, metaphors, similes, or jokes may be especially difficult for language disabled children. Often figurative language is interpreted literally" (Oyer et. al., 1987, 67).

**Intonation System.** By two years of age, most children have mastered the adult intonation system. Thus, they can listen to subtle tone changes and can predict if adults and other children feel angry, happy, or sad even if they cannot understand the words they may say. Many learning-disabled children lack mastery of the intonation system, and experience difficulty interpreting emotions by listening to the intonation of someone's voice.

These "children may have difficulty adjusting language and tone of voice to a specific social situation. They may fail at integrating either accurate or adaptive feelings or emotions with expressive language. Their intonation and word choice, for example, might suggest anger and hostility when this is not actually the case, leading to misunderstanding and sometimes rejection by peers" (Levine, 1987, 158).

**Pragmatics.** Related to deficits in the intonation system are deficits in the pragmatics system. "Pragmatics refers to the use of language in a social context for a particular purpose" (Oyer et. al., 1987, 60). In order to maximally use language, children must (1) learn how to initiate a conversation, (2) take turns in conversation, (3) maintain a conversation topic, (4) change conversational topics and choose a conversation, (5) address different people by modifying their language, and (6) talk in different situations (Oyer et. al., 1987).

Numerous studies have indicated that learning disabled children, adolescents, and adults experience difficulty in the area of pragmatics which negatively affects social interactions. "Children who have difficulty with pragmatics may not consider the listener's ability to follow the speaker's train of thought" (Oyer et. al., 1987, 68). "The language disabled tend not to couch their speech in polite terms or to show consideration for others in their language use" (Oyer et. al., 1987, 69). Learning disabled children have been observed to more frequently make nasty statements to their peers, and in turn, they receive more statements of rejection from their peers (Bryan & Bryan, 1986).

Communicative incompetence reduces the social effectiveness of children who are learning disabled. Learning disabled boys appear to experience significant difficulty in adapting messages to the needs of the listener and in interpreting and responding to subtle nonverbal feedback (Knight-Arest, 1984). Learning disabled children appear to be less conversationally persuasive than non-LD peers, and more conversationally compliant, thus do not regulate the flow of dialogue (Lovitt, 1989, 159).

In addition to being widely misunderstood or misinterpreted, such children unintentionally commit many faux pas.

"As children approach adolescence, increasing social demands are made by their peers. Language disabilities may prevent children from meeting these demands (e.g., appropriate use of slang terms or coy, flirting behaviors with the opposite sex), resulting in social maladjustment, which in turn may cause increasing academic problems. Maladjustment may be manifested through anxiety, frustration, lack of motivation, or withdrawal" (Oyer et. al., 1987, 71). Research indicates that LD adolescents and adults experience difficulty in situations requiring extensive language interactions and in maintaining a conversation (Johnson & Blalock, 1987).

### Social Skills Problems

Numerous explanations for the social skills problems of learning disabled students have been postulated including the following: (1) cognitive and social cognition deficits, (2) communication deficits, (3) social imperceptiveness, (4) lack of empathy and role-taking ability. Learning disabled children and youth experience a wide variety of cognitive and communication deficits which make understanding social situations very difficult.

**Social Imperceptiveness.** The social and emotional problems of some learning disabled youngsters are due to their social imperceptions, their lack of skill in perceiving accurately the feelings and subtle responses of others (Bryan, 1977). For many learning disabled students attention deficits, impulsivity, and hyperactivity interfere with socialization efforts. It is rare to find a child with significant attention deficits near the top of the popularity poll at school because affected children who are generally inattentive to detail may have real trouble reading the social scene (Levine, 1987). "One can readily imagine how easy it would be to misinterpret inattentiveness in a social interchange as disinterest or negativism" (Hallahan & Kauffman, 1988, 124). "Children who are impulsive may also have trouble predicting social consequences, generating appropriate interactional strategies, and controlling aggressive outbursts. All of these shortcomings are apt to predispose children to rejection" (Levine, 1987, 262).

Learning disabled youngsters experience significant difficulties in interpersonal exchange and in understanding the affective states of other's because of an inability to interpret nonverbal and verbal communication.

Some learning disabled students do not "react appropriately to others' facial expressions, hand and arm gestures, posture, tone of voice, or general moods" (Mercer, 1987, 447). Numerous studies indicate that learning disabled students often do not grasp the significance of nonverbal communication including judging emotions and assessing affective expressions (Bryan, 1977).

Learning disabled children who are unable to infer emotions from verbal and nonverbal communication also have difficulty taking the perspective of others. "They lack awareness or ability to understand the emotions, motives, and intentions of other people" (Mercer, 1987, 452). "Children who are overly preoccupied with their own needs and appetites may have real trouble sharing, compromising, and in particular, taking the perspective of another child. This can seriously thwart any efforts at sustained interaction" (Levine, 1987, 261). "People with social disabilities appear to be less attuned than their peers to the feelings of others. They may use inappropriate behavior or language because they do not know if the person to whom they are reacting is sad or happy, approving or disapproving, accepting or rejecting" (Lerner, 1989, 471).

**Social Disability.** Learning disabled "students may behave inappropriately because of social cognition problems. They may not clearly understand the demands of the situation and may, for example, misread others' behavior or fail to consider others' perspectives. Thus, the source of the problem lies in cognitive limitations or misunderstandings" (Pullis, 1988, 87). "Social cognition generally refers to a child's ability to understand social interaction processes. Social cognition can involve a wide variety of cognitive processes such as perspective taking, empathy, and knowledge of social conventions of behavior. It is their knowledge base that helps direct children's social behavior or tactics" (Pullis, 1988, 86).

"Children with learning disabilities often have social and emotional behavior problems. The child with social problems may be unable to behave appropriately with peers in social situations (teasing, withdrawing, interrupting conversations)" (Mercer & Mercer, 1989, 146). They may show aggressive behavior toward a victim, throw temper tantrums, and use inappropriate language as a result of frustration over lack of academic success (Mercer, 1987). There is increasing evidence that learning disabled children experience problems in social relationships whether interacting with parents, teachers, peers, or strangers (Bryan & Bryan, 1986).

Many learning disabled students are said to have a social disability.

"Students with such deficits have been described in general as performing poorly in the kinds of independent activities expected of students of the same chronological age, inept in judging moods and attitudes of people, insensitive to the atmosphere of a social situation, displaying inappropriate behaviors, and making inappropriate remarks" (Lerner, 1989, 470).

**Peer relationships** are difficult for learning disabled individuals. Researchers have indicated that "the social life of LD youngsters is different from that of other students. They are more often ignored when attempting to initiate a social interaction. Their socially different behavior is even noted by strangers, who are able to detect reliably differences between learning disabled and non-learning disabled youngsters after viewing interactions for only a few minutes (Bryan, 1986).

Several authorities believe that learning disabled children elicit negative reactions from others because they lack social comprehension skills (Weiss, 1984). Learning disabled children tend to be either rejected or ignored by their peers, and evidence indicates that learning-disabled girls are even more at risk for social rejection and isolation than are learning-disabled boys (Hallahan & Kauffman, 1988). Research suggests that some of the negativeness emitted toward learning disabled youngsters may be due to not making appropriate eye contact with other people during conversations (Bryan, et. al., 1980).

"In conversation learning disabled students make more nasty and competitive statements and receive more rejections than non-learning disabled youngsters. When working with a partner, they tend to resist the initiatives of the partner for cooperative work.

Studies of the social skills of learning disabled adolescents showed that although many learning-disabled adolescents are not social isolates, they tend to engage in fewer activities related to extracurricular events and go out with friends less frequently than non-learning disabled adolescents (Deshler & Schumaker, 1983). "Even adolescents who have had opportunities for peer interactions and modeling as children may have failed to learn social skills. Many learning handicapped youngsters have as much difficulty learning social skills as they have with reading, writing, and arithmetic. They reach adolescence with inadequate social tools to choose the right clothes to wear, the right things to say, the right things to do" (Silverman et. al., 1983, 168).

Zigmond (1978) indicates that learning disabled adolescents do not seem to develop a broad enough repertoire of social behaviors to react differently to different situations. As a result, their behavior is often inappropriate. They also seem to lack social judgment, so are continuously getting themselves and their peers into trouble, both in school and in the community. Learning disabled "students do not seem to understand the role they play in influencing the consequences that accrue to them. They need to be taught explicitly that their classroom behaviors have an impact on how the teacher responds to them and that, depending on the behaviors they display, the teacher's response will be positive or negative" (Silverman et. al., 1983, 169).

Some learning disabled adolescents use egocentric reasoning strategies and are less able than their peers to make moral decisions based on group norms and expectations (Derr, 1986). Investigators have found that, even though learning-disabled students are aware of social norms, they admit that they are more willing than nonhandicapped peers to violate social norms by committing antisocial acts (Bryan, et. al., 1982). Learning disabled adolescents do not appear to have the skills of social metacognition which would allow them to analyze and reflect consciously on personal social ability; analyze themselves, the social scene, and its requirements (Flavell, 1985).

**Parents and teachers** view learning disabled students more negatively than their than non-learning disabled children (Lerner, 1989). Research indicated that teachers, parents, and peers rated mainstreamed LD students as deficient in task-related, interpersonal, and self-related social skills (e.g., accepting authority, helping others, expressing feelings, and having positive attitudes); and that LD children were more poorly accepted by peers in play and work situations (Gresham & Reschly, 1986). LD youngsters are likely to be rejected by parents, teachers, and peers because of their numerous problems in social behavior, language, and temperament (Bryan, 1986).

## SENSE OF PERSONAL CONTROL

### Metacognitive Deficits

Metacognition is interpreted by educational and psychological researchers as involving two processes: (1) cognitive self-awareness or knowledge about one's own cognitions, and (2) the regulation and control of the strategic aspects of cognition or one's ability to control his/her cognitions (Mann & Sabatino, 1985, 220).

Recent research has suggested qualitative and quantitative differences between mildly handicapped and average children and youth on a variety of information processing variables, including (1) efficiency of learning (capacity), (2) availability of prior knowledge (knowledge base), (3) strategies for processing information, and (4) metacognitive operations used by the learner to direct the learning process (Reschly, 1987; Reid, 1988). Learning disabled "students often fail to develop efficient and effective strategies for learning" (Reid, 1988, 16). The memory deficits of learning disabled youngsters appears to be a production deficit, or mediation deficit in which they do not automatically produce appropriate strategies for learning (Robinson & Deshler, 1988). "Similarly, LD children may not have developed a rich knowledge base as their more academically successful peers. Inadequacies in the knowledge base may be both a cause of subsequent learning problems and a symptom of LD students' failure to access existing knowledge" (Reid, 1988, 16).

"The impulsive behavior of learning-disabled students may be basically due to a lack of alternative cognitive strategies. These students respond impulsively because they do not have other ways readily at hand for coping with the learning task" (Mercer, 1987, 189). A characteristic of learning-disabled students is that they lack functional cognitive strategies. They do not know how to control and direct their thinking to learn, how to gain more knowledge, or how to remember what they learn (Mercer, 1987).

Metacognition can be divided into categories according to specific cognitive processes including metamemory, metalistening, metacomprehension, and metaattention (Hallahan et. al., 1985). These specific categories of metacognitive skills continue to involve the student's specific knowledge of his/her abilities in that area and the strategies necessary for organizing, planning, and learning the specific skills involved in memory, listening, reading comprehension, etc. and controlling one's attention for better task focus. Learning disabled children frequently experience difficulty in all areas of metacognition.

Much research has been conducted in metacomprehension in reading. This research indicates that many learning disabled children are deficient in the following metacomprehension strategies: (1) clarifying the purpose of reading, (2) focusing on the important content of passages, (3) monitoring one's understanding of the material, (4) rereading and scanning, and (5) using external sources (e.g., dictionary). It has also been found that while many poor readers lack effective cognitive strategies, others may be fully capable of exercising strategies but do not know when or how to best use them (Hallahan et. al., 1985). These readers are metacognitively deficient. They do not understand that different strategies are needed to achieve different goals (Mann & Sabatino, 1985). Metacognition distinguishes many good readers from poor readers. Poor readers acquire skills, but they seldom apply them independently in reading contexts; and they lack the self-management skills that help them know when to use a strategy and how to adapt it to ever-changing reading situations (Reid, 1988).

Research (Englert & Thomas, 1987) indicates that (1) Learning disabled students tend to produce poorly organized compositions and recalls because they have difficulty organizing their expository ideas, sustaining their expository writing, and summarizing information from single or multiple sources; (2) The performance gaps found in students' reading and writing performance were also found in their metacognitive knowledge about text organizations; (3) When planning questions learning disabled students focused exclusively on details rather than categories or groups of ideas; (4) When editing questions, learning disabled students demonstrate little or no awareness of the broader conceptual categories related to text structures that could be used to predict, generate, and monitor text ideas.

## Motivation Deficits

Recent research has established significant differences in motivation, attention, social skills, and locus of control between mildly handicapped and average learners (Reschly, 1987, 42). Teachers and parents often note that learning-disabled students do not have the motivation needed for learning academic tasks (Lerner, 1989).

**Cognitive Prerequisite Deficits.** Motivation can be viewed as goal-directed activity that involves different ways of thinking (Ames, 1984b). From a quantitative perspective, goal-directed activity is translated into time-on-task or academic engaged time (Ames, 1984b). From a qualitative perspective, goal-directed activity involves specific cognitive-mediational processes such as information processing, metacognitive processes, and attributions (Ames, 1984b, 236). Thus, motivation is a complex, multifaceted entity.

The literature is replete with information regarding learning disabled students' lack of task focus and attention difficulties. Research, also, indicates that learning disabled youngsters experience information processing difficulties including reduced speed or efficiency in elementary information processing operations; problems integrating knowledge from previous learning; difficulty using strategies in acquisition, memory, and problem-solving; and, lack of automaticity in metacognitive processes (Palinesar & Brown, 1987). Thus, LD youngsters may lack the cognitive prerequisites to maintain or increase academic engaged time (quantitative perspective of motivation), or to utilize cognitive-mediational processes (qualitative perspective of motivation) in sustaining motivation.

**Inconsistent Motivation.** Learning disabled children and youth frequently experience difficulties in consistently maintaining motivation and often experience a loss of motivation. Like all humans, children with deficits of attention and intention have little difficulty performing under conditions of high motivation (Levine, 1987).

> The real issue is how effectively a child concentrates and produces under moderately motivating conditions. This is indeed what separates children with intention problems from those without such problems. The former are less able to be productive unless the content and/or potential rewards are intensely compelling (Levine, 1987, 32).

Thus, inconsistent performance may relate to variations in levels of motivation (Douglas, 1983).

**Lack Independence.** "One characteristic of children with learning disabilities is that they do not develop a schema that promotes active, independent learning" (Beckman & Weller, 1990, 26). Due to lack of automaticity in metacognitive skills, learning disabled children are frequently unable to plan and organize for task completion whether a daily assignment or a term paper. They lack the ability to monitor their progress toward task completion and plan needed time allotments. They frequently are unable to monitor their own errors, and to evaluate the accuracy of task performance once the assignment is completed. This lack of metacognitive skills often results in a student who is dependent on others to plan and organize academic tasks and to depend on others to determine if the finished product is accurate. Many learning disabled individuals lack the motivation needed to complete tasks and reach goals independently. Because of these problems, they frequently must rely on others for motivation, direction, and approval (Beckman & Weller, 1990).

**Visual Image Deficits.** Learning disabled students frequently do not appear to be motivated by the rewards associated with appropriate academic behavior. "Verbal descriptions of motivational systems are often ineffective because exceptional learners are unable to maintain a mental image of them. To perform at their maximum potential, these students need concrete, visible examples of the contingency arrangement" (Raschke & Dedrick, 1989, 62).

**Lack or Loss of Motivation.** This lack of motivation may be the consequence of chronic academic failure. When students learn to doubt their intellectual abilities, they come to view their achievement efforts as futile" (Lerner, 1989, 475). "Each LD student, by definition, has experienced significant and often prolonged academic failure" (Pullis, 1988, 78). Negative feelings about the self in the student role are often manifested in two areas—lack of motivation on tasks and classroom misbehavior (Pullis, 1988). Children who have developed negative feelings about their academic performance often will not be very task oriented because their school experiences cause them to anticipate failure, feelings of incompetence, and embarrassment (Pullis, 1988).

Children who appear to lack motivation may engage in numerous avoidance behaviors to prevent failure and feelings of incompetence such as not starting tasks without several reminders, asking many questions about the quality of their work, or looking busy without actually finishing any academic tasks. Some students' avoidance behaviors may involve withdrawal in terms of "excessive daydreaming, psychosomatic illnesses, truancy, or even fear of school," while other students may resort to acting out behaviors "such as excessive talking during work periods, out-of-seat behavior, aggression toward peers, and conflicts with the teacher concerning compliance with rules or assignments" to such a degree that the student is removed from the classroom. (Pullis, 1988, 82).

Personal priorities can affect motivation. For some learning disabled children and youth, completing academic tasks in school rank low in their priorities. "Their perception that what they are being asked to memorize is irrelevant, remote from their current interests and future plans, makes it especially hard for them to consolidate such data in a meaningful manner" (Levine, 1987, 123). Some children may be motivated to strive for success in one subject area or situation and not in others, which may also be a coping strategy to avoid failure. "If a particular goal requires too much effort or too much delay of gratification, or if it greatly exceeds the capacity of a child's attention, it may be abandoned" (Levine, 1987, 424). Thus, it is not unusual for children who have experienced continual frustration in the classroom to merely "give up" trying to meet the demands of the school situation.

Children rapidly lose motivation when they perceive the likelihood of success as minimal. Children have little tolerance for failure and are commonly drained of motivation when they are least likely to succeed. They have a common, innate sense that it is better not to try at all than to make an effort and fail. This is true in the classroom, on the playing field, and in social settings (Levine, 1987, 424).

### Attribution Deficits

Studies of motivation in learning-disabled students often involve an analysis of the students' style of attribution or their ideas concerning the causes of their academic successes and failures (Lerner, 1989). "Good students tend to attribute their successes and failures to their own efforts or actions (reflecting an internal locus of control). They persevere on difficult tasks, delay gratification, and are actively involved in the learning situation" (Lerner, 1989, 475).

"There is considerable evidence that children's causal attributions (personal analyses of reasons) for failure are good predictors of their responses to difficulties in achievement situations" (Levine, 1987, 425). Learning-disabled "students often attribute their successes and failures to factors outside of their control (reflecting an external locus of control). They attribute success to luck or to the teacher, and they blame failures on their lack of ability or the difficulty of the task" (Lerner, 1989, 475). Children "who believe somehow that uncontrollable forces, such as their innate inability, caused them to fail are likely to respond in a helpless fashion. This is typically accompanied by a loss of motivation, a sense of diminished expectancy from goals" (Levine, 1987, 425). LD children and youth have been labeled "at risk for developing learned helplessness" (Hallahan & Kauffman, 1988, 125), a belief "that one simply does not have the ability to succeed and therefore any intensification of effort would be doomed to failure" (Levine, 1987, 425).

> Research "points to the learning-disabled child as one who does not believe in his or her own abilities (learned helplessness), has an inadequate grasp of what strategies are available for problem-solving (poor metacognitive skills), and is unable to produce appropriate learning strategies spontaneously. The picture we get is of a child who does not actively involve himself or herself in the learning situation" (Hallahan & Kauffman, 1988, 125).

Several researchers found that the locus of control orientation may effect the success of specific teaching strategies. Pascarella et. al., (1983) found that students with internal locus of control made greater progress using the low structure independent teaching strategy, while the students with external locus of control made greater reading progress using high structure and a direct-teaching strategy. Rogers & Saklofshe (1985) found that learning disabled children with external locus of control orientation (general and academic) and high academic self-concepts were rated as more successful in their special programs than those with internal orientations and low academic self-concepts.

> Learning disabled children appear to have a distinctive and different set of affective characteristics in comparison with normally achieving children. These characteristics are marked by low self-perceptions of ability, reflecting relatively negative academic self-concept, along with tendencies toward learned helplessness and lower expectations for future success in school. LD children therefore have relatively little confidence in their ability and expect to achieve at lower levels, but when success does occur, they see it as being caused by a teacher's assistance or easy work (Chapman, 1988, 362).

In essence, the attribution studies indicate that learning disabled children differ from their more successful peers on many personality variables considered important for school learning. "Special program teachers, in particular, should be aware of varied affective characteristics among learning disabled children. This variation may hold important implications for planning and implementing special programs (Rogers & Saklofshe, 1988, 276).

## SELF-CONCEPTS OF LEARNING DISABLED STUDENTS

Recent research and literature focusing on the affective characteristics of learning disabled students specify the need to consider a number of affective characteristics rather than just a general self-concept. These affective characteristics include general and academic self-concepts, locus of control, performance expectations, and social characteristics.

### General Self-Concept

Self-concept, the general way in which one sees oneself, has been investigated in numerous studies comparing learning disabled students to other handicapped and nonhandicapped students. "In general, the investigation of self-concept differences between learning disabled and normally achieving children has yielded inconsistent results" (Gresham,

1988, 294). Numerous researchers have reported that learning disabled students have significantly lower or more negative self-concept scores than nonhandicapped or normally achieving peers (e.g., Jones, 1985; Rogers, 1983; Battle, 1981). Other researchers, however, reported no significant differences between the general self-concepts of the learning disabled and normative populations (Silverman & Zigmond, 1981; Vallecorsa, 1980).

Conceptually, there are a number of possible reasons for inconsistent self-concept results. (1) Constructs such as self-concept or self-esteem are vaguely defined and do not point to any clear operational definitions (Harter, 1978). (2) A bewildering array of operational definitions, hypotheses, and instruments are utilized in self-concept research. (3) The definition of learning disabilities is operationalized in numerous ways, thus, the populations may not truly be comparable. (4) Different investigators have employed different research designs, studied a wide range of ages, and made use of numerous different tests and measures, which further restricts the possibility of arriving at comparable conclusions (Pringle, 1964).

As previously mentioned (Chapter 1), the self-concept is currently viewed as complex and multifaceted. A number of factors are considered relevant to the development of the student's self-concept including athletic skill, personal physical attractiveness, social attractiveness, special aptitudes, intelligence, academic performance, peer acceptance, moral code, and leadership qualities. Thus, individuals may simultaneously have positive and negative perceptions regarding various aspects of their personality and their abilities to function in their world. More consistent research results may be achieved by analyzing the separate factors of self-concept rather than trying to determine a generalized self-concept.

## Self-Concept of Academic Achievement

An extensive body of literature indicates that success and failure in school is influenced not only by cognitive abilities, but also by various affective and motivational variables (Dweck, 1986). Several researchers have revealed that the correlations between intelligence test performance and scholastic achievement account for only 25 to 50 percent of the variance associated with predicting achievement from intelligence quotients alone (Zigler, 1966). Accordingly, the effect of noncognitive variables on academic achievement accounts for 50 to 75 percent of the variance. In fact, at the kindergarten level a self-concept evaluation is a more accurate predictor of second grade reading achievement than a mental age evaluation (Wattenberg & Clifford, 1964).

## Academic Self-Concept

The cognitive-motivational characteristics of learning disabled children including academic self-concept, locus of control, and achievement expectations appear to be significantly related to success and failure in school (Chapman, 1988). Research has suggested that the academic self-concept was formed before the end of the third grade and that it quickly stabilized as patterns of school success and failure were established (Battle, 1981). Studies with learning disabled children suggest that decrements in academic self-concept occur by age 8 or 9 (around Grade 3) and remain relatively stable through at least Grade 10 (Chapman, 1987).

Numerous studies indicate that learning disabled children tend to report significantly lower academic self-concepts than do non-learning disabled or normally achieving peers (e.g., Chapman, 1987; Bryan & Bryan, 1986). Academic self-concept appears to be consistently stronger in predicting grades and academic achievement than academic locus of control and achievement expectations for both learning disabled and nonlearning disabled students (Chapman, 1988).

## Locus of Control

Reviews of the literature on locus of control suggest that the non-disabled child is external for both success and failure at the age of 4 to 5 years, becomes internal for success by age 6 to 7 years, and finally becomes internal for both success and failure by the age of 10 to 11 years (Lawrence & Winschel, 1975). Children with learning disabilities do not follow this typical pattern and are more external in their orientation than nondisabled children of the same age (e.g., Rogers, 1983; Snyder, 1982). Additionally, when internality does develop for learning disabled children, it is internality for failure (a result of their behavior) and not for success (chance or action of others) (Chapman & Boersma, 1979). Learning disabled children take significantly less responsibility for their academic successes and failures than normal achievers (Rogers & Saklofske, 1985).

## Achievement Expectations

Learning disabled children have been portrayed as lacking confidence in their ability to positively influence learning outcomes (Bryan, 1986), as having more negative perceptions of their ability (Chapman, 1988), and as having relatively low expectations for future successful achievement outcomes (Rogers & Saklofske, 1985). It would "seem likely that negative self-concepts, external locus of control beliefs and low academic performance expectations should have a detrimental effect on persistence and effort in learning situations, leading to failure experiences" (Rogers & Saklofske, 1985, 276). The relationship between academic failure experiences and negative affective characteristics is likely one of reciprocal interaction.

## Social Deficits

"Deficits in academic self-concept usually co-exist with poor peer acceptance/rejection, deficits in positive social behaviors, and excessive negative social interaction patterns" (Gresham, 1988, 295). Collectively, this suggests that students with learning disabilities are paying a high social-psychological price for their poor academic achievement.

Gresham & Reschly (1986) studied perceptions of teachers, parents, and peers for learning disabled and non-learning disabled youngsters using rating scales. The results indicated that teachers, parents, and peers rated mainstreamed learning disabled students as deficient in task-related, interpersonal, and self-related social skill domains. "LD children's social interaction problems may exacerbate their academic problems. If they are not able to interact effectively with their classmates or teachers, their school experiences (which may already be marked by severe academic failure can become even more negative)" (Pullis, 1988, 86).

## Anxiety

One of the few characteristics that all learning disabled students have in common is failure in school. The failure to learn leads to adverse emotional responses including feelings of self-derision, poor ego perception, and anxiety which augment the failure to learn syndrome (Lerner, 1989). "Within the social learning theory, anxiety is often viewed as a series of responses indicative of low-expectancy of success in a valued-need area" (Margalit & Zak, 1984, 537). High anxiety levels are considered to be related to low self-concept scores (McCandles, 1967), and to reduced efficiency of the cognitive processes (Tobias, 1979).

Learning disabled students experienced significantly negative self-concepts in comparison to other handicapped and nonhandicapped children, and high anxiety levels due to their perceived intelligence and school status, and physical characteristics and attributes (Jones, 1985).

Various studies of learning disabled children have suggested that a loss of self-esteem, high levels of performance anxiety, and even clinical depression are further complications of learning disabilities (Levine, 1987). "Success is essential for normal development. Children who are achieving mastery in no area, those with no recent triumphs, are very much at risk" (Levine, 1987, 426). Childhood depression is a common psychiatric complication of developmental dysfunction as between 10 percent and 20 percent of children with learning disabilities have been found to have significant depression (Stevenson & Romney, 1984).

## SUMMARY

The federal definition of specific learning disabilities contains five major components or concepts including (1) Psychological Processing Component, (2) Academic Component, (3) Exclusionary Component, (4) Severe Discrepancy Component, and (5) Language Component. In operationalizing the federal definition numerous approaches have been used, however, most include an academic component and a severe discrepancy component. Therefore, a student is considered to have a specific learning disability if s/he does not achieve at the proper age and ability levels when provided appropriate learning experiences, and demonstrates a severe discrepancy between intellectual ability and achievement in one or more of the following areas: Oral expression, listening comprehension, written expression, basic reading skills, reading comprehension, mathematics calculation, mathematics reasoning, and/or pre-academic skills.

The major characteristics of elementary and secondary learning disabled students can be categorized into three areas: (1) academic deficits, (2) cognitive deficits (attention, perceptual, motor, memory, problem-solving, metacognition), (3) social and emotional problems (hyperactivity, self-concept, learned helplessness, social imperception, distractability, motivation). It is difficult to identify preschool children as learning disabled because they have not as yet failed academically. During kindergarten and first grade potential learning disabled students frequently experience difficulty in academic readiness skills (alphabet knowledge, quantitative concepts, directional concepts), language, perceptual skills, motor, attention, and social skills.

The social-emotional problems of learning disabled students may be their most serious weakness. The social behaviors of many learning disabled students are less acceptable than their nonhandicapped peers as they evidence (1) less ability to predict the consequences for their behaviors, (2) greater misinterpretation of social cues, (3) more difficulty adapting their behaviors to the characteristics of their listeners, and (4) more frequent performance of inappropriate social behaviors. Numerous explanations for the social skills problems of learning disabled students have been postulated including the following: (1) cognitive and social cognition deficits, (2) communication deficits, (3) social imperceptiveness, (4) lack of empathy and role-taking ability. Learning disabled adolescents do not seem to develop a broad enough repertoire of social behaviors to react differently to different situations.

Research indicates that learning disabled youngsters demonstrate a reduced sense of personal control in all aspects of their lives as compared to nonhandicapped peers. Metacognitive deficits render them less aware of their own cognitive abilities, and unable to regulate and control strategic aspects of their cognition. Thus, they often fail to develop efficient and effective strategies for learning. They do not know how to control and direct their thinking to learn, to gain more knowledge, or how to remember what they learn. Learning disabled youngsters frequently experience difficulties in consistently maintaining motivation and often experience loss of motivation. Learning disabled children who have developed negative feelings about their academic performance often will not be very task-oriented because their school experiences cause them to anticipate failure, feelings of incompetence, and embarrassment. Learning disabled youngsters often attribute their successes and failures to factors outside of their control (reflecting an external locus of control), thus, they do not believe in their own abilities and do not understand the role of their effort in the success or failure.

# Chapter Seven

# MILDLY MENTALLY RETARDED STUDENTS

*A major requirement for acceptance by society is appropriate social behavior. One of the major problems in individuals with intellectual deficits is a parallel deficit in social behavior* (Kramer et. al., 1988, 48),

---

"Mental retardation generally refers to delayed intellectual growth and is manifested in inappropriate or immature reactions to one's environment and below average performance in the academic, psychological, physical, linguistic, and social domains" (Patton et. al., 1990, 33). In its Eleventh Annual Report to Congress, the United States Department of Education (1989) indicated that over 601,288 mentally retarded youngsters between 6 and 21 years of age were being educated in America's public schools. Fifteen percent of the handicapped children served under P.L.94–142 were labeled mentally retarded.

## Definitions and Classifications of Mental Retardation

"Mental retardation definitions have varied considerably over the years and between disciplines" (Drew et. al., 1988, 7). The 1973 definition of mental retardation by the American Association on Mental Deficiency was incorporated into P.L. 94–142.

### Definitions of Mental Retardation

The American Association on Mental Deficiency (AAMD) definition of mental retardation has undergone several changes with major educational ramifications. "Three major components have consistently (with certain revisions) appeared in all of the AAMD definitions: subaverage general intellectual functioning, impairments in adaptive behavior, and manifested during the developmental period" (Morrison, 1988, 142).

The 1959 and 1961 AAMD definitions by Heber stated, "Mental retardation refers to subaverage general intellectual functioning which originates during the developmental period and is associated with impairment in adaptive behavior" and indicated that subaverage general intellectual functioning was "greater than one standard deviation below the mean" (Patton et. al., 1990, 46) or below IQ 85 on the Wechsler scales. Additionally, impairment in adaptive behavior refers to the effectiveness of the individual to adapt to the natural and social demands of his environment which may be reflected in (1) Maturation, (2) Learning, and (3) Social Adjustment (Patton et. al., 1990), and the condition must be manifested during the first 16 years of life (Morrison, 1988).

The 1973 American Association on Mental Retardation (formerly AAMD) revised definition stated, "Mental retardation refers to significantly subaverage general intellectual functioning existing concurrently with deficits in adaptive behavior, and manifested during the developmental period" (Grossman, 1973, 11). However, the 1973 definition specified that significantly subaverage general intellectual functioning was "two or more standard deviations below the mean" (Patton et. al., 1990, 46) or measured intelligence below IQ 70. Adaptive behavior was "defined as effectiveness or degree with which the individual meets the standards of personal independence and social responsibility expected of his age and cultural group" (Patton et. al., 1990, 46). The developmental period was extended to age 18 years.

"According to the 1961 AAMR definition, almost 16% of the general population could have been identified as mentally retarded from a purely psychometric perspective," while the 1973 definition considered "less than 3% of the population" as mentally retarded (Patton et. al., 1990, 44). This change in definition "resulted in the technical declassification of approximately 13% of the total [mentally retarded] population by lowering the ceiling IQ score from 85 to 70 (Wechsler scales)" (Polloway & Smith, 1988, 9). By complementing IQ with adaptive behavior, the 1973 definition clearly decreased the potential number of individuals who could accurately be identified as mentally retarded (Polloway & Smith, 1988, 10). Thus, "the 1973 revision of the definition resulted in a reduction by more than eighty-five percent of the number of individuals who could be identified as mentally retarded" (Patton et. al., 1990, 44).

The 1973 AAMD definition of mental retardation was accepted and implemented into P.L.94–142, the Education for All Handicapped Children Act. "The 1983 AAMR definition suggests using a flexible upper IQ range of 70 to 75 rather than an exact cutoff of 70" and the developmental period was extended to the "period of time between conception and 18 years of age" (Patton & Polloway, 1990, 200). Adaptive behavior was considered to involve several major perspectives depending on age ranges including the following: **Infancy and Early Childhood** —sensory-motor skills, self-help skills, communication skills, and socialization; **Childhood and Early Adolescence** —application of basic academic skills in daily life, and application of reasoning and judgment in mastery of the environment, social skills; **Late Adolescence and Adult Life** —vocational and social responsibilities and performances (Grossman, 1983). In practice the IQ score continues to be granted the greatest weight in determining if a child is labeled mentally retarded, although adaptive behavior scales are usually administered as confirming evidence.

## Classifications of Mental Retardation

"Mental retardation can be classified in numerous ways: the two most common methods are (1) by etiology, and (2) by severity" (Patton & Polloway, 1990, 202).

**Classification by Etiology.** "There are essentially two major groups of causes: biological and psychosocial. Biological causes, frequently easier to identify than psychosocial causes, have traditionally been associated with moderate, severe and profound forms of retardation" (Patton & Polloway, 1990, 207). "Although the specific cause of severe retardation can be isolated in most cases, specific causation can be attributed in very few cases of mild retardation" (Cartwright, 1989, 232). "Psychosocial causes play a significant role in many cases of mild retardation and are hypothesized to interact with inherited traits" (Patton & Polloway, 1990, 207).

The AAMR has designated the following ten categories for classifying the causes of mental retardation: (1) *Infections and intoxicants* (e.g. rubella, drugs, alcohol); (2) *Trauma or physical agent* (e.g. anoxia birth injury, irradiation); (3) *Metabolism or nutrition* (galactosemia, hypoglycemia, PKU); (4) *Gross brain disease* (e.g. tumors, Huntington's chorea); (5) *Unknown prenatal influence* (e.g. spina bifida, hydrocephalus); (6) *Chromosomal abnormality* (Down's syndrome, fragile X syndrome); (7) *Gestational disorder* (prematurity, low birth weight); (8) *Psychiatric disorder* (e.g. psychosis); (9) *Environmental influences* (e.g. psychosocial disadvantage, severe neglect); (10) *Other Conditions* (e.g. blindness, deafness) (Cartwright et. al., 1989).

**Classification by Severity.** Classifying retardation by severity is frequently used by a wide range of disciplines. The classification system cited most often is the AAMR system which uses the terms **mild** [IQ 56–70], **moderate** [IQ 41–55], **severe** [IQ 26–40], and **profound** [IQ 25 and below]" (Patton & Polloway, 1990, 202).

"Historically, terms such as **educable** and **trainable** (corresponding to **mild** and **moderate,** respectively) have often been used in school environments and in the literature" (Patton & Polloway, 1990, 202). The educator's classification scheme contains three subgroups: (1) educable mentally retarded (EMR) with IQs from about 50 or 55 to 70; (2) trainable mentally retarded (TMR) with IQs from 30 or 35 to 55; and (3) severely and profoundly mentally handicapped (SPH) with IQs of about 30 or lower (Cartwright et. al., 1989).

"The cause of most cases of mild retardation is unknown" (Thomas & Patton, 1990, 198). The mildly retarded typically come from low socioeconomic status circumstances. This is true regardless of race or ethnicity, and has been reported in studies conducted throughout the Western world" (Reschly, 1988).

## Characteristics of the Mildly Mentally Retarded

"While the slower rate at which these children develop motor, social, and language skills may be noticeably different from their peers', mild retardation is often not suspected until the children enter school" (Thomas & Patton, 1990, 199). "They do not exhibit any physical stigmata suggestive of mental retardation or any other handicap. They are usually regarded as functioning within broadly defined normal limits by other members of their family" (Reschly, 1988, 23). The first indication of mild retardation is often a combination of difficulty with academic subjects and behavioral problems which results in repeated failure in educational settings (Thomas & Patton, 1990). Most students classified as mildly mentally retarded obtain IQ scores between about 55 and 75, and have been retained one or more times prior to being formally classified as mildly mentally retarded (Reschly, 1987, 23).

## Cognitive and Language Learning Problems

"By definition, mentally retarded individuals have delayed intellectual functioning. Of interest to those working with these individuals is . . . the impact it has on the way the children learn and on their ability to perform the skills critical to functioning in real-life situations later on" (Morrison, 1988, 154). In many ways, the intellectual problems of children with retardation are reflected in lessened rate and capacity for learning, and for acquiring new concepts and information (Cartwright et. al., 1989). Mildly retarded individuals progress at one-half to three-fourths the rate of their average-intelligence peers; they appear to have a higher "forget rate"; and they do not reach the academic levels of average nonhandicapped peers. Research regarding the cognitive functioning of mildly retarded children and youth has generally focused on the subprocesses of cognitive functioning including attention, information processing, learning efficiency, transfer generalization, and level of learning.

**Attention.** Persons who are retarded seem to have significant difficulty in the three major components of attention: (1) attention span; length of time on task; (2) focus: inhibition of distracting stimuli; and (3) selective attention: discrimination of important stimulus characteristics (Patton & Polloway, 1990). Thus, mildly mentally retarded individuals have short attention spans, and attend to task for only brief periods before being distracted by extraneous stimuli. They experience difficulty in tuning out noises, movement, and other classroom activities in order to concentrate on their assignment. Frequently, they are unable to determine what they should pay attention to—teacher talking to another group, their neighbors whispering, or their partners in a collaboration activity. Mentally retarded individuals are deficient in the number of dimensions that can be attended to at any one time (Morrison, 1988). For example, a primary grade mildly mentally retarded child may categorize by two dimensions simultaneously—color (red and blue) and shape (blocks), but be unable to categorize by several examples of size, shape, and color simultaneously.

**Information Processing.** "The ability to remember is critical to the cognitive functioning of any individual" (Morrison, 1988, 155). Research studies of the information processes of the mentally retarded reveal that these individuals are deficient in information processing skills involving sensory input, speed, attention, short-term memory, transfer, and access to memory. It is suggested that at least part of the information processing deficit in mildly retarded individuals is due to sensory input limitations in the visual cortex which processes less visual information and at a slower rate than nonhandicapped students (Saccuzzo & Michael, 1984).

**Short-term memory** problems appear to be characteristic of retarded individuals and arise primarily from their inability to automatically use rehearsal strategies such as verbal rehearsal, and image rehearsal (Mercer & Snell, 1977). Mentally retarded individuals fail to spontaneously use strategies that facilitate transfer of information through the memory systems (Morrison, 1988). The capacity of the short-term or working memory is smaller among retarded individuals than among normal persons (Brown, 1974), thus, the amount of information placed in long-term memory storage is reduced as well. Most researchers contend that once learned, information is retained over the long term about as well by those with retardation as those without (Patton & Polloway, 1990).

In addition, **long-term memory** deficits among the retarded have been observed in capacity and access to long-term memory. "Differences in knowledge (contained in long-term memory) clearly influence what will be attended to, what will be perceived, and the likelihood of passing new information into long-term memory" (Kramer et. al., 1988, 45). Mentally retarded children appear to have less information stored in long-term memory and, therefore, have fewer concepts that can be related to and integrated with new information. Access to long-term storage may be significantly reduced if mentally retarded individuals forget labels for concepts and categories, and thereby, be unable to retrieve information.

**Learning Efficiency.** "Mentally retarded individuals are, as a group, inefficient learners. It is this characteristic more than any other that distinguishes them from their nonretarded peers" (Kramer et. al., 1988, 43). Mentally retarded learners are generally characterized as passive learners who do not spontaneously use appropriate strategies (Loper, 1980). "Not only are retarded individuals less efficient in formal learn-

ing situations, many believe that these individuals are especially deficient in acquiring information and skills in informal or naturally occurring
situations" (Kramer et. al., 1988, 43).

Incidental learning is not an effective means of gaining information
for retarded children. "Children who are retarded often do not acquire
information that is peripheral or incidental to the main point of attention.
They do not seem to be able to handle as many different pieces or kinds
of information at one time as normal children can. Consequently, information not directly relevant to the task being performed may not be
acquired" (Cartwright et̃. al., 1989, 236).

**Transfer Generalization.** "Students who are retarded tend to show
deficiencies in the ability to apply knowledge or skills to new tasks,
problems, or stimulus situations" (Patton & Polloway, 1990, 210). "The
ability to profit from experiences and to generalize is poor for individuals who are retarded. Therefore, it takes more time for them to form a
learning set (a systematic method of solving problems)" (Cartwright et.
al., 1989, 236). In order to facilitate generalization, students must be
expected to perform similar tasks in various settings, using numerous
learning materials, and with various teachers.

**Level of Learning.** "Most authorities agree that children who are
retarded perform better on learning tasks that are straight forward and
concrete rather than highly abstract" (Cartwright et. al., 1989, 236). "The
ability to engage in abstract thinking or to work with abstract materials is
usually limited. Symbolic thought, as exemplified by introspection and
hypothesizing, is restricted. It is a common assumption that individuals
who are mildly retarded will not reach Piaget's (1970, 1971) level of
formal thought and thus even as adults will be limited to engaging in
thought consistent with the stage of concrete operations" (Patton & Polloway,
1990, 210).

Studies reveal that a critical difference between retarded and nonretarded learners is the ability to reason (plan ahead, exhibit foresight,
and understand relations); and that mentally retarded individuals are
behind not only their chronological-age nonretarded peers, but also
their mental-age nonretarded peers (Spitz, 1979).

**Language Deficits.** The development of speech and language is closely
associated with intellectual development; therefore, it is not surprising
that mentally retarded individuals display more problems in these areas
than nonhandicapped students (Patton & Polloway, 1990). "Where environment appears to play a large role in the etiology of the retardation, as

it does for many who are mildly retarded, language deficits may be related to such factors as absence of or limited adequate speech and language models and less encouragement to use language" (Thomas & Patton, 1990, 219). Research indicates that nearly 90 percent of students labeled mildly retarded have speech and language disorders (Epstein et. al., 1989).

Mentally retarded students experience a higher prevalence of speech problems especially in articulation areas of substitution and omission of sounds which decrease the intelligibility of speech. Articulation and voice problems are probably a result of marked delays in motor development (Edwards & Edwards, 1970).

Delayed language development is associated with mental retardation (Morrison, 1988). These language delays are cognitive, not developmental (Bowerman, 1976), and are similar to the language development found in younger children who are of the equivalent mental age (Morrison, 1988). This delayed language development has been evidenced in a number of language areas including the following: restricted vocabulary development, auditory discrimination, incorrect grammatical structure and usage, and sentence length; pragmatic language; delayed oral language development.

Language difficulties experienced by mildly retarded students include the following receptive language difficulties: (1) Problems understanding verbal receptive language; (2) Inability to determine main idea of orally presented information; (3) Experiences difficulty in discriminating similar sounding words; (4) Problems repeating a series of words or digits that were orally presented; (5) Problems understanding abstract information and directions; (6) Experiences attention deficits in processing verbal directions (Patton & Polloway, 1990; Wallace et. al., 1989). Expressive language difficulties of mentally retarded children include the following: (1) Difficulties with verbal expression; (2) Experiences problems maintaining a conversation (pragmatics); (3) Responds inappropriately to verbal questions (semantics); (4) Prefers verbal tasks that require little listening; (5) Experiences difficulty retelling a story that was previously read aloud; (6) Omits common prefixes and suffixes (morphology); (7) Experiences difficulty understanding pronoun antecedents; (8) Difficulty with gramatical structure (syntax) (Patton & Polloway, 1990; Wallace et. al., 1987).

"Academic or intellectual tasks that are dependent on language or verbal learning will often be difficult for children who are retarded. . . . Due to the high correlation between cognitive and language abilities, severe language delays may be a sign that a child is not progressing at a satisfactory rate" (Cartwright et. al., 1989, 237). Language skills deficits may be one of the greatest obstacles that individuals with mild mental retardation must overcome if they are to be integrated fully into society (Polloway & Smith, 1982).

## Academic Achievement

Mildly retarded children, whose learning rate is approximately one-half to three-fourths the rate of nonhandicapped children, exhibit deficits and delays in all academic areas. In general, mildly mentally retarded children enrolled in the primary grades (1st–3rd) will be functioning at preschool and readiness levels; intermediate age-grade level mildly retarded students will be at the primary grade level just beginning real academics; and Jr. High age-grade level mildly retarded students will focus on functional academics rather than academic skills foundations.

The majority of students who are mildly retarded read at a lower level than would be expected for their MA, and of the various aspects of reading, comprehension appears to be the most difficult for these students. Since retarded students appear to have a higher "forget" rate than nonhandicapped students, they may spend years "learning, forgetting, and relearning" the same sight vocabulary words, thus, progress to successively higher levels of academic achievement may proceed very slowly. The child who is mildly mentally retarded may attain some understanding of phonics skills in order to decode unfamiliar words (Snell, 1983). The difficulties retarded children have in understanding and using language severely impact reading comprehension. Comprehension of anything but literal level is difficult for retarded children. Since they will cognitively attain no higher than the concrete operational level, any higher level comprehension skill (e.g., inference, evaluation) will require beginning with the concrete and real-life situations and moving to the abstract.

"In mathematics, the majority of students with mild retardation can learn the basic computations" (Thomas & Patton, 1990, 218). The performance of mildly retarded students in computation tasks is more consistent with their mental age (Whorton & Algozzine, 1978). However, they must be taught using concrete and practical experiences due to deficits in cognition. Mildly retarded students experience significant difficulties in mathematics reasoning and "word" problems. Since generalization is difficult for them, mildly retarded students will need to be taught functional use of mathematics.

While the mildly retarded may learn functional writing skills, they will probably experience significant difficulty in creative writing or writing a report because they do not possess automaticity in the underlying skills of penmanship, language processing, creative thinking, grammar, punctuation and capitalization, paragraph organization, paragraph transition, and mechanics of paper writing. Programs for mildly retarded students will usually focus on functional writing skills such as letters and applications.

"Adaptive behavior deficiencies in school settings are associated with coping behavior, social skills, language development, emotional development, self-care, and applied cognitive and academic skills" (Drew et. al., 1988, 252). The remediation of adaptive behavior deficiencies is extremely important in assisting a child to reach "normalization." Appropriate behaviors in adaptive skills areas is frequently the determining factor in not labeling a "high" functioning student as mildly mentally retarded.

### Social Learning Problems

"One of the major problems in individuals with intellectual deficits is a parallel deficit in social behavior" (Kramer et. al., 1988, 48). Research clearly indicates that children and adolescents who are mildly mentally retarded display more social and behavioral problems than their non-handicapped counterparts (Epstein et. al., 1989). Mildly retarded individuals often develop patterns of behavior that further distinguish them from nonretarded peers because of their experiences in dealing with an environment in which they are less able to cope (Thomas & Patton, 1990). "Children who are retarded may not fully comprehend what is expected of them and may respond inappropriately not so much because they lack the particular response required as because they have misinterpreted the situation" (Cartwright et. al., 1989, 239). For many mildly retarded individuals, it is the lack of social competencies rather than intellectual deficits which bring unwanted attention (Kramer et. al., 1988). Mildly retarded students experience difficulties in social sensitivity and insight, social communication, self-concept and self-esteem, and social interactions (Patton & Polloway, 1990).

**Social Sensitivity and Insight.** Social and cognitive skills are interrelated in that the development of such skills as role-taking, self-awareness, interpersonal skills, social communication skills reflect both social and cognitive development (Kramer et. al., 1988). Research clearly indicates that mentally retarded children display a significant delay in demonstrating the ability to understand another person's point of view or engage in social perspective-taking. Additionally, they do not perceive others in as many ways, view others in more egocentric terms, and demonstrate limited insight into the motives and characteristics of others (Kramer et. al., 1988).

During middle childhood intermediate grades, 4th–6th, ages 9–12 years, nonhandicapped children make significant growth in the area of social perspective-taking (role-taking). Since mildly mentally retarded same-aged peers would be cognitively functioning like children of 6–8 years old or 1st–3rd graders, their social development would also reflect delayed development.

Social comprehension and moral judgment are two areas of social ability that depend to a great extent on the cognitive functioning level. "As with other areas of social development, mildly retarded individuals have demonstrated difficulty in developing moral judgment and are perceived to have difficulties dealing with more than one aspect of a moral dilemma" (Kramer et. al., 1988, 51).

**Social Communication and Problem-Solving.** "Referential communication requires skills in taking the perspective of the potential learner (role-playing) as well as communication and language skills" (Kramer et. al., 1988, 51). Mildly mentally retarded individuals experience deficits in both cognition and language which significantly reduces their functioning level and rate of acquisition of social skills.

> Children who do not have the verbal and communication skills of their age mates may withdraw from interpersonal relationships or seek attention in a variety of inappropriate ways. These children may misbehave because they cannot clearly distinguish between acceptable and unacceptable standards of behavior. Problem behavior can also result from the frustrations of scholastic failure or as an attempt to gain acceptance from other children, who might encourage deviant behavior. Much inappropriate social behavior that occurs is a result of repeated failures (Thomas & Patton, 1990, 199).

Mildly retarded children and youth experience significant difficulties in problem-solving due to their reduced cognitive abilities. They appear to have limited interpersonal problem solving strategies and fail to see sequential relationships among a series of interactions (Asher & Renshaw, 1981). Thus, mildly retarded individuals experience difficulty in most aspects of social functioning including social sensitivity (role-taking & social inference), social insight (social comparison & moral judgment), and social communication (referential communication & social problem-solving) due to reduced cognitive and language capacities. "Clearly, personal and social characteristics are intertwined. An individual's personal-social status is affected by his or her own competencies and by significant others' reactions to those competencies" (Morrison, 1988, 158).

**Social Interaction.** Individuals who are mildly retarded frequently have poor interpersonal relationships and are more often rejected than accepted by their peers (Polloway et. al., 1986). The reasons for this reduced social status seem to reside in a complex interaction of the characteristics exhibited by the mentally retarded children including reduced cognitive competence, lack of social competencies, and inappropriate communication and behavior (MacMillan & Morrison, 1980).

"The differences between young children who are retarded and their normal peers seem to be related to behavior: that is, children with mild retardation act like normal children who are younger in chronological age" (Cartwright et. al., 1989, 238). Developmentally delayed preschoolers exhibit a general lack of success in initiating social interactions and an absence of individual social behaviors that are closely associated with peer-related social competence such as attempting to influence the behavior of others (Guralnick & Groom, 1987). Although mildly mentally retarded children demonstrate a higher frequency and quality of interactions than moderately and severely retarded, levels of solitary play and limited exchanges are the predominant behaviors observed (Morrison, 1988). Thus, at a very early age, limited social interchange is apparent in mentally retarded children.

These social differences among retarded and nonhandicapped children and youth appear to escalate with age as social appropriateness becomes more important. The concept of the six-hour retarded child (President's Committee on Mental Retardation, 1970) involved mildly retarded children with IQs 70–85, prior to the AAMD definition change. The "new" EMRs, IQs 50–70, experience more difficulty in social and recreational activities than previously labeled higher functioning retarded students. Past mainstreaming efforts failed to achieve increased social interaction, social acceptance, and behavioral modeling by handicapped students (Gresham, 1988). Integrative efforts with the "new" EMRs are likely to be more successful after students learn prosocial behaviors and correct inappropriate behaviors, since generalization is so difficult for mildly mentally retarded students, it cannot be assumed that exposure to nonhandicapped peers alone would be sufficient to facilitate social interaction (Kehle & Barclay, 1979).

"Mildly mentally retarded students as adults have serious adjustment problems, often related to the specific domains of behavior that led to the initial referral, classification, and placement. These domains of behavior have to do with abstract thought, application of concepts of time and number, and literacy skills" (Reschly, 1987, 31). Thus, mildly mentally retarded persons, the "new" EMRs, do not magically disappear as normal adults into the community (Edgerton, 1984).

## Sense of Personal Control

### Metacognitive Deficits

"Efficient problem solvers use metacognitive knowledge to select, monitor, and create problem-solving strategies" (Kramer et. al., 1988, 53). The literature has long indicated the failures of mentally retarded individuals to spontaneously use cognitive strategies such as mneumonics (Ellis, 1970). Additionally, retarded children have difficulty selecting, modifying, and sequencing strategies and they experience problems in the area of self-questioning (Borys, 1979; Campione & Brown, 1977).

"There is solid evidence that educable mentally retarded students can learn and maintain task-specific cognitive strategies" (Kramer et. al., 1988, 53). The accumulated evidence from numerous early training efforts made it clear that strategies such as verbal elaboration, repetitive rehearsal, visual imagery, and self-instruction could be learned and used to improve performance on specific tasks (Kramer et. al., 1980).

However, numerous studies revealed that mildly retarded learners have failed to generalize the use of trained task-specific cognitive strategies to new situations (Kramer & Engel, 1981). The difficulty that retarded individuals have in generalizing new information is well documented (MacMillan, 1982). Recent studies aimed at improving the intellectual abilities of mildly retarded students have also failed to result in generalization (Kramer et. al., 1988, 53). Attempts to train mildly retarded individuals to use cognitive strategies to improve social skills, academic skills, or general problem-solving skills have also revealed failure to generalize.

Thus, "retarded students can be trained to use task-specific cognitive strategies and they will continue to use these strategies when presented with the training task. Attempts to modify more general memory monitoring or problem-solving skills have met with little success" (Kramer et. al., 1988, 53). It appears that for generalization to occur, students must demonstrate the effective use of the executive skills (metacognition) such as strategy selection and monitoring (Borkowski and Varnhagen, 1984). The literature clearly indicates, then, that mildly retarded individuals are unable to use metacognitive skills effectively in strategy selection, in monitoring their learning, and in generalizing learning to new situations.

## Attribution Deficits

Attributions involve the reasons children and youth give for their success or failure in academic situations, and the amount of personal control they perceive as having over their successes or failures. "Research has shown that many retarded individuals do not believe they are in control of their own destinies; they believe they are controlled by external or outside forces. They tend to think that things happen to them by chance and that they can do little to change anything (Hallahan & Kauffman, 1988). External control is considered to be a debilitating orientation, as it keeps the child/youth from accepting responsibility for his/her own successes and failures and impedes the development of self-reliance (Thomas & Patton, 1990).

"Popular belief indicates that mentally retarded students are more likely to expect to fail because of the belief that they encounter a higher rate of failure in their natural environments and a lower rate of success than normal children of the same age" (Kramer et. al., 1988, 49). Mentally retarded individuals react to failure by decreasing their efforts on tasks following failure experiences (Logan & Rose, 1982). When given negative feedback on cognitive tasks they were performing, retarded children stopped looking for effective strategies (Weiss, 1984). In contrast, successful experiences lead to increases in performance and expectations of success (Ollendick, et. al., 1971). Thus, it appears that motivation to learn and positive expectancies for success can be enhanced by minimizing the failure experiences of mentally retarded youngsters and maximizing the successes.

## Motivation Deficits

"Given that experiential factors for mentally retarded children differ substantially from that of normal children, it is not surprising that a retarded individual's motivation differs from that of a nonretarded individual of the same mental and chronological age" (Kramer et. al., 1988, 49). Little research has been conducted regarding the motivations of mildly retarded youngsters. However, considering the results of attribution research that mentally retarded individuals tend to be outer-directed, it is not surprising that tangible reinforcers such as candy, stickers, toys, etc. are more effective in motivating mentally retarded students than verbal reinforcers or grades.

## Self-Concepts of Mildly Retarded Students

### General Self-Concepts

Most of the research regarding the self-concept of the mentally retarded has been concerned with identifying behavioral differences between the retarded and the normal (Gardner, 1974). Prior to 1960 there were very few research studies pertaining to the self-concept of the mentally retarded. Ringness (1959) was among the first to conduct research regarding the self-concept of mentally retarded students. His study revealed mentally retarded children have less well-differentiated and less realistic self-concepts than average or bright children, accompanied by unrealistic levels of aspiration.

Schurr et. al. (1970) reviewed the self-concept research concerning mentally retarded subjects published prior to 1970 and concluded differences in subject samples and instrumentation, as well as inconsistent results, precluded any generalizations about the self-concept of the typically mentally retarded person. However, research conducted since 1973 utilizes the "new" EMRs with IQs of 50–70, while the research conducted prior to 1973 used EMR subject populations with IQs 70–85. Therefore, the research results prior to 1973 cannot be compared to results since 1973 without considering the different subject populations.

Robinson and Robinson (1976) found the retarded as a group tended to be more anxious than nonretarded children, and their self-concepts more negative and more defensive than those of nonretarded children. Cline (1975) reported primary level educable mentally retarded students had significantly higher self-concept scores than Junior High level retarded students, but normal children had higher self-concept scores than retarded students at all levels. Stangvik's (1979) results indicated that pupils of low ability have lower self-concepts than average pupils, but the low ability pupils generally indicated higher ideal self-concepts than pupils of average ability.

Jones' (1985) results indicated that educable mentally retarded students (ages 10–13 years) possess significantly more negative phenomenal (conscious) and nonphenomenal (unconscious) self-concepts than emotionally disturbed (ED), learning disabled (LD), speech/language impaired (S/L), and nonhandicapped students (NH). "The mean performance scores of the EMR students were significantly lower than the NH students on five of the six cluster scores and on the total score of the Piers-Harris Scale, indicating high anxiety levels and negative feelings regarding their intelligence and school status, popularity, happiness, and behavior" (35).

A number of studies were conducted to determine if placement impacted on the self-concept of mildly mentally retarded students, the "new" EMRs. Luftig (1980) reviewed research on the effects of placement on the self-concept of the "new" EMRs, and concluded that they maintain higher levels of self-concept in special classes.

> The vast majority of what we know about how mentally retarded students perceive themselves has been derived or inferred from how these children and youth have responded to stimulus situations such as self statements and role-play situations. The limitations in their language and communication skills has made examination of self-awareness particularly difficult. While other individuals can explain their cognitive responses, the mentally retarded people have a more difficult time organizing and expressing their thoughts (Kramer et. al., 1988, 48).

The relevant literature on self-concept has generally indicated that students who are mildly retarded report lower levels of self-efficacy than do their peers who are not retarded (Simeonsson, 1978). It can be concluded that students who are mildly retarded do not hold strong, positive feelings about their own abilities and potential. However, there is considerable correlation between negative self-concept and chronic failure (Patton & Polloway, 1990). The level of self-esteem remains an important consideration in teaching the mentally retarded, given the vulnerable status of their competencies in relation to others in their environments (Morrison, 1988).

### Self-Concepts of Academic Achievement

The self-image of the retarded child is intricately linked to his academic success. Being viewed as academically successful by one's teacher is of utmost importance (Richmond, 1973). In evaluating self-concept differences between low and high achieving mildly retarded adolescents, Lawrence and Winschel (1973) found a positive relationship between adequate self-concept and high achievement of retarded children. Children of lower than average ability have more difficulty than other children in gaining feelings of achievement and in developing favorable attitudes (Andrews, 1971).

Research revealed retarded children tended to be more anxious than nonretarded children (Jones, 1985). Many retarded children expect failure and learn to defend themselves against it; as a result, their self-concepts are more negative and defensive than those of nonretarded children (Robinson & Robinson, 1976). Low ability pupils are met by more negative attitudes from others both in school and society (Guskin & Jones, 1982). Due to a history of failure and of dependency oriented treatment, mentally retarded individuals have become especially sensitive to others' evaluations of them (Stangvik, 1979).

Jones' (1983) results indicated that educable mentally retarded students viewed their intelligence negatively, perceived their school status to be low, experienced high anxiety, low popularity, and low happiness levels. Thus, the results suggested that educable mentally retarded students exhibited a negative "school-related self-concept" or negative academic achievement self-concept.

## Summary

The 1961 AAMD definition of mental retardation required subaverage general intellectual functioning (1 standard deviation below the mean or IQ below 85), which originated during the developmental period (birth to 16 years), and was associated with deficits in adaptive behavior. The 1973 AAMD definition, however, declassified 13% of the school-aged population who were labeled mildly retarded, when it changed the subaverage general intellectual functioning to −2 standard deviations below the mean or IQ below 70; and required concurrent deficits in adaptive behavior. Students previously labeled moderately retarded, IQs 50–70, were re-labeled as mildly mentally retarded. The declassified students attended regular education classes, some were reclassified learning disabled, some received Chapter I reading and math services, while many were left to flounder on their own with no specialized assistance.

The etiology of most mild forms of mental retardation are unknown or environmental (e.g., low socioeconomic homes). Mildly retarded students experience deficits and delays in cognition in the areas of attention, information processing, learning efficiency, transfer generalization, and level of learning. Reduced and/or unfocused attention, restriction to the cognitive operational development level, inability to learn automatically and incidentally, and inability to generalize significantly reduces the child's functioning level in academics as well as language acquisition and usage.

In general, mildly mentally retarded children enrolled in the primary grades (1st–3rd) will be functioning at preschool and readiness levels; intermediate age-grade level mildly retarded students will be at the primary grade level just beginning real academics. The majority of mildly retarded students read at a lower level than would be expected for their mental age, experiencing deficits in comprehension. They can learn mathematics computations, but experience significant difficulty in math reasoning. Adaptive behavior deficiencies in school settings are associated with coping skills, social skills, language development, emotional development, self-care, and social interaction.

Mildly retarded students are unable to use metacognitive skills effectively in strategy selection, in monitoring their learning, and in generalizing learning to new situations. Mildly retarded children believe they are controlled by external or outside forces, that things happen to them by chance and they can do little to change anything. Mildly retarded individuals react to failure by decreasing their efforts on tasks following failure experiences.

Most of the literature on self-concept of mildly retarded students indicates that they do not hold strong, positive feelings about their abilities and potential. Retarded students appear to have a low self-concept of academic achievement including negative feelings about their intelligence, school status, and popularity. They appear to experience significant anxiety about school-related situations and activities.

# Chapter Eight

# BEHAVIOR DISORDERED STUDENTS

*Children who are troubled—and who cause trouble for their parents, brothers, sisters, teachers, and peers—are often diagnosed "emotionally disturbed." They are in conflict with self and others* (Whelan, 1988, 184).

---

These children are referred to by a variety of terms including the following: emotionally disturbed, socially maladjusted, psychologically disordered, emotionally handicapped, emotionally impaired, behaviorally impaired, socially/emotionally handicapped, behaviorally/emotionally handicapped, seriously behaviorally disabled, personal and social adjustment problems, or even psychotic or schizophrenic if their behavior is extremely abnormal or bizarre (Heward & Orlansky, 1988; Shea & Bower, 1987). Generally, the term behavior disorders is preferred by most educational professionals. Using a behavioral perspective, one views behavior disorders more in terms of learned behavior that is problematic (Paul, 1987). "The term, *emotionally disturbed,* communicates a psychodynamic perspective and stresses behavior as a manifestation of disturbed thoughts and feelings" (Shea & Bower, 1987, 6).

Regardless of the term used to describe these children, there are a

155

significant number of children who are displaying severely inappropriate behaviors in the classroom. *The Eleventh Annual Report to Congress* (U.S. Department of Education, 1989), indicates that 374,730 seriously emotionally disturbed children and adolescents, ages 6–21 years, or 9.1% of the total special education population, received special education services during the school year 1987–88.

## Definitions of Behavior Disorders

"Currently, there is no definition of behavior disorders that is generally agreed on" (Heward & Orlansky, 1988, 169). "Lack of a reliable and widely accepted definition has caused difficulties in identifying and estimating the prevalence of children with behavior disorders" (Paul, 1987, 15). There is general agreement among the professionals that behavior disorders refers to behavior that is significantly or extremely different from usual, the problem is a long standing chronic condition, and the behavior is unacceptable because of social or cultural expectations (Hallahan & Kauffman, 1988). "Behavior disorders usually involve familiar behaviors that occur with a frequency, duration, and/or intensity that is too great or too small relative to the educator's expectations" (Cullinan & Epstein, 1990, 158). Lerner et al. (1987) define behavioral and emotional disorders as follows:

> Children with emotional and behavioral disorders are in conflict with themselves or with others. Their behavior deviates significantly from that of the normal child over a substantial period of time. Their coping skills are poor or nonexistent. For some children, the behavior problems appear during the preschool years; for others, the problem becomes evident in later years. Very severe emotional disorders include childhood schizophrenia (34).

### P.L.94-142 Definition

Seriously emotionally disturbed children are defined as follows:

(i) The term means a condition exhibiting one or more of the following characteristics over a period of time and to a marked degree, which adversely affects educational performance.

(a) An inability to learn which cannot be explained by intellectual, sensory, and health factors;

(b) An inability to build or maintain satisfactory relationships with peers and teachers;

(c) Inappropriate types of behavior or feelings under normal circumstances;

(d) A general pervasive mood of unhappiness or depression; or

(e) A tendency to develop physical symptoms or fears associated with personal or school problems.

(ii) The term includes children who are schizophrenic or autistic. The term does not include children who are socially maladjusted unless it is determined that they are seriously emotionally disturbed

(Federal Register, 1977, 42478).

## Etiology of Behavior Disorders

The etiology of behavior disorders/emotional disturbances (BD/ED) involves the interaction of multiple factors or contributing factors. "It is extremely unusual to find a single cause that has led directly to disturbed behavior" (Hallahan & Kauffman, 1988, 171).

Whelan (1988, 200) indicates the causes of emotional disturbance may be divided into two major categories—biogenic and psychogenic. Biogenic refers to the physical, biological, and hereditary insults that diminish an individual's capability to cope with environmental demands; and are more evident in the severe types of emotional disturbance. Psychogenic describes internal conflicts raging within a child and the relationship of these conflicts to external, complex, and environmental events; and are associated with the relationship between the child and the environment over time.

Hallahan & Kauffman (1988) summarized many of the different theories regarding the origin, nature, and cure of disturbance in children as follows:

1. *The Biological Approach:* the view that genetic, neurological, and biochemical factors may cause disturbed behavior.

2. *The Psychoanalytic Approach:* the view that traditional psychoanalytic concepts can be used to find the underlying causes of disturbance.

3. *The Psychoeducational Approach:* the view that discovering why children behave as they do is important, but so is the acquisition of academic and daily living skills.

4. *The Humanistic Approach:* the view that behavioral disorders are symptomatic of a child's being out of touch with self and feelings.

5. *The Ecological Approach:* the view that ED/BD results from poor interaction of the child with elements of the social environment.
6. *The Behavioral Approach:* the view that all behavior is learned; therefore, ED/BD represents inappropriate learning (163–164).

## Characteristics of Behavior Disordered Students

The inappropriate and maladaptive behaviors exhibited by behavior disordered children and adolescents are manifested as deficits in academic learning, cognitive development and social interactions.

### Cognitative and Academic Learning Problems

Due to the significant focus on the inappropriate behaviors engaged in by behavior disordered children, discussions of academic and cognitive functioning are frequently omitted from texts on behavior disorders, and are seldom researched. Obviously, the presenting problem—the deviant behavior—must be brought under control as a prerequisite to adequate academic functioning. Disturbed behaviors are frequently categorized as mild-moderate behavior disorders and severe-profound behavior disorders. Additionally, mild-moderate behavior disorders are described in terms of two major dimensions: (1) Conduct Disorders or aggressive (externalizing) behavior, and (2) Personality Disorders or withdrawn (internalizing) behavior (Rizzo & Zabel, 1988).

Children who are mildly to moderately behavior disordered can live at home and attend school during the day (Cartwright et. al., 1989). These children are usually educated in self-contained classrooms, and are gradually mainstreamed into regular education classrooms as they learn to control their inappropriate behaviors. Students with mild-moderate behavior disorders often show some degree of learning disorders— cognitive and academic.

Cognitively, the average mildly or moderately behavior disordered youngster has an IQ in the dull-normal range (around 90); very few behaviorally disordered children score above the bright-normal range (Hallahan & Kauffman, 1988). "Compared to the normal distribution of intelligence, many more behavior disordered children fall into the slow learner and mildly retarded categories" (Hallahan & Kauffman, 1988, 178). The low normal IQs for mild-moderate behavior disordered children and adolescents indicate delays in learning to perform academic

tasks that nonhandicapped peers can perform successfully, and the failure to gain adequately from their environmental experiences.

Academically, mild-moderate behavior disordered students are underachievers when considering both chronological age and mental age.
Their behavior at school interferes with attending to task and completing the required academic assignments. For some children the pattern of
failure in academic situations is so severe and long-standing that they do
not have the skills to handle academic situations (Cartwright et. al.,
1988).

Mild-moderate behavior disordered students perform behind nonhandicapped peers in reading, arithmetic, and spelling (Kauffman et.
al., 1987). They frequently experience difficulty in written composition
assignments due to interference from attention deficits, and lack of
automaticity in the prerequisite skills necessary to produce a written
assignment. Of significant concern is the fact that academic retardation
increases with age or grade level, and increased failure in academics
produces even more deviant behavior (Whelan, 1988). Research, however,
indicates that behavior disordered students function at higher academic
levels in reading, math, and other academics than learning disabled
peers (Epstein & Cullinan, 1983).

The aggressive "child who is refusing to work, swearing at teachers,
knocking materials off other children's desks, and performing all sorts of
inappropriate behaviors obviously is not a participant in instruction"
(Cartwright et. al., 1989, 290). The significantly withdrawn child who
retreats into fantasy and depression, refuses to talk in class or complete
assignments, experiences "illnesses" and phobic reactions at school, appears
extremely anxious and nervous when asked to perform, also, is not an
active learner.

**Attention Deficits.** Attention deficits including selective attention and
selective intention significantly impact the ability of the mild-moderate
behavior disordered student to progress academically in the regular
classroom. Children with selective attention deficits have erratic focus
and concentration, preferring to focus on incidental nonrelevant factors
(Levine, 1987). They always know what their classmates are doing, whose
class is at recess, what's going on in the hall. They evidence very poor
ability to utilize the cues from their teacher that indicates their behavior
is inappropriate and that they should modify their behavior. Children
with selective attention problems also experience selective intention
deficits such as failure to monitor what they say; poorly planned and

inappropriate action; inconsistent performance on tasks they do complete shows sacrifice of accuracy for speed; and failure to learn from experience (Levine, 1987).

The seriously withdrawn or depressed behavior disordered child or youth also possesses selective attention deficits. Their overriding anxiety and depression, avoidance of possible failure in academics, daydreaming or "existing in another time and space" severely impair their ability to focus attention on classroom tasks at hand.

Aggressive mild-moderate behavior disordered youngsters frequently demonstrate characteristics of attention deficit hyperactive disorder (AD/HD) (American Psychiatric Association, 1987) including impulsivity, overactivity, not persisting on tasks, easily distracted, inadequate decision-making skills, interrupting others, and aggression. Hyperactive children are frequently at odds with their teachers. Their high energy level often finds them out of their seat and off-task, when at their desk they may be hanging upside down half-way under the desk, reaching to touch or look at their neighbor's paper or book. During classroom discussions they blurt-out answers before the teacher finishes the question, when waiting their turn they may sit on their knees in the seat and wave their arms frantically to be called on—often forgetting what they were going to say when they are called on to provide an answer or response. During reading group seatwork, while teacher is busy with another group, they will be out of their seat, off-task, engaging in minor mischief with anyone who will participate and "picking fights," pulling pig-tails, sharpening all of the pencils, and continuously talking and cruising the classroom. When teacher verbally reprimands or physically attempts to take the student to his desk, he becomes hostile and aggressive. As a result these students seldom complete assignments, and they interfere with the ability of peers to complete their assignments.

**Information Processing Deficits.** Information processing skills of mild to moderate behavior disordered youngsters reveal significant deficits. Their initial problem is paying enough attention to lessons to even get the process started. Additionally, since their attention span is so short they may not pay enough attention to gain all salient features required in order to perform the lesson correctly. For example, they may read the directions just enough to learn that they are to indicate an answer (or guess and not read the directions at all), but they may not have attended well enough to the directions to note that specific items are to be underlined or circled. Attention deficits, also, reduce the amount of information processed in the short-term memory and stored in the long-term memory. Information that is stored may be composed of only partially accurate information due to lack of attention to detail. Information may be difficult to retrieve because of lack of labeling and integrating with the long-term memory store. The use of working memory may be very minimal due to lack of metacognitive skills to manage the organization and use of information. Some behavior disordered youngsters may be able to process information appropriately, but experience extreme anxiety about the school setting, the subject, and/or life in general, which may "short circuit" the whole process, and significantly reduce learning.

Behavior disordered children who are also learning disabled may experience perceptual difficulties producing inaccurate information, experience deficits or delays in understanding complexities of language — syntax and semantics, or may experience significant fine motor skill deficits that limit the child's ability to demonstrate learning through written responses. Due to short attention span, the behavior disordered student, aggressive or withdrawn, will not be able to attend to task and concentrate long enough to produce a viable report or creative story.

Learning efficiency among behavior disordered children and adolescents may be almost nonexistent. Those youngsters who are also learning disabled may not spontaneously use strategies, such as verbal rehearsal and clustering, to help themselves remember. Since behavior disordered children and adolescents, both aggressive and withdrawn, fail to use metacognitive skills to monitor and adjust their behavior, it is unlikely that they will be able to use metacognition to monitor their memory processes and academic functioning.

**Automatization Deficits.** Automatization is another skill very important to effective and efficient learning. Mild-moderate behavior disordered youth, both aggressive and withdrawn, are so involved with themselves and the deviant behaviors that rule their lives that they may have little time, inclination, or patience and concentration to develop prerequisite academic skills to a level required for automaticity. Behavior disordered children may lack a fluent automatic reading vocabulary which is a prerequisite to reading comprehension. They may lack automaticity with basic math facts which impairs their ability to perform algorithms (math processes). The frustration of attempting to perform a task for which they do not possess the basic prerequisites may increase the aggressive or withdrawn behaviors of these children, thus, interfering with skill acquisition.

## Social and Behavioral Learning Problems

In normal development there is a close relationship among cognitive and social/emotional development. Thus, as a child/youth develops cognitively, s/he acquires more mature ability in social developmental skills including the following: social perspective-taking, social regulation, moral development, social problem solving, and social relationships. The normal child and youth, also, matures emotionally in terms of self-knowledge (beliefs, commitments, attitudes, values), self-competence, and self-evaluation as s/he develops cognitively. These complex social and emotional skills depend on abstract thinking, the use of logic, and automaticity in self-monitoring.

"The emotionally disturbed child and adolescent (as well as the adult) is likely to differ from peers in terms of greater egocentricity and lack of decentration in cognitive and social tasks" (Monson & Simeonsson, 1987, 67). In other words, the emotionally disturbed or behaviorally disordered youngster is more self-centered, less able to engage in social perspective-taking, and empathize with others. These weaknesses severely hamper abilities to form satisfying interpersonal relationships, engage in socially appropriate behavior, and understand his/her role in the success or failure of social situations.

**Interpersonal Relationships.** "Peer interaction is a central aspect of child development, providing opportunities for companionship, social status, self understanding, personal maturing, and adjustment to society" (Cullinan & Epstein, 1990, 161). Children and youth exhibiting mild-moderate behavior disorders in interpersonal relationships frequently engage in aggressive behaviors against peers or completely withdraw from them. "These children cannot develop normal social interactions and are deprived of normal kinds of approval and satisfaction from others" (Lerner et. al., 1989, 35).

> Behavior disordered children are seldom really liked by anyone—their peers, teachers, brothers or sisters, even parents. Sadder still, they often do not even like themselves. They are difficult to be around, and attempts to befriend them may lead only to rejection, verbal abuse, or even physical attack (Heward & Orlansky, 1988, 169).

"**Aggressive behavior** is defined as behavior that inflicts physical or psychological injury on another person. It includes physical assaults, such as hitting, kicking, biting, and shoving, and verbal assaults, such as making threats, hurling insults, and name-calling" (Epanchin, 1987,

111). Aggressive behaviors may lead to the destruction of property. They usually are of the excessive type; the behaviors occur often and with great intensity repeatedly violating the rights of other persons and socially accepted norms for appropriate ways of behaving (Whelan, 1990: Epanchin, 1987). It is not surprising, then that aggressive children of this nature in regular elementary and secondary classrooms are seldom socially accepted by peers. They are seldom allowed to participate very long in community activities such as Little League ballgames and scouting due to the aggressive and hostile behavior toward other children. "It appears that aggressive behavior patterns have already become a major component of the child's behavioral repertoire by the age of 10 years" (Griffin, 1985, 251).

**Withdrawn behavior** involves too little social interaction; "children are unusually quiet, having few emotional highs or lows. Preferring to be alone, they will avoid group activities. . . . These children will not spontaneously initiate conversation. Often they will try to avoid verbal contacts" (Lerner et. al. 1987, 34). "They are social isolates who have few friends, seldom play with other children their own age, and lack the social skills necessary to have fun. Some retreat into fantasy or daydreaming; some develop fears that are completely out of proportion to the circumstances" (Hallahan & Kauffman, 1988, 183).

Obviously, neither the mild-moderate aggressive behavior disordered youth, nor the mild-moderate withdrawn behavior disordered youth, experience appropriate, satisfying interactions with peers. Many children who experience difficulty with peer interactions lack insight into the reciprocal nature of interactions or lack critical social-cognitive developmental skills (Youniss, 1978). Though the behavior disordered youngster may accept their peers' dislike as unchangeable, they may not see the relationship between their behavior and the social rejection.

Studies have revealed that behavior disordered children lack social-evaluation ability (Jurkovic & Selman, 1980). Mild-moderate behavior disordered youth frequently made errors in interpreting peers behavior toward them in that they perceived peers to be hostile whenever the peers' intentions were ambiguous, and they reacted aggressively to the perceived hostile behavior (Dodge & Frame, 1982). Behavior disordered youngsters appear to be less knowledgeable about appropriate ways to be helpful to peers in situations of need.

**Inappropriate Behavior. Aggressive** children and adolescents with conduct disorders tend to be disruptive, impulsive, angry, destructive, and aggressive (Rizzo & Zabel, 1988). Aggressive behavior is probably the most common presenting problem among youngsters classified as emotionally and behaviorally disturbed (Epanchin, 1987). Aggressive conduct disorders involve repeated episodes of violent confrontation with others, including acts of physical assault, robbery or theft involving physical confrontation, or sexually assaultive behavior (Rizzo & Zabel, 1988).

Within the school setting disorders of aggression may involve cruelty, bullying peers, threats, petty extortion, fighting on the playground, screaming, tantrums, hostile resistance; disrespect, disobedience, and threatening teachers (Cullinan & Epstein, 1990). Unpredictable outbursts and threats disrupt the class and interfere with other children's concentration, frequently all day long (Epanchin, 1987).

"From a social learning perspective, conduct disorders in children and adolescents result either from a failure to learn appropriate social skills, or from learning inappropriate social behaviors or both" (Rizzo & Zabel, 1988, 130). Many behavior disordered children have problems determining when and where certain behaviors are appropriate (Heward & Orlansky, 1988). Additionally, aggressive children learn many aggressive responses through observation and imitation of family members. Children are more likely to be aggressive when they are victims of physical assault, verbal threats, taunts, insults; and/or when positive reinforcement decreases or ends (Epanchin, 1987). It is the conduct-disordered (hyperaggressive) child or youth whose adulthood is most likely to be characterized by socially intolerable behavior (Kazdin, 1987).

Griffin (1985) compared three groups of behavior disordered adolescents: (1) violent and aggressive, (2) graduates of the treatment center, (3) random subjects selected from the total treatment program, all of whom were at one time enrolled in a short-term residential treatment program for emotionally disturbed children. The results indicated that aggressive youth are different in childhood than their behavior disordered peers. As a group, they exhibit a significantly greater number of conduct-disordered behaviors, developmentally related organic factors, and academic problems prior to age nine than the comparison subjects in the other two groups. These results highlight the necessity for screening "at-risk" students and beginning intervention programs immediately.

**Personality disorders** involving extreme cases of worry, self-consciousness, insecurity, fears, depression, and anxiety often result in inappropriate and deviant behaviors. "Periods of withdrawal may alternate with angry outbursts, tantrums, crying, or running away" (Rizzo & Zabel, 1988, 90).

Withdrawn behavior disordered youngsters often retreat into their own daydreams and fantasies; some regress to earlier developmental stages and demand constant help and attention (Heward & Orlansky, 1988).

A major concern regarding withdrawn behavior disordered adolescents is depression—a condition that may include mood disturbances, inability to think or concentrate, lack of motivation, sadness, apathy, poor self-esteem and pervasive pessimism (Hallahan & Kauffman, 1987). Depression has frequently been linked to suicide among teens. "Obviously, these behavior patterns limit the child's chances to take part in and learn from the school and leisure activities that normal children participate in" (Heward & Orlansky, 1988, 187). "It seems self-evident that social incompetence reduces the developing individual's opportunities for friendships and other important chances for profiting from classroom and informal learning activities (Cullinan & Epstein, 1990, 169).

"For the child with personality problems, disappointment, self-blame, and hopelessness are constant life companions" (Rizzo & Zabel, 1988, 91). A pattern of immature and withdrawn behavior together with school failure is predictive of poor adjustment in adulthood for girls" (Cartwright et. al., 1989, 292).

## Sense of Personal Control

"Many behavior disordered children think they have little control over their lives. Things just seem to happen to them, and being disruptive is their means of reacting to a world that is inconsistent and frustrating" (Heward & Orlansky, 1988, 200).

### Metacognition Deficits

Mild-moderate behavior disordered children and youth are under-achievers, academically, and many are also learning disabled; thus, they experience numerous social, emotional, and cognitive deficits that interfere with adequate functioning. Similarly, as their handicapped peers (learning disabled, educable mentally retarded, language disordered), the behavior disordered children and youth experience difficulties with the metacognitive aspect that regulates and controls strategic aspects of cognition or their ability to control their cognitions (Mann & Sabatino, 1985).

Behavior disordered children and youth are deficient in the meta-cognitive operations to direct the learning process, and to monitor and control their behavior. Schloss (1985) indicates major concerns regarding behavior disordered children and youth include the following: (1) Skill deficits: the absence of a response in the student's repertoire; (2) Motivational deficits: the students' failing to perform a behavior even though the prerequisite skills are present in his repertoire; and (3) Discrimination deficits: result when an individual has the skill and motivation necessary to engage in the desired behavior, but is not aware of appropriate conditions for performing it.

Behavior disordered children and youth experience attention deficits similar to those of learning disabled students including problems with focusing attention and sustaining attention, poor concentration, impulsivity, and overactivity which inhibit information processing and using the metacognitive skills. These youngsters lack functional cognitive strategies to control and direct thinking, learning, and remembering, and lack monitoring skills to determine if their responses (academic and social) are correct or appropriate. Youngsters who have mild-moderate behavior disorders experience difficulty with both academic and social problem-solving, and problems with drawing inferences. They frequently lack the automaticity in prerequisite skills to fluently perform academic tasks, and paired with the lack of metacognitive skills relegates them to focusing on the subskills unable to understand the process.

The lack of metacognitive abilities in social areas significantly interferes with the social acceptability of the behavior disordered student. The lack of social perspective-taking interferes with the youngster's ability to form mutually satisfying social relationships as s/he can not understand the other person's reasoning, can not empathize, can not feel happy at the friend's good fortune, and thus is relegated to immature egocentric behaviors. The lack of self-monitoring and social-evaluation in social situations renders the behaviorally disordered youth unable to determine when his/her behaviors are socially appropriate or inappropriate; thus, s/he can not monitor accuracy or effect and change the behaviors when social responses indicate that the behavior is inappropriate. Since they can not understand behaviors from the perspective of the other person, they will not understand why they are ignored, not asked to parties, not included in "the group" activities, nor why they are no longer friends. The lack of metacognitive skills means that the behavior disordered youth will be unable to engage in social problem-solving, will be socially incompetent, and will continue to function at an immature moral development stage.

The lack of metacognitive abilities renders the child unable to control his/her behavior. This deficit means that the hostile, aggressive child continues to rampage until his energy is spent; and the withdrawn, anxiety-inferiority obsessed child will be unable to halt the destructive emotions of depression and fear. This lack of self-control is far more devastating than just academic deficits or just behavioral deficits, for the lack of self-control interferes with independence and appropriateness in all functioning areas: social, emotional, cognitive, and academic.

## Motivation/Attribution Deficits

"Students with long histories of academic failure and a weak need for achievement typically attribute their success to easy questions or luck and their failures to lack of ability" (Biehler & Snowman, 1986, 482). Similarly, research regarding children's beliefs about failure in social situations revealed that low-accepted children tended to attribute rejection to their own personal incompetence rather than to peer compatibility or rejection traits (Geotz & Dweck, 1980).

> Because low achieving students attribute failure to low ability, future failure is seen as more likely than future success. Consequently, satisfactory achievement and reward may have little effect on the failure avoiding strategies that poor students have developed over the years . . . It may be, then, that rewards will not motivate low-need achievers to work harder so long as they attribute success to factors that are unstable and beyond their control (Biehler & Snowman, 1986, 482).

Severely anxious and withdrawn children often display learned helplessness—a belief that nothing they do can change the bad situations in their lives. Learned helplessness results in severe deterioration in performance after failure because the failure just serves to reinforce in them that there is nothing they can do to change things (Kirk & Gallagher, 1989). The inability to change the bad situations in their lives, and to gain love and respect from parents, who frequently are themselves disturbed, adds to feelings of helplessness and reinforces low self-image and low self-worth.

Unruh et. al. (1987) studied the differences between emotionally disturbed/behavior disordered 9-to-13-year-old elementary students as compared to peers on measures of perception of locus of control and found no significant differences among the groups. However, Nowicki & DiGirolamo (1989) studied emotionally disturbed and nondisturbed subjects ages 9–11 years-old and found that an external locus of control and poorer performance in decoding voice tone and facial expression were associated with emotional disturbance.

Perna et. al. (1983) studied the relationship of internal locus of control, academic achievement, and IQ in emotionally disturbed boys ages 10–15 years. Results indicated that subjects with a higher degree of internal locus of control made greater gains in academic achievement; and chronological ages and IQ scores did not affect their degree of internal locus of control.

Morgan (1986) studied the locus of control in children labeled learning disabled, behaviorally disordered, and learning disabled with significant behavioral disorders. Children labeled learning disabled were found to be significantly more internally controlled than children labeled behaviorally disordered or than children labeled learning disabled with behavioral disorders.

Luchow et. al. (1985) studied learned helplessness and perceived effects of ability and effort on academic performance among emotionally handicapped and learning disabled/emotionally handicapped children. Results indicated that EH children took significantly more personal responsibility for academic failure than did LD/EH, although the two groups did not differ significantly in taking responsibility for academic success. LD/EH children attributed success to effort and failure to a lack of effort; EH children attributed success to ability, but failure to both a lack of ability and a lack of effort. Among EH children, significant positive correlations were found between report card grades and perceived internality for success. Among LD/EH children, significant negative correlations were found between report card grades and perceived lack of effort as the cause of failure.

King et. al. (1986) conducted a study to differentiate conduct disorder from depressive disorders in school age children. Results indicated that depressed children often have a depressed parent; receive harsh, power-assertive discipline from their parents; have a rigidly adaptive family style; have a more internal locus of control; and tend to internalize aggression more than do non-depressed conduct disordered children.

A profile of unsuccessful academic performance, in combination with inadequate social coping behaviors, portrays a typical emotionally disturbed child or youth" (Whelan, 1988, 210). Thus, all major facets of emotionally disturbed children's lives (internal and external) are chaotic. "The ways that children cope with internal and external chaos are as varied as the children who display them . . . Deficit and excessive behaviors are ways of avoiding circumstances associated with pain and failure, of coping with problems from within and without..." (Whelan, 1988, 204).

Research reported in Whelan (1988, 205) indicates three general behavioral coping styles of children and youth with behavior disorders:

Type 1: The child who can succeed but will not invest energy in task completion.... the probability of pain through failure poses too high a risk.

Type 2: The child accepts an assigned task but either does not complete it or makes many errors ... this coping style functions to avoid personal investment. To invest and still fail is a proposition too devastating to risk ... the child can avoid the painful consequences of inappropriate aggression by placidly using up allotted task time in a nonproductive fashion.

Type 3: The child is described as having given up, characterized by the absence of behavior, a withdrawal from fighting expectations, or even the semblance of attempting to meet requests for performance (Gallagher & Whelan, 1972).

Successful interventions depend on the ability of the teachers and school psychologist to determine the coping style of each behavior disordered child and youth. Most intervention methods include a combination of experiences designed to enhance social-cognitive and behavioral skills and motivation as well as to provide positive peer experiences (Rose-Krasnor, 1980).

## Self-Concepts of Behavior Disordered Students

Much of the early research regarding the self-concepts of behavior disordered/emotionally disturbed children and youth has concerned children who were severely emotionally disturbed. The behaviors, emotions, motivation, attributions, academic success of behavior disordered youngsters are compared to those of the average nonhandicapped child or youth of the same age.

Mental health specialists agree that the mentally healthy child is happy most of the time, builds lasting and positive relationships with other people, has an accurate perception of reality, is able to organize thoughts and actions to accomplish reasonable goals, achieves academically at a level close to his or her potential, has mostly good feelings about himself or herself, and behaves as expected for a child of a given age and sex (Hallahan & Kauffman, 1988, 162).

A picture of the behavior disordered or severely emotionally disturbed youngster is in most ways the direct opposite of that of the mentally healthy child described above.

## General Self-Concept

"All human beings have a perspective, or point of view, through which they interpret the world. This personal and unique perspective includes the individual perception of self and personal actions as well as a perception of others and their actions and places, objects, and events that make up the world" (Shea & Bauer, 1987, 18). Much of the research regarding the general self-concept of emotionally disturbed youngsters indicates an over-evaluated delusional self-concept or a significantly lower self-concept than that of nonhandicapped youth.

**Low Self-Concepts.** Bloom et. al. (1979) disclosed the self-concept scores for behaviorally disordered children were significantly lower than the self-concept scores of normal and able youngsters. Politino (1980) also found the self-concept of emotionally disturbed children lower than for normal.

Jones (1985) found that emotionally disturbed students, in public school settings mainstreamed for at least part of the day, possessed significantly more negative phenomenal (conscious) and nonphenomenal (unconscious) self-concepts than nonhandicapped students ages 10–13 years old. Additionally, the emotionally disturbed students indicated experiencing high anxiety levels.

Sweeney & Zionts (1989) examined differences between regular education and emotionally disturbed early adolescents with respect to self-concept, body image, and selected uses of clothing. Their findings revealed that emotionally impaired were less likely to use clothing to influence mood than were regular education students.

## Self-Concept of Academic Achievement

Although the intelligence quotient is generally agreed to be an excellent predictor of school success and achievement, caution must be used in predicting the achievement level of emotionally disturbed students.

Achievement is a significant factor in emotional disturbance; however, the cause and effect relationship has not been determined (Shea, 1979, 11).

Stennett (1966) found the more years an emotionally disturbed child stayed in school, the further educationally he was behind his non-handicapped peers. Grossman (1965) indicated being in the classroom was a threatening experience for students with emotional problems. Many of them had not acquired the educational skills necessary to meet the educational demands imposed upon them. Their emotional problems interfered with their ability to use even those skills they had developed. Even when their lower-than-normal IQ scores are taken into account, most disturbed children are underachievers, as measured by standardized tests (Hallahan & Kauffman, 1988).

Shea (1978, 50) indicated the poor self-concept of emotionally disturbed children manifests itself as a lack of self-confidence, fear of the unfamiliar, feelings of inferiority, hypersensitivity to criticism, resistance to independent functioning, and reluctance to attempt many activities.

Jones (1985) found that emotionally disturbed students perceived their behavior to be significantly less acceptable to adults and peers than nonhandicapped students. They, also, perceived their intellectual ability, school status, and popularity more negatively than did nonhandicapped students.

Anxiety-withdrawn behavior disordered children have such low self-concepts that failure in a school task or a social setting only confirms for them their worthlessness and helpless in the face of an unfriendly environment (Seligman & Peterson, 1986). Their performance in the classroom may be much worse than they are capable of doing simply because they are so pessimistic about themselves and their ability. "Low self-esteem seems to be at the heart of much of the underachievement of anxious-withdrawn children" (Kirk & Gallagher, 1989, 406).

Hardt (1988) indicates that passive-aggressive behavior in an emotionally disturbed child affects the child's progress and affects peer interactions in classroom settings. Passive-aggressive personalities are typically helpless, dependent, impulsive, overly anxious, poorly oriented to reality, and procrastinating. The passive-aggressive child uses numerous tactics to control the classroom environment, such as selective vision, selective hearing, slow-down tactics, losing objects, and the destructive volunteer tactic. Passive-aggressive children fail to develop satisfying interpersonal relationships and possess a negative self-esteem.

Thus, the research indicates that the general self-concepts and academic self-concepts of behavior disordered children are significantly negative and interfere with their functioning in all aspects of life. Their external locus of control and expectancy for failure perpetuates a severely negative cycle.

## Summary

Behavior disordered students, both aggressive and withdrawn, are a significant concern of the public school system in terms of their social, emotional, cognitive, and academic progress, but also, on the effects they have on other children in the classroom. The Federal definition used in PL94–142 refers to severely emotionally disturbed children who experience an inability to build or maintain satisfactory relationships with peers and adults, who engage in inappropriate types of behavior or feelings under normal circumstances, who possess a general pervasive mood of unhappiness or depression, and who reveal a tendency to develop physical symptoms or fears associated with personal or school problems.

The etiology of behavior disorders involves the interaction of multiple factors or contributing factors. Generally, causes are either biogenic (biological, physical and hereditary causes) or psychogenic (conflicts raging within the child). At least six theories have been proposed regarding the origin, nature, and cure of disturbance in children including the Biological Approach, the Psychoanalytic Approach, the Humanistic Approach, the Psychoeducational Approach, the Ecological Approach, and the Behavioral Approach. The inappropriate and maladaptive behaviors exhibited by behavior disordered children and adolescents are evident in deficits in academic learning, cognitive development, and social interactions. Disturbed behaviors are frequently categorized as mild-moderate behavior disorders (aggressive behaviors, withdrawn behaviors) and severe-profound behavior disorders.

Mild-moderate behavior disordered children are usually educated in the public school systems in self-contained classrooms, gradually mainstreaming to the regular classroom as they learn to control their behaviors. Though most mild-moderate behavior disordered students possess normal-range IQ (around 90) they experience many cognitive delays including metacognitive skills, attention deficits, information processing deficits, inefficiency in learning, and lack automatization. These deficits interact to prevent higher level cognitive functioning and academic success. They also experience significant deficits in terms of self-concept and have expectancies for failure.

# Unit Three
## CURRICULAR PERSPECTIVES

## Chapter Nine

# ASSESSMENT AND PROGRAM PLANNING FOR ENHANCING SELF-CONCEPTS

*"Since we have no direct access to a person's self-concept, it must be inferred from stimuli, verbal or nonverbal, which the student emits"* (Stangvik, 1979, 91).

Generic Assessment Information
Assessing Infants and Preschoolers
    Social and Emotional Development
    Infant and Preschool Children's Social Interactions
    Play Skill Development
    Self-Awareness and Pre-Self-Concept Development
Assessing Middle Childhood-Aged and Adolescent Students
    Social and Emotional Development
    Self-Concept During Middle Childhood and Adolescence
Changing Self-Concepts
Planning the Individualized Education Program
Summary

---

"T"he social and emotional growth and development of a child does not occur in isolation. . . . Social and emotional growth and development are closely linked with all aspects of child development into a synergistic relationship" (Jones, 1988, 241). Educators and parents are becoming increasingly aware that a child's acquisition of necessary social and emotional (affective) skills is critical for the student's mental and emotional health, both in and out of school (Cartledge & Milburn, 1986). Affect is difficult to quantify (Swanson & Watson, 1989).

## GENERIC ASSESSMENT INFORMATION

"Assessment is a process of collecting information about a student that will be used in forming judgments and making decisions concerning that student. . . . The most important goal of assessment, however, is to gather information that helps plan for instruction to improve the student's learning" (Lerner, 1989, 54). Five general types of decisions or reasons for assessing special needs children include the following: (1) Screening, (2) Diagnosis (Classification), (3) Educational Assessment (Instructional Planning), (4) Monitoring Pupil Progress, and (5) Program Evaluation. Peterson (1987) defined the purposes of assessment as follows:

1. Screening: To identify children who are not within normal ranges of development and need further evaluation and who may be candidates for early intervention programs.
2. Diagnosis: To conduct an in-depth evaluation to verify if a problem exists; to determine the nature and severity of the problem and prescribe the treatment or type of intervention services needed.
3. Educational Assessment: To identify a child's specific level of functioning across each of the developmental areas and to gather other performance data for developing the Individualized Education Program (IEP).
4. Performance Monitoring: To track or monitor each child's performance mastery of new skills as a result of the special instructional or therapeutic activities in the intervention program.
5. Program Evaluation: To evaluate the quality of the overall intervention program and to document its impact upon the children or parents it serves (285–286).

Assessment information may be obtained from a number of procedures and instruments, the selection of which often depends on the purpose of the assessment. It is suggested that teachers, the school-based assistance team, and the multidisciplinary evaluation team administer a variety of procedures and instruments including the following: norm-referenced tests, criterion-referenced tests, informal diagnostic tests, systematic observational techniques, and curriculum-based assessments, as well as collecting pertinent case history information.

Avoiding test bias is a major concern of P.L.94–142, and it mandates a multidisciplinary, nondiscriminatory evaluation. Numerous problems concerning testing bias have risen including the following: reliability and validity of the tests, test administration and interpretation by a trained tester, administered in the primary language of the child, using the test for its designed purpose. "These problems have their roots in inappropriate use and interpretation of tests in making social and educational decisions about the futures of children, regardless of their ethnic or socioeconomic backgrounds" (Swanson & Watson, 1989, 384). Thus, during the assessment/evaluation process elimination of test bias is crucial in arriving at an accurate diagnosis.

## ASSESSING INFANTS AND PRESCHOOLERS

"Assessing infants and preschoolers with handicaps is a necessary and fundamental activity for teachers, therapists, and other professionals in early intervention" (Bailey & Wolery, 1989, 1). "The early childhood years are crucial for all children, but for the child who deviates from the norm in terms of physical, mental, behavioral, motivational development or learning characteristics, these years are especially critical" (Lerner, 1989, 231). "Infants and young children with handicaps frequently have delays or disorders in social development severe enough to suggest that intervention should occur" (Bailey & Wolery, 1989, 391).

### Social and Emotional Development of Infants and Preschoolers

"Social and emotional development are difficult areas to evaluate in terms of normal behavior because there is such a wide variance in normal behavior" (Jones, 1988, 262). "The behavior of young children is extremely variable depending upon the setting, the time of day, who is present, and other factors" (Fallen & Umansky, 1985, 339). Therefore, using a single instrument or observation to document a child's behavior is not advised. "A multimodal approach uses a combination of strategies for collecting information, which may include systematic observations in various settings, interviews, rating scales, and paper pencil tests" (Fallen & Umansky, 1985, 340).

#### Screening Instruments

"The administration of developmental screening measures to individual children is the major event in the early-identification process" (Neisworth & Bagnato, 1987, 150). Numerous preschool and primary grade screening tests are available. Fallen and Umansky (1985) describe forty-three general and specific screening tests. Frequently used multidimensional developmental screening instruments which contain a social-emotional subtest include the following:

*Denver Developmental Screening Test* (1 mo.–6 years) (Frankenburg et. al., 1981)

*Developmental Profile* (0–9 yrs.) (Alpern et. al., 1981)
*Developmental Indicators for the Assessment of Learning-Revised (DIAL-R)* (2–0 to 5–11 years) (Mardell-Czudnowski & Goldenberg, 1983)

Developmental screening instruments are generally short, quick to administer, and inexpensive as they may be used to screen 50–100 children a day in a Child Find screening situation.

Screening instruments designed to assess children who appear to have social, emotional, self-concept, and/or behavioral problems include the following:

*Revised Child Behavior Checklist* (4–0 to 16–0) (Achenbach, 1982, 1983)
*Joseph Preschool and Primary Self-Concept Screening Test* (3–6 to 9–11 years) (Joseph, 1979)
*Preschool Behavior Rating Scale* (3–0 to 5–11 years) (Barker & Doeff, 1980).

**Evaluation Instruments**

"Several types of data are sought during the evaluation process including developmental data which can be compared to norms to determine the child's functioning abilities in relation to normal same-aged peers. These data are valuable in determining the level of the child's adaptive behavior—a crucial concern of any diagnosis, especially in a diagnosis of mental retardation" (Jones, 1988, 262–263).

**Norm-Referenced Assessments.** Diagnostic analysis with norm-referenced measures results in scores that gauge the child's functional levels (e.g., mental age, developmental age, IQ, DQ, percentiles) in the various developmental areas (Neisworth & Bagnato, 1987). Frequently administered norm-referenced developmental batteries which contain a social and emotional measure include the following:

*Gesell Developmental Schedules* (Knobloch & Pasamanick, 1974)
*Vineland Adaptive Behavior* (Sparrow, et. al., 1984)
*Vineland Social Maturity Scale* (Doll, 1985)

A norm-referenced test designed to assess the social and emotional development of children (aged 3–0 to 7–11 years) is the *Test of Early Socio-Emotional Development* (Hresko & Brown, 1984).

"NRA [norm-referenced assessment] is important in the process of determining levels of skill development; but used alone, it provides only general information for the initial phase of curriculum planning" (Neisworth & Bagnato, 1987, 163). Norm-referenced testing is used to pinpoint developmental areas of weakness and are useful in writing Individualized Education Program (IEP) annual goals.

**Criterion-Referenced Assessment.** Criterion-referenced assessment measures the child's progress in learning by determining his/her initial level of functioning and skill development in hierarchies or task-analyzed sequences of developmental skills. Criterion-referenced assessments provide entry level skills and specific information for setting Individualized Education Program objectives and teaching sequences. Frequently used developmental criterion-referenced assessments containing a social and emotional subtest include the following:

> *Portage Guide to Early Education* (Portage Project, 1976)
> *Callier-Azusa Scale* (Stillman, 1974)
> *Early Intervention Developmental Profile* (Schaefer & Moersch, 1981)
> *BRIGANCE Diagnostic Inventory of Early Development* (Brigance, 1983)

These developmental diagnostic instruments provide information regarding a child's functioning in all of the major developmental areas. The skills assessed are task-analyzed and provide valuable information regarding entry level functioning. This is especially important to the classroom teacher in planning the short-term objectives and teaching sequences on the Individual Education Program.

**Informal-Observational Assessment.** A published observational instrument for assessing social-emotional functioning of a child in an early childhood program is the *Scales of Socio-Emotional Development* (0–3 years) (Lewis & Michalson, 1983). Additional sources for gaining an overview of the social and emotional development of young children involves using checklists for comparing a child's behaviors to normal social and emotional developmental hierarchies.

## Infant and Preschool Children's Social Interactions

"The child expresses social and emotional skills at play, in interactions with other children and adults, and in problem-solving and other challenging situations" (Fallen & Umansky, 1985, 332).

### Sensorimotor Stage Instruments and Techniques

**Interactions with Adults/Children/Environment.** "Interactions between the caregiver and the young child should produce an empathic bond or secure attachment that promotes a clear concept of self-identity in the child" (Fallen & Umansky, 1985, 333). "Some infants with handicaps experience disrupted social relationships with their parents, and preschoolers with handicaps display poor social interaction skills and achieve less social acceptance by peers than normally developing children in their peer group" (Bailey & Wolery, 1989, 392–393).

Systematic observation appears to provide the most accurate diagnostic information regarding the social skills of young children due to their variability.

> Numerous instances of systematic observation in various settings (e.g., classroom, playground), at different times during the day, in different sized activity groupings (e.g., individual, small group), or in structured and unstructured activities may provide much information regarding the child's responsiveness and initiation of interactions. Systematic observation requires a means to organize data derived from numerous observations of the child in his/her interactions with adults, other children, and the environment (Jones, 1988, 263).

A systematic observation form to record many observations of the child in social interactions can be created by using a social development skills checklist and transferring the skills to a grid. An example is the *Systematic Observation Form: Social Development Interactions with Adults/ Children/Environment* (TABLE 1). Using this systematic observation form, it can be readily ascertained if the sensorimotor stage child's interactions are primarily responsive or self-initiated; and if the interactions occur mainly with adults, other children, or the environment. Continued weekly use of the Systematic Observation Form and other similar forms provides an excellent means of monitoring the child's performance and progress in the various developmental areas.

**Social Interactions at Home.** Severely handicapped and young children may behave differently at home than at school. With older, higher functioning children, parents can be interviewed regarding their child playing with neighborhood children, associations in community activities and clubs, home chores, and following family rules (Jones, 1988, 263). These activities are beyond the capabilities of many young and special needs children.

Many adaptive behavior scales begin at age two or three years, so the behaviors indicated are above the capabilities of the child functioning within the sensorimotor stage. Home adaptive behavior (social skills) can be assessed by having parents respond to or check the social development skills on a checklist or by using the systematic observation forms created with the same skills (e.g., TABLE 1) or by using the same skills in a "yes-no" questionnaire format.

TABLE 1

SYSTEMATIC OBSERVATION FORM: SOCIAL DEVELOPMENT:
INTERACTIONS WITH ADULTS / CHILDREN / ENVIRONMENT

| | Date / Place | | | | | | | | | | | |
|---|---|---|---|---|---|---|---|---|---|---|---|---|
| **Responsive Interactions with Adults** | No awareness of adults. | | | | | | | | | | | |
| | Smiles at familiar adult. | | | | | | | | | | | |
| | Attends to adult. | | | | | | | | | | | |
| | Cooperates passively. | | | | | | | | | | | |
| | Responds to adult interaction. | | | | | | | | | | | |
| | Smiles to activity with adult. | | | | | | | | | | | |
| | Responds to mother. | | | | | | | | | | | |
| | Stranger anxiety. | | | | | | | | | | | |
| | Attends to name spoken. | | | | | | | | | | | |
| | Responds to 2 interactions. | | | | | | | | | | | |
| | Stops activity at "No." | | | | | | | | | | | |
| **Initiative Interactions with Adults** | Attracts attention. | | | | | | | | | | | |
| | Identifies familiar adults. | | | | | | | | | | | |
| | Likes action manipulation. | | | | | | | | | | | |
| | Imitates simple actions. | | | | | | | | | | | |
| | Plays games with adults. | | | | | | | | | | | |
| | Maintains contact with familiar adult. | | | | | | | | | | | |
| | Seeks continued interactions. | | | | | | | | | | | |
| | Shows preference for adults. | | | | | | | | | | | |
| | Actively seeks attention. | | | | | | | | | | | |
| | Leader in play with adult. | | | | | | | | | | | |
| | Seeks adult's help. | | | | | | | | | | | |
| | Initiates dialogue with adults. | | | | | | | | | | | |
| | Seeks adult for play. | | | | | | | | | | | |
| | Seeks adult for play chosen by child. | | | | | | | | | | | |
| | Non-family adult preference. | | | | | | | | | | | |
| **Responsive Interactions to Children** | Ignores other children. | | | | | | | | | | | |
| | Responds to other child's presence. | | | | | | | | | | | |
| | Responds to familiar children. | | | | | | | | | | | |
| | Attends to confrontations. | | | | | | | | | | | |
| | Responds to play attempts. | | | | | | | | | | | |
| | Shows sympathy, affection, pity, guilt. | | | | | | | | | | | |

TABLE 1 (Continued)

| | Date / Place | | | | | | | | | | |
|---|---|---|---|---|---|---|---|---|---|---|---|
| Initiative Interactions with Children | Vocalizes to child's face. | | | | | | | | | | |
| | Explores other child tactiley. | | | | | | | | | | |
| | Shows interest in some object. | | | | | | | | | | |
| | Offers toy to child. | | | | | | | | | | |
| | Plays game with child. | | | | | | | | | | |
| | Prefers other child. | | | | | | | | | | |
| | Reverses play role. | | | | | | | | | | |
| | Seeks other child's help. | | | | | | | | | | |
| Responsive Interactions with Environment | Aware of light, sound, touch. | | | | | | | | | | |
| | Shows preferred eating schedule. | | | | | | | | | | |
| | Responds to touch, warm temperatures. | | | | | | | | | | |
| | Aware of body movements. | | | | | | | | | | |
| | Differentiates environments. | | | | | | | | | | |
| | Responds to environment changes. | | | | | | | | | | |
| | Frustration causes temper tantrums, etc. | | | | | | | | | | |
| Initiative Interactions with the Environment | Anticipates familiar events. | | | | | | | | | | |
| | Attempts to change position. | | | | | | | | | | |
| | Self-stimulation without objects. | | | | | | | | | | |
| | Vocalizes to show discomfort. | | | | | | | | | | |
| | Makes different vocalizations. | | | | | | | | | | |
| | Expresses preferences in foods. | | | | | | | | | | |
| | Shows interest in objects. | | | | | | | | | | |
| | Reaches out to explore. | | | | | | | | | | |
| | Shows curiosity and explores. | | | | | | | | | | |
| | Inappropriate use of objects. | | | | | | | | | | |
| | Shows object preference. | | | | | | | | | | |
| | Seeks object for comfort. | | | | | | | | | | |
| | Uses object for function. | | | | | | | | | | |
| | Locates objects in room. | | | | | | | | | | |
| | Threatens wrong behavior. | | | | | | | | | | |

The home adaptive behavior information serves several purposes including providing a "biased, nonobjective" assessment of the child's functioning at home which can be compared to school functioning. The questionnaire also allows parents to be involved in the evaluation process and to understand the difficulty in assessing young and/or handicapped

TABLE 1 (Continued)

| | Date / Place | | | | | | | | | | | |
|---|---|---|---|---|---|---|---|---|---|---|---|---|
| Initiative Interactions with the Environment | Plays on object alone. | | | | | | | | | | | |
| | Indicates need to toilet. | | | | | | | | | | | |
| | Knows not to throw food. | | | | | | | | | | | |
| | Knows not to identify objects as "own." | | | | | | | | | | | |
| | | | | | | | | | | | | |
| | | | | | | | | | | | | |
| | | | | | | | | | | | | |
| | | | | | | | | | | | | |

KEY:
X- Behavior Present   E- Behavior Emerging
N- Behavior Not Present

TIME:
A- AM
P- PM

LOCATION OF OBSERVATION:
C- Classroom     P- Playground
G- Group Activity     F- Free Play     S- Structured

Source: Jones, C. 1988. p. 248-249.

children. It provides parents some insights into the amount of consideration by many professionals that is involved in the evaluation of their
child.

## Preschool Social Interaction Assessments

"Preschool-aged children with handicaps exhibit substantial social
interaction deficits" (Bailey & Wolery, 1989, 394). "Young children with
special needs often show unique behaviors in their interactions with
others or when faced with a problematic task" (Fallen & Umansky, 1985,
332).

Assessing the social interactions of preschool-aged children is frequently easier than assessing the social interactions of infants and toddlers.
Nonhandicapped preschool-aged children possess motor skills and communication skills that facilitate reactions and interactions which are
more observable than the often subtle reactions and interactions of
infants. Additionally, numerous norm-referenced and criterion-referenced
assessments, and informal instruments and procedures have been designed
for use with preschoolers.

Preschool-aged children who are functioning within the sensorimotor
stage should be assessed using the same procedures as those used with
chronological-aged sensorimotor stage functioning children. The norm-

referenced and criterion-referenced assessments previously mentioned were designed to assess preschool-aged and preschool level functioning children, to provide adequate information for diagnosis of social deficits and preparation of goals and objectives for the Individualized Education Program.

**Peer Interactions.** Social interaction or social reciprocity with preschool-aged children can be assessed by looking at "the number of social behaviors that a child directs to his peers and the number directed to him from his peers" (Bailey & Wolery, 1989, 395). Teachers assessing social behaviors or misbehaviors may wish to determine the frequency and/or duration with which the behaviors occur. Frequency is usually determined by counting the number of times a behavior occurs within a given time period. Duration of a given social interaction or misbehavior can be determined by using a stopwatch to measure the time span covered by the interaction.

At the toddler or preschool level, peer preferences or relationships can be determined by observing the frequency with which children mutually interact and seek each other for play. At the preschool level, social relationships with peers are most often measured by the use of a sociometric assessment (Bailey & Wolery, 1989).

**Home Adaptive Behavior.** The preschool-aged child's home adaptive behavior is generally derived by interviewing the parents regarding how well the child plays and cooperates with other neighborhood children and siblings; how well s/he follows family rules and obeys parents; how well the child shows responsibility by performance of self-help skills, picking up his/her toys, taking care of possessions, and performing daily chores; and how well the child gets along with significant others.

## Play Skills Development

Numerous theorists have proposed various definitions of play and prepared varied play skills hierarchies. "The most recent views of play, however, are in accord with the psychoanalytic and cognitive perspectives, emphasizing play as a medium for cognitive and social-emotional growth" (Beers & Wehman, 1985, 408). "For obvious reasons, norm-referenced measures of play do not exist" (Beers & Wehman, 1985, 436). Many developmental scales assess cognitive or motor skills prerequisites necessary to engage in play activities. Evaluation of play skills should result in determination of a developmental skills functioning level and specific strengths and weaknesses to be used in programming.

Some criterion-referenced or curriculum-based assessments that may be useful in assessing play skills of children include the following:

*Play Assessment Scale* (0–3 years) (toy play) (Fewell, 1986)
*Symbolic Play Scale Checklist* (9 mo.–5 years) (Westby, 1980)
*Peer Play Scale* (2–7 years) (peer play) (Howes, 1980)

## Play Skills of Infants and Toddlers

"For young handicapped children with mild and moderate delays, one of the most effective ways to assess the level of play development is through observational assessment" (Fallen & Umansky, 1985, 431). Systematic observation is also one of the most effective means of evaluating the play skills of severely handicapped children.

The determination of specific strengths and weaknesses requires a criterion-referenced instrument or task-analyses of various play skills. Few formal criterion-referenced instruments specifically assess play skills as a separate area; usually play skills are included in other developmental areas such as socialization and motor skills. Specific strengths and weaknesses in play skill development can be determined utilizing systematic observation in various settings, at different times during the day, over a several-week period to gain a pattern of behavior. For best success with observation, the observational factors should be carefully delineated. Thus, a programming play skills sequence can be very helpful in determining the child's level of play (e.g., Practice Play, Emerging Symbolic Play), type of play in which the child engages (e.g., Exploratory Play, Action/Object Play, Learned Movements/New Situations), and the specific play skills displayed by the child (e.g., Engages in sensory exploration of own body).

Frequent monitoring of the child's progress in play skill development, through systematic observation, can be facilitated by transferring the play skills to a data collection grid, *Systematic Observation Form: Play Skills* (TABLE 2). Thus, monitoring the Individualized Educational Program can easily be an ongoing and frequent activity within the classroom. Analyses of Systematic Observation Form data provide a continuous assessment by quickly indicating within which level of practice play or emerging symbolic play the child is functioning. The child's program can then be easily planned or modified, based on the hierarchy of play skills.

TABLE 2

SYSTEMATIC OBSERVATION FORM: PLAY SKILLS

| | Date / Place / Time: | | | | | | | | | | |
|---|---|---|---|---|---|---|---|---|---|---|---|
| Exploratory Play | Sensory exploration of own body | | | | | | | | | | |
| | Repeats pleasant body actions | | | | | | | | | | |
| | Explores objects using senses | | | | | | | | | | |
| | Manipulates objects | | | | | | | | | | |
| | Pulls at dangling toys | | | | | | | | | | |
| Action / Object Play | Shakes toys repeatedly | | | | | | | | | | |
| | Makes mobiles swing | | | | | | | | | | |
| | Bangs objects on table | | | | | | | | | | |
| | Grasps dangling objects | | | | | | | | | | |
| | Uncovers a hidden toy | | | | | | | | | | |
| | Squeezes doll to squeek | | | | | | | | | | |
| Learned Moves New Situation | Rolls ball in imitation | | | | | | | | | | |
| | Holds crayon, imitates scribbling | | | | | | | | | | |
| | Stacks rings on pegs | | | | | | | | | | |
| | Dumps objects from container | | | | | | | | | | |
| | Scoops with spoons | | | | | | | | | | |
| Experimentation / Ritualized Play | Solitary or onlooker play | | | | | | | | | | |
| | Initiates play | | | | | | | | | | |
| | Scribbles with crayon | | | | | | | | | | |
| | Puts objects in/out container | | | | | | | | | | |
| | Pulls wheeled toy | | | | | | | | | | |
| | Carries or hugs doll | | | | | | | | | | |
| | Puts pegs in pegboard | | | | | | | | | | |
| | Throws objects from playpen | | | | | | | | | | |
| | Drops toys / watches fall | | | | | | | | | | |
| | Crawls pushing toy car | | | | | | | | | | |

## Preschool Play Skills

Previous discussion indicated that there were few, if any, norm-referenced play assessments for preschool age or functioning level children, and suggested several scales to use in the play skill assessment of children. Scales or assessment instruments for young children often question the caregivers about the child's functioning level. Questionnaires provide a static assessment based on an adult's memory of the child's behaviors.

## TABLE 2

### SYSTEMATIC OBSERVATION FORM: PLAY SKILLS

| | Date / Place / Time: | | | | | | | | | | | |
|---|---|---|---|---|---|---|---|---|---|---|---|---|
| **Familiar Actions/ New Objects** | Throws small ball | | | | | | | | | | | |
| | Paints with large brush | | | | | | | | | | | |
| | Puts sized rings on peg | | | | | | | | | | | |
| | Builds block tower | | | | | | | | | | | |
| | Plays with clay | | | | | | | | | | | |
| | Transports blocks in wagon | | | | | | | | | | | |
| | Strings beads | | | | | | | | | | | |
| | Pounds pegs in pegboard | | | | | | | | | | | |
| | Pulls string to activate toy | | | | | | | | | | | |
| | Turns handle to activate toy | | | | | | | | | | | |
| | Rocks on a rocking horse | | | | | | | | | | | |
| | Swings in a swing | | | | | | | | | | | |
| | Takes objects apart | | | | | | | | | | | |
| **Concrete Pretend** | Rides a broom horse | | | | | | | | | | | |
| | Plays house | | | | | | | | | | | |
| | Moves (dances) to music | | | | | | | | | | | |

KEY:   X   Behavior Present
       E   Behavior Emerging
       N   Behavior Not Present

TIME:   A   AM
        P   PM

LOCATION OF OBSERVATION:
   C   Classroom
   P   Playground
   F   Free Play
   G   Group Activity
   S   Structured

Source: Jones, C. 1988, p. 268-269.

Informal assessment and systematic observation of children in action provide a dynamic picture of the child's play skills. The determination of specific strengths and weaknesses requires numerous observations in various settings (e.g., preschool classroom, playground, lunchroom, individual or group settings), at various times during the day, over a several week period to determine "baseline" behavior.

## Self-Awareness and Pre-Self-Concept Development

The development of self awareness and the various self-concepts emerge in early childhood and continue to define and redefine the self throughout life.

### Infants and Toddlers

The self-concept growth process during the sensorimotor stage focuses primarily on the child's awareness of his/her own body, recognition of the attention provided by others, and understanding of body image. Few, if any, self-concept instruments exist to assess the self-concept functioning levels of sensorimotor stage children. The pre-self-concept skills of infants and toddlers are best assessed through systematic observation of the child at scheduled times throughout the day and over a several week period.

Monitoring the sensorimotor stage child's self-awareness development should involve numerous observations weekly. Numerous systematic observations can be recorded on a systematic observation form created by transferring the skills to a grid, such as *Systematic Observation Form: Self-Awareness (TABLE 3)*.

### Self-Concepts of Preschoolers

As the young child moves into the preschool years, s/he demonstrates mastery of the sensorimotor stage concepts of Body Awareness, Recognition of Attention, and Body Image (TABLE 3). During the preschool years the child begins to develop self-concepts by becoming aware of his/her strengths and weaknesses in gross motor play activities, personal physical attractiveness, social attractiveness, intelligence, special aptitudes, preacademic performance, and peer acceptance.

There are very few assessment instruments that seek to determine the self-concept of preschool-aged children. The *Joseph Preschool and Primary Self-Concept Screening Test* (3–6 to 9–11 years) (Joseph, 1989) can be used to gain an overview of the child's self-concept and to determine the child's areas of personal strengths and weaknesses. In general at the preschool age, social and emotional assessments provide adequate information that can be generalized to ascertain if the child has primarily a negative or positive self-concept orientation.

## TABLE 3

### Systematic Observation Form: Self Awareness

| | Date / Time / Place | | | | | | | | | | | |
|---|---|---|---|---|---|---|---|---|---|---|---|---|
| **Body Awareness** | Responds with total body movement. | | | | | | | | | | | |
| | Shows awareness of own body. | | | | | | | | | | | |
| | Visually explores own body. | | | | | | | | | | | |
| | Explores with hands, mouth, eyes. | | | | | | | | | | | |
| | Studies self in mirror. | | | | | | | | | | | |
| **Recognition of Attention** | Recognizes others paying attention. | | | | | | | | | | | |
| | Responds to others, attempts to play. | | | | | | | | | | | |
| | Stops action when told "No." | | | | | | | | | | | |
| | Recognizes own name. | | | | | | | | | | | |
| | Differentiates +/- attention. | | | | | | | | | | | |
| **Body Image** | Holds objects placed in hands. | | | | | | | | | | | |
| | Differentiates self from objects / others. | | | | | | | | | | | |
| | Concept of size of self. | | | | | | | | | | | |
| | Sense of self in space. | | | | | | | | | | | |
| | Understands directionality. | | | | | | | | | | | |
| | Recognizes body parts on doll. | | | | | | | | | | | |
| | Touches body parts on cue. | | | | | | | | | | | |
| | Aware of sex roles. | | | | | | | | | | | |
| | Identifies with same sex parent. | | | | | | | | | | | |
| **Concept of Abilities** | Socially attractive. | | | | | | | | | | | |
| | Aware of physical attractiveness. | | | | | | | | | | | |
| | Aware of special aptitude. | | | | | | | | | | | |

Source:    Jones, C. (1988).

## ASSESSING MIDDLE CHILDHOOD AGED AND ADOLESCENT STUDENTS

Handicapped students frequently exhibit social and emotional behavior problems which interfere with successful academic performance. "Assessment of social/emotional functioning is required by the regulations implementing PL 94–142 for classification of students as seriously emotionally disturbed" (Helton, 1988, 406). "Assessment of adaptive behavior is required by the regulations implementing PL 94–142 for classification of students as mentally retarded, in which students must demonstrate significantly deficient functioning in both intelligence and adaptive behavior" (Helton, 1988, 407). Determining social/emotional functioning may also be necessary to ascertain if students' school problems are primarily the result of a learning disability or of emotional disturbance or if they are experiencing both handicapping conditions simultaneously (Helton, 1988).

### Assessing Social-Emotional Development

"Assessing a student's social skills and emotional status is difficult" (Lerner, 1989, 483). This difficulty includes a number of problems with the validity and reliability of procedures and assessments usually utilized in assessing affective functioning including the following: (1) Social behaviors are situation specific and are not generalizable between situations; (2) People's ideas of what constitutes acceptable behavior differ greatly; (3) The results of the assessment often depends on the person doing the assessing and the reporting (Luftig, 1988); and (4) There are more than 340 different self-concept, and social/emotional measures reported in the literature (Mitchell, 1985).

The social and emotional functioning of students is multifaceted including social interactions with family and peers, social competence, social perspective-taking, moral development, sense of personal control (attributions, motivation), and self-concepts. Therefore, it appears logical to assume that such varied affective factors as social, emotional, adaptive, and self-concept behaviors should be assessed, using multiple methods and sessions of data collection (Cartledge & Milburn, 1986). "Indeed, it would seem appropriate to assess a child's self-concept, locus of control beliefs, and academic performance expectations at the time of diagnosis and when planning academic programs and placements" (Rogers & Saklofske, 1985).

Several levels of information regarding a child's various areas of affective functioning is often collected including classroom screening to identify "at-risk" students in comparison to peers in various settings; and evaluation for individual behavior and personality deviances from the norm. General approaches for assessing social and emotional functioning include the following: (1) behavior checklists or rating scales, (2) interview instruments, (3) self-report instruments, (4) direct behavioral observations of a student, and (5) projective techniques (Helton, 1988; Lerner, 1989).

### Screening

Direct observation of students in the classroom is perhaps the most frequently used screening method. Teachers keep anecdotal records, logs, notations on specific deviant or problem behaviors with special considerations given to the type of behavior and its frequency, intensity, and duration (Mercer, 1987). These informal notations assist the teacher in identifying social-emotional behavior problems that require immediate attention. The teacher also needs to be concerned with antecedent and consequent behaviors that allow her to predict when and where certain students will experience difficulty and will require intervention assistance.

### Evaluation: Behavior Problems

The purpose of an individual multidisciplinary evaluation is to determine if the student has a severe enough discrepancy from the norm in affective behaviors as to require assistance in order to be successful. A multidisciplinary approach, a number of assessors using a number of assessment instruments in varied settings, is especially necessary in the area of affective development in order to avoid test bias.

**Behavior Checklists and Rating Scales.** Checklists and rating scales are "devices which provide methods for obtaining and recording judgments of teachers, students, peers, and parents concerning undesirable social-emotional behavior. Checklists generally are used to record the presence or absence of specific characteristics or behaviors" (Mercer, 1987, 454). Rating scales are designed to indicate the frequency of a particular behavior or the degree to which the selected attitude or behavior is present (Mercer & Mercer, 1989). There are numerous norm-referenced and informal rating scales and checklists available for use by teachers and diagnosticians.

Norm-referenced checklists and rating scales frequently used to assess social skills during middle childhood and adolescence "provide data on the relative severity of a student's behavior problems for classification purposes" (Helton, 1988, 406), and include the following:

*The Walker Problem Behavior Identification Checklist* (K–6) (Walker, 1983)
*Child Behavior Checklist* (ages 4–16) (Achenbach & Edelbrock, 1983)
*The Social-Emotional Dimension Scale* (5–18 years) (Hutton & Roberts, 1986)

**Interview Instruments.** Interview instruments require the interviewer (school psychologist, social worker, guidance counselor, etc.) to follow systematic procedures as s/he interviews one or several persons (e.g., family members, peers, other teachers) who know the student (Mercer & Mercer, 1989). Norm-referenced interview instruments commonly used to assess adjustment in the social, behavioral, and adaptive areas during the middle childhood and adolescent years include the following:

*Behavior Rating Profile* (grades 1–12) (Brown & Hammill, 1983)
*Scales of Independent Behavior* (infant–adult) (Bruininks et. al., 1985)

### Evaluation: Adaptive Behavior

Adaptive behavior or social competence is a person's ability to cope with the social demands of the environment. "According to most definitions, for individuals to be labeled retarded, they must exhibit problems in social adaptation" (Patton et. al., 1990, 98–99). Norm-referenced assessment instruments often used in evaluating a student's adaptive behavior include the following:

*Social Skills Rating System* (ages 3–18; preschool–Grade 12) (Gresham & Elliott, 1990)
*The AAMD (Adaptive Behavior Scale-School Edition)* (3–16 years) (Nihira et. al., 1981)
*Vineland Adaptive Behavior Scales* (birth–18 years) (Sparrow et. al., 1984)

### Evaluation: Environment

A number of environmental influences such as general school climate, nature of the school curriculum, teacher behaviors, peer influences, and home influences should be considered when making programming decisions (Helton et. al., 1982). Most environmental assessments consist of checklists. Formal environmental evaluation instruments include the following:

*Ecological Assessment of Child Problem Behavior* (Wahler et. al., 1976).

## Evaluation: Peer and Adult Interactions

"Apparently, a significant proportion of at-risk children do not learn requisite social and affective skills on their own, and they suffer from poor peer relationships, loneliness, and poor self-concept" (Luftig, 1988, 417). Some of the formal assessment instruments previously indicated have subtests or subscales that evaluate social interactions including the following:

*The Walker Problem Behavior Identification Checklist* (disturbed peer relationships) (Walker, 1983)
*Weller-Strawser Scales of Adaptive Behavior* (social coping and relationships, 6–12 and 13–18 years) (Weller & Strawser, 1981)
*Behavior Rating Profile* (behavior with peers) (Brown & Hammill, 1983)
*Vineland Adaptive Behavior Scales* (socialization) (Sparrow et. al., 1984)
*Social-Emotional Dimension Scale* (avoidance of peer and teacher interaction) (Hutton & Roberts, 1986)

## Evaluation: Student Perceptions of Competence

A student's perceptions of his/her own social competence and sense of personal control dramatically effect motivation, confidence in academic and social situations, and ultimately academic progress and social adjustment. Thus, the evaluation of a student would be significantly enhanced by determining the student's own perceptions of his/her skills and abilities. Specific assessments that have been developed to assist in ascertaining students' own perceptions of their social competence and their sense of personal control include the following:

*Nowicki-Strickland Locus of Control Scale* (Nowicki & Strickland, 1973)
*Kohn Social Competence Scale* (Kohn et. al., 1979)
*Projected Academic Performance Scale* (Chapman & Boersma, 1978)
*Perceived Competence Scale for Children* (grades 3–6) (Harter, 1982)

## Systematic Observation

"Direct, systematic observation of student behavior can provide information and insights about the child's social-emotional skills" (Mercer, 1987, 453). The teacher should observe the behaviors, the conditions under which the behavior occurs, the frequency of occurrence in varied settings and at varied times; and the impact on the student's engaged learning time (on-task rate), completion rate, and accuracy rate. The at-risk student should be observed in comparison to same-sex peers to determine degree of deviancy from peers.

The use of direct, systematic observation helps to provide the teacher or other observers with more objectivity than anecdotal records. Direct, systematic observation requires an organized procedure and an organized form on which to record data. The *Systematic Observation Form: Classroom Behaviors* (TABLE 4) was created to provide a means of quantifying inappropriate classroom behaviors, and to observe an at-risk student in comparison to peers.

The behavior variables utilized in TABLE 4 are described as follows:

1. **Noise** (N): Any sounds created by the child that distract either another student or the teacher from the current work/activity. The noise may be generated vocally (including "talk outs" or unintelligible sounds) or nonvocally ("tapping a pencil" or "snapping fingers") (Germann & Tindal, 1985, 258–259).

2. **Out of Place** (OP): Any movement beyond either the explicitly or implicitly defined boundaries in which the child is allowed movement. If a child is seated at a desk, then movement of any sort out of the seat is "out of place" (Germann & Tindal, 1985, 259).

3. **Physical Contact** (PC): Any contact with another person or that person's property that is unacceptable to that person. Kicking, hitting, pushing, tearing, breaking, and taking are categorized as physical contact or destruction (Germann & Tindal, 1985, 259).

4. **Off-Task** (OF): Any movement off of a prescribed activity that does not fall into one of the three previously defined categories. "Looking around," "staring into space," "doodling," or any observable movement off the current task/activity at hand is included (Germann & Tindal, 1985, 259).

5. **Lack of Social Behavior** (LB): A behavioral deficit in which the student is withdrawn and socially isolated (Germann & Tindal, 1985).

6. **On Task** (OT): On-task scores represent the percentages of time the student was actually engaged in task related behavior such as attending to his/her assignments (Gickling & Thompson, 1985, 213).

7. **Task Completion** (TC): Completion scores are determined by the number of items attempted whether right or wrong. These scores represent the total number of response efforts made by each student per task (Gickling & Thompson, 1985, 213).

8. **Task Accuracy Rate** (ACC): Task accuracy rates will be determined

**Table 4**

SYSTEMATIC OBSERVATION FORM: CLASSROOM BEHAVIORS

Target Student: _____ Observer: _____ Date: _____

Observation #: _____ Summary: Target:    OT _____ TC _____ ACC _____
                                             Class Ave: OT _____ TC _____ ACC _____

| Students | Observation Frames (20 Frames) Off-Task Behaviors | | | | | | | | | | | | | | | | | | | | ALT | | |
|---|---|---|---|---|---|---|---|---|---|---|---|---|---|---|---|---|---|---|---|---|---|---|---|
| | | | | | | | | | | | | | | | | | | | | | OT | TC | ACC |
| Target Student | | | | | | | | | | | | | | | | | | | | | | | |
| Peer #1 | | | | | | | | | | | | | | | | | | | | | | | |
| Target | | | | | | | | | | | | | | | | | | | | | | | |
| Peer #2 | | | | | | | | | | | | | | | | | | | | | | | |
| Target | | | | | | | | | | | | | | | | | | | | | | | |
| Peer #3 | | | | | | | | | | | | | | | | | | | | | | | |
| Target | | | | | | | | | | | | | | | | | | | | | | | |
| Peer #4 | | | | | | | | | | | | | | | | | | | | | | | |
| Target | | | | | | | | | | | | | | | | | | | | | | | |
| | | | | | | | | | | | | | | | | | | | | | | | |
| | | | | | | | | | | | | | | | | | | | | | | | |
| | | | | | | | | | | | | | | | | | | | | | | | |

KEY:  Behaviors
    N    Noise
    OP   Out of Place
    PC   Physical Contact
    OF   Off-Task
    LB   Lack of Social Behavior
  Other  Specify

Academic Learning Time (ALT)
    OT   On-Task Behavior Rate
    TC   Task Completion Rate
   ACC  Accuracy Rate

REFERENCES: Gickling & Thompson, 1985; Germann & Tindall, 1985.

by the number of correct items compared to the total number of task items.

"In the initial assessments, an observation is conducted over several days for 20 to 30 minutes, with each session implemented at different times of the school day" (Germann & Tindal, 1985, 259). The observation of the target student and his/her peers is systematically rotated at intervals of one minute providing six 10-second intervals of data (TABLE 4). Thus, if Johnny is the target student he will be observed for one minute (note behaviors every 10 seconds in separate frames), then observe a randomly selected same-sex peer (Boy #1) for one minute and record the behavior on TABLE 4. "This process is repeated (focusing on first the target and then a different same-sex peer) until all of the same-sex peers in the classroom have been observed.

For each behavior, a discrepancy is calculated between the target student's rates of behavior and the average of the same-sex peers' rates of behavior. When the target student shows behavior 2X (two times) discrepant from the class average, a significant problem in social skills should be suspected and a referral for Special Education consideration should be initiated. For example, if the average "noise" behaviors of the boys in the classroom is 25% of the observation time, but Johnny was engaged in inappropriate noise-making 75% of the observation period, his behavior is at least two times discrepant from the average for boys in his classroom.

## Informal Evaluation

Teachers can sometimes engineer procedures (e.g., writing autobiographies, group discussions, thinking exercises in moral dilemmas) during which the student will reveal social and emotional developmental milestones, metacognitive skills, social perspective-taking, and social problem-solving.

## Projective Tests

"Projective techniques continue to be used widely by testing practitioners despite controversy over their validity, reliability, and general usefulness" (Jackson & Pavnonen, 1980). Psychologists frequently administer projective tests aimed at discerning unconscious motives, feelings, and attitudes. Frequently administered projective instruments and procedures include the following: (1) Human Figure Drawing Test (Koppitz, 1968), (2) Draw-A–Person Test (Urban, 1963), (3) Rorschach Psycho-

diagnostic Plates (Rorschach & Huber, 1954), (4) Educational Apperception Test (Thompson & Somes, 1973), (5) Children's Apperception Test
(Bellak & Bellak, 1949), and (6) Rhode Sentence Completion Test (Jensen,
1967). The training for administration and interpretation of projective
tests often takes years. In public school assessment projective tests results
do not play a major role in determining a diagnosis.

### Evaluation: Summary

With so many methods, instruments, and techniques available for
social and emotional evaluation, the teacher may be confused regarding
which instruments to use. Several factors should be kept in mind in
selecting evaluation techniques including the following:

1. What is the purpose of the assessment? (Screening? Evaluation?)
2. How will the information collected be utilized? (Diagnosis? Programming?)
3. What types of information are needed? (Social? Emotional? Adaptive?)
4. How much time will be allotted for assessment?
5. What is the age and intellectual ability level of the students to be
   tested?
6. Who is the tester? (Classroom teacher? Diagnostician?)

Generally, an evaluation of social and emotional development will
require a norm-referenced instrument to determine deviance from same-
aged peers, a task-analyzed skills hierarchy for programming, an environmental assessment to determine causes or contributory factors, an assessment of social interactions which may be part of a norm-referenced
developmental instrument: and an evaluation of the child's own perceptions of his/her competence, attributions, motivation, and expectations.

## Assessing Self-Concepts During Middle Childhood and Adolescence

There is no way to actually derive the true self-concept (Gergen, 1971).
Since we have no direct access to a person's self-concept, it must be
inferred from stimuli, verbal or nonverbal, which the student emits
(Stangvik, 1979, 91). More than 340 self-concept and personality measures
are reported in the literature (Mitchell, 1985), and for most of these
measures the degree of reliability of the instrument has not been determined (Wylie, 1974).

Most authors of self-concept instruments adhere to the theory of the multidimensional nature of the self-concept, and they have composed their tests accordingly. Thus, while most self-concept assessment instruments assess the general self-concept, they also yield specific self-concept scores in such areas as academic, physical, and peer group self-concepts (Luftig, 1988, 429–430).

## Self-Reporting Instruments

Self-reporting is probably the most common means of obtaining a measure of self-concept. Self-reporting measures are instruments which require the subjects to make judgments concerning their behaviors or their feelings toward themselves (Jones, 1983, 66). The advantage of self reporting is the provision of an inside view of the person based on the person's experience and knowledge of himself (LaBenne & Greene, 1969). Self-reporting seems to be the best method of measuring the individual's conscious world (Wylie, 1961), though self-reporting measures are weak in external validity due to the possibility that some reports can be faked and some students are incapable of making accurate evaluations of themselves (LaBenne & Greene, 1969, 11).

Self-report self-concept instruments frequently used in the assessment of middle childhood-aged and adolescent students includes the following:

*Coopersmith Self-Esteem Inventories* (elementary age) (Coopersmith, 1981)
*Piers-Harris Children's Self-Concept Scale* (3rd–12th grade) (Piers & Harris, 1969, 1984)
*Tennessee Self-Concept Scale* (12 years plus) (Fitts, 1965)

The Piers-Harris is probably the most popular of all the self-concept assessment instruments available today (Luftig, 1988). The Piers-Harris yields seven types of self-concept (self-perception) scores including the following: (1) Intellectual ability and School status, (2) Behavior, (3) Physical Appearance and Attributes, (4) Anxiety, (5) Popularity, (6) Happiness and Satisfaction, and (7) Total Self-Concept score. The "Piers-Harris appears to be the best children's self-concept measure currently available. It is highly recommended for use as a classroom screening device, as an aid to clinical assessment, and as a research tool" (Jeske, 1985, 961).

The Piers-Harris, then, provides a general self-concept and insight into which areas may be significantly weak. Specific self-concept areas, especially areas of weakness, could be probed using more indepth evaluation instruments. For example, if the Piers-Harris reveals significant weakness in the area of intellectual and school attributes, specific information regarding the academic self-concept, academic locus of control, and academic achievement expectations might be ascertained by administering the following:

*Perception of Ability Scale for Students* (academic self-concept) (Boersma & Chapman, 1988)

*Intellectual Achievement Responsibility Questionnaire* (academic locus of control) (Crandall et. al., 1965)

*Projected Academic Performance Scale* (academic achievement expectations) (Chapman & Boersma, 1978).

Through factor analysis of the *Perception of Ability Scale for Students* (Boersma & Chapman, 1988) additional information can be derived regarding the academic self-concept including the following: (1) Perception of General Ability, (2) Perception of Arithmetic Ability, (3) General School Satisfaction, (4) Perception of Reading and Spelling Ability, (5) Perception of Penmanship and Neatness, and (6) Confidence in Academic Ability (Chapman, 1988, 359). This additional specific information about the areas in which the student feels incompetent is valuable in planning the Individual Education Program

### Informal Assessment of Self-Concept

Numerous text books contain informal self-concept assessments including sentence completion, forced-choice words, and forced-choice statements such as "Which sentence is most like me? (a) Nothing gets me too mad. (b) I get mad easily and explode" (Swanson & Watson, 1989, 422). These assessments are especially useful at the beginning of a school year in assisting the teacher in getting to know her students. The teacher must remember, however, that the responses are situation specific and may not represent the child's global feelings.

## CHANGING THE SELF-CONCEPT

Overall, research evidence has clearly illustrated a persistent and significant relationship between the self-concept and academic achievement (Purkey, 1970). This relationship has suggested the important role of the school in the development and/or change in the self-concept. The self-concept appears to be pliable during the elementary school years (Yamamoto, 1972). Thus, the elementary school teachers play an extremely important role in the development of the child's self-image.

That there can be change in the self-concept of the individual is widely accepted (Wylie, 1961).

The high degree of stability of the self-concept makes it resistant to change by causing the self to ignore aspects of experience which are inconsistent with it and by selecting perceptions which confirm the self-concept (Combs & Snygg, 1959, 159). Research findings show scholastic self-concept to be a relatively stable dimension of personality for both early and middle adolescents (Harris, 1971).

> Repeated instances of success or failure in a particular area may quickly result in a self-concept as adequate or inadequate with respect to that matter in a child who has no preexisting concepts. The same experiences of success or failure experienced by a child who already has strong perceptions of self in that area may result in no appreciable change in the self-concept whatever (Combs & Gordon, 1967, 159).

A self-concept resulting from many experiences over a long period of time may take an equally long time to change. Self-concepts formed as a result of long and adverse experiences do not change quickly, nor do they change as the result of words alone. Changes in the fundamental concepts of self usually change slowly and gradually.

Research indicates that the aspects of the self-concept involved in perception of one's ability to handle learning and increased knowledge can be altered through careful environmental design (Muller & Spuhler, 1976).

Several studies collectively suggest that the self-concept is a significant component in motivation for learning in students ranging in age from 4–75, from all socio-economic backgrounds, urban or rural areas, ghetto or private schools, regardless of ethnic background (Eklof, 1973; Dewey, 1978; Hill & Ruhe, 1977). A student's efforts to obtain knowledge and skill is dependent on his perceptions of his ability to succeed. Conceptualizing the self as a capable learner is critical to the presence of motivation for learning (Ballif, 1978).

In a longitudinal investigation of approximately 5,500 students in 72 schools, the results indicated that neither the school organization nor types of teacher affected the development of self-concept in above-average ability students, but did affect the self-image of average and below-average ability students (Lunn, 1970). Children of average ability were especially influenced by teacher-type in developing academic self-concepts (Lunn, 1970).

"Generally speaking, the more closely related an experience is perceived to the phenomenal self, the greater will be its effect upon behavior" (Combs & Snygg, 1959, 149). In other words, for education to be effective the educator must find ways of helping people to discover the personal meanings of events for them. It is only when events are seen as having some relationship to the person that behavior is changed.

Relevance in education is contingent first upon understanding the student, and, secondly, upon individualizing the educational process (Yamamoto, 1972). Understanding the student is derived from knowledge of how the student perceives himself. This self-conception includes effects of environmental, social, emotional, and physical conditions of paramount influence in the life of the student. Individualization of an educational program is dependent, not only upon the child's current performance level and measured potential, but also upon the child's concept regarding his/her ability and achievement potential. "It is crucial that adequate assessment of self-concept be included in the special needs student's Individualized Assessment Program" (multidisciplinary evaluation) (Luftig, 1989, 429).

## PLANNING THE INDIVIDUALIZED EDUCATION PROGRAM

"One of the major provisions of P.L. 94-142 is the requirement that an individualized education program (IEP) be formulated for each student identified as handicapped" (Lerner, 1989, 55). The Individualized Education Program serves two primary purposes: (1) It is the curriculum for a specific exceptional student, and (2) It is a management tool for monitoring the student's progress through his/her specially designed curriculum. The Individualized Education Program must include the following factors:

(1) The child's present functioning levels
(2) Annual and short-term instructional objectives
(3) The special services and to what extent regular classroom participation
(4) The projected date for initiation and anticipated duration of such services
(5) Criteria, evaluation procedures, and schedules for determining progress (Mercer, 1987, 145).

Individualized Education Programs frequently include behavioral objectives to reduce inappropriate behaviors such as "talk outs," "hitting," "temper tantrums"; sometimes the IEP may specify "improve the self-concept" without implementation means.

## Individualized Education Program Development: Affective

For illustrative purposes, we will utilize the generic results of Jones' (1985) study, in which The Piers-Harris was administered to four categories of handicapped children (educable mentally retarded, emotionally disturbed, speech/language impaired, and learning disabled) and non-handicapped children ages 10–13 years old. All four categories of handicapped students scored significantly lower on the total self-concept score than nonhandicapped students. Additionally, handicapped students scored lower on the following cluster scales: (1) Educable Mentally Retarded: anxiety, intellectual ability and school status, popularity, behavior, happiness; (2) Emotionally Disturbed: anxiety, intellectual ability and school status, popularity, behavior; (3) Speech/Language Impaired: anxiety, intellectual ability and school status, popularity; (4) Learning Disabled: anxiety, intellectual ability and school status, physical appearance and attributes.

Jones' (1985) concluded that the evidence did not support a self-concept indigenous to all handicapped students, a "handicapped self-concept," but the results did suggest a negative "school-related" self-concept common to handicapped students. For students who reveal such a negative "school-related" self-concept, the teacher or diagnostician should administer several additional assessments:

(1) Academic self-concept test: To determine specific subjects (e.g., math, reading) the student feels negative toward
(2) Academic locus of control: To determine if the child is inner-motivated or requires motivational assistance (outer-directed)
(3) Academic achievement expectations: To determine if the child expects success or failure in the future

Paired with the results from the academic testing, the systematic observations, and academic performance in the classroom, the teacher possesses a good picture of the student which enables him/her to plan remediation strategies for improving the student's "school-related" or academic self-concept. Thus, the preparation of the affective portion of the Individualized Education Program is predicated upon information from a multidisciplinary evaluation in all areas of suspected disability and related areas. In the social, emotional, and self-concept areas, the assessments administered will depend on the suspected/actual disability and obvious problems of the student.

## Case Study: Joey

Joey is an eleven-year-old educable mentally retarded student, whose self-concept was assessed using The Piers-Harris. Joey appears to experience anxiety about his intellectual abilities and school status, popularity, and behavior. To determine the sources of Joey's anxiety and negative feelings, he was administered an academic self-concept test, a locus of control test, and a projected performance scale. The results indicated low perceptions of his general ability and his academic ability; low perceptions of his reading and spelling abilities; expectations of continued failure; and that he is outer-directed.

Joey's academic testing revealed difficulties in all language arts areas. Observations and teacher reports indicated immature and inappropriate social and academic behaviors for age and grade, short attention span, short periods of time-on-task, and lack of independence in seatwork. The IEP Team planned Joey's academic IEP to include developmental/ remedial assistance in language arts areas. In planning the affective portion of the IEP, the Team referred to information regarding normal social and emotional development. Since Joey is eleven years old, but educable mentally retarded, in many ways he is similar in social skills and behaviors to an eight year old (his mental age). The IEP Team decided that if Joey was taught social perspective-taking, pragmatics, and social regulation skills that he would be more acceptable to same-aged peers; and if he was taught independence and coping skills he would improve his academic performance and reduce anxiety.

*Joey's Individualized Education Program (Affective)*
Summary of Present Performance

A. The *Piers-Harris* deficit areas: Total score, anxiety, intellectual ability and school status, popularity, behavior, and happiness
B. *Perception of Ability Scale* deficits: Perception of general ability, academic ability, reading and spelling ability
C. *Intellectual Achievement Responsibility:* Outer directed locus of control
D. *Projected Academic Performance Scale:* Continued expectations of failure

**Goal I: Joey will improve peer interactions and popularity.**

Objective A: Joey will increase perspective-taking skills in the following areas:

(1) Express his own feelings

(2) Understand a peer's feelings

(3) Express concern for a peer

(4) Anticipate how one would react in various hypothetical situations (social inference) using role play, discussion of hypothetical situations, discussion of daily life situations during 4 out of 5 small group sessions on 3 successive data days as monitored by systematic observation implemented by the teacher.

Objective B: Joey will increase pragmatic language skills in the following areas:

(1) Asking a favor

(2) Asking for and offering help

(3) Beginning and ending conversations

(4) Verbally negotiating

(5) Joining in an activity already begun

(6) Sharing using role play

(7) Directed practice in daily situations that arise verbally describing the process during 4 out of 5 daily small group sessions on 3 successive data days as monitored by systematic observation implemented by the teacher

**Goal II: Joey will improve social-regulation (self-control) and moral development skills**

Objective A: Joey will demonstrate that he understands and uses the following social-regulation concepts:

(1) Appropriate behavior differs in social situations

(2) One must conform to several sets of social behavior rules (e.g., home, school, library, church)

(3) One must regulate their own behavior according to agreed-upon social rules and/or rule-governed play

(4) One should participate appropriately in activities requiring public comparison and/or competition

using role play, discussion of case study samples, discussion of actual daily events during 4 out of 5 daily small social skills group sessions on 3 successive data days monitored by systematic observation implemented by the teacher.

Objective B: Joey will demonstrate using self-control in the following situations:
(1) Temptation to take another's possessions
(2) Victim of teasing and name-calling
(3) Under false accusations
(4) Rough physical encounters (e.g., fighting, unsupervised wrestling)
(5) Losing or being left out of a game
(6) Embarrassment
(7) Reactions to failure, anger, fear
using role play, discussion of case studies, discussion of actual daily events during 4 out of 5 daily small group social-skills group sessions on 3 successive data days monitored by systematic observation implemented by the teacher.

**Goal III: Joey will improve self-competence and independence in the classroom**

Objective A: Joey will demonstrate using the following self-competence skills:
(1) Listening attentively to instructions
(2) Asking for assistance appropriately
(3) Completes assignments and self-corrects errors
(4) Demonstrates teacher pleasing skills
using listening centers and/or lab, during daily encounters, role-play episodes during 4 out of 5 daily small group social-skills sessions on 3 successive data days monitored by systematic observation implemented by teacher.

Objective B: Joey will improve feelings regarding intellectual abilities through improving time on-task behaviors and completion rates using learning and study strategies, role-play, demonstration practice during 4 out of 5 small group sessions on 3 successive data days monitored by systematic observation implemented by teacher.

Objective C: Joey will improve self-competence by setting realistic goals of work completion, using organizational strategies and independence skills self-recorded on a daily planning sheet after role-playing and modeling during 4 out of 5 daily small group sessions on 3 successive data days monitored by systematic observation implemented by teacher.

## SUMMARY

In Special Education, assessment is a process that includes screening, diagnosis, educational assessment, performance monitoring, and program evaluation. Screening identifies "at-risk" students, who may need an indepth evaluation for diagnosis. The educational assessment provides the teacher with specific information regarding the student's entry level skills. P.L. 94-142 requires periodic monitoring of student progress to determine if the child is progressing, and at least annually the IEP is evaluated for appropriateness.

Unbiased testing/assessment is an area of major concern. P.L. 94-142 requires a nondiscriminatory, multidisciplinary evaluation. In order for testing situations to be unbiased the following situations must exist: (1) The tester must be trained to administer and interpret tests; (2) Tests must possess appropriate reliability and validity; (3) Tests must be administered in the primary language of the child; (4) A team of testers using a variety of assessment instruments must be used.

A number of assessment instruments and procedures have been designed to screen and evaluate (diagnose) social, emotional, and self-concept behaviors. These assessment techniques include norm-referenced instruments, criterion-referenced instruments, systematic observation, and informal tests. The norm-referenced instruments are usually used to determine diagnosis information, while criterion-referenced and systematic observation provide specific entry level information for planning the Individualized Education Program.

Research indicates that the self-concept is pliable during the elementary school years; however, it tends to be resistant to quick change. In order to design an effective Individualized Education Program to change the negative "school-related" self-concept, the teacher also needs to know about the student's academic self-concept, academic locus of control, and academic achievement expectations. The affective IEP, then, is the social and emotional skills curriculum for the exceptional student.

# Chapter Ten

# METHODS, PROCEDURES, STRATEGIES FOR ENHANCING ACHIEVEMENT AND SELF-CONCEPT

*"A major factor in successful teaching is the instructor's ability to implement educational strategies that increase a student's motivation to perform while assisting in the development of appropriate classroom behavior"* (Polloway et. al., 1989, 96).

---

Professionals in the fields of psychology, sociology, and education are continually engaged in research regarding the functioning of children within the schools. From the results of these studies, many psychoeducational interventions have been proposed for use by teachers to enhance achievement and self-concept within the classroom. Psychoeducational interventions are those which address the psychological and educational needs of students by supplementing the curriculum in many ways including the following: (1) Cognitive: thinking, reasoning, problem-solving, and decision-making; (2) Affective: temperament, self-image, self-control, enthusiasm; (3) Socialization: friendship, interactions with peers, teachers, parents; (4) Academic: reading, language arts, mathematics, social studies; (5) Physical: walking, running, endurance, coordination, nutrition; (6) Vocational Preparation: Career awareness and goals, specific job skills, vocational opportunities (Maher & Zins, 1987).

## ENHANCING SELF-CONCEPTS IN EARLY CHILDHOOD AND INFANCY

Jersild (1952) contended that for many young children the school is second only to the home as an institution which determines the growing child's concept of himself and his attitudes toward self-acceptance or self-rejection. Combs and Snygg (1959) concurred that what happens to an individual at school is important to the production of an adequate personality. These learnings occur whether the teachers plan for their occurrence or not. "The essential point is that the student, to acquire a satisfactory feeling of competence and acceptability, must grow up having success experiences and being accepted" (Combs & Snygg, 1959, 377).

> Self-concept development is an important aim of education for several reasons. It is an important quality of the existential situation of the person, and it may be an important predictor of behavior and achievement (Stangvik, 1979, 11).

Epstein (1981) studied people's emotional responses to events that raised or lowered self-esteem. He noted that when self-esteem was raised, high levels were reported for happiness, security, affection, energy availability, alertness, calmness, clear-mindedness, singleness of purpose, lack of restraint, and spontaneity. Epstein also noted that when self-esteem was lowered, high levels were reported for anger, unhappiness, feelings of threat, weariness, withdrawal, nervousness, disorganization, conflict, feelings of restraint, and self-consciousness.

Educators are becoming more aware of the importance of social skills and affective functioning during the school years. The acquisition of adequate social skills and a healthy mental outlook and self-concept have been shown to affect people throughout their school years and into adulthood (Luftig, 1988). The activities provided in this chapter are examples of activities in various categories at numerous age levels rather than an exhaustive accumulation.

"The child who seems himself as socially adept, emotionally self-possessed, physically skilled, and intellectually able feels secure and masterful—ready to cope with changes in his environment as they occur—ready to relish life and welcome new experiences" (Hendrick, 1990, 11). The important dimensions of self-concept are body self (or self-image), cognitive self, social self, and self-esteem (which is the evaluative aspect of the self-concept) (Horrocks & Jackson, 1972).

## Encouraging a Positive Body Image

"The body image dimension of the self-concept includes the value an individual puts on his physical, sexual, and racial characteristics" (Samuels, 1987, 226). A child feels more comfortable and gains more control over himself/herself and the environment when s/he becomes aware of their body and can experiment with it in relationship to space, objects, and other persons (Yawkey, 1980). Physical activity offers rich opportunities for the development of all the selves (Hendrick, 1990).

> Obviously the body benefits—and so does the emotional self, as the child acquires feelings of competence through the acquisition of new skills, or uses physical activity as an acceptable channel for aggressive feelings, or involves herself in creative dance to explore a wide range of emotions. The cooperative interplay between children and the satisfaction of doing things together develops the social self. The cognitive self is enhanced as children learn about body image and spatial relationships, and the creative self is provided with opportunities for original thinking that are encouraged by movement exploration activities and also nourished by the marvelous creative opportunities inherent in dance experiences (Hendrick, 1990, 127).

### Tactile-Kinesthetic-Vestibular Activities

Body image can be promoted through tactile-kinesthetic-vestibular activities from infancy in several levels of activities: (1) Awareness and Attention, (2) Recognition and Discrimination, and (3) Orientation in Space (Jones, 1988, 100–101).

**Awareness and Attention Level.** At the awareness and attention level, "the child learns to attend to textures, temperatures, vibrating surfaces, and varied stimuli" (Jones, 1988, 99). Activities at the awareness and attention level for the nonambulatory student include the following:

*Hands/Feet Activities*
- Rub with blanket/towel
- Rub with smooth/rough, soft/hard, light/heavy, cool/warm, sticky/slick textures
- Warm/cold blow dryer

*Body Activities*
- Lying in a hammock
- Lying on a carpeted surface
- Roll child up in a blanket and unroll
- Bathe child in small swimming pool
- Lying on a vibrating pad
- Massage
- Rubbing body/trunk with baby powder (Jones, 1988, 101)

**Recognition and Discrimination Level.** "Between the developmental ages of 10 and 18 months the child enters the recognition and discrimination phase of tactile-kinesthetic-vestibular sensation programming. Movement is required at this level of functioning" (Jones, 1988, 102).

Movement appears to stimulate cognitive development as the child begins to have an impact on his/her environment. Exploration through movement assists the child in understanding causality, object function, and object permanence. The child's cognitive functioning improves to allow matching and classification of objects by size, shape, textures. The child's beginning ideas about body image allow him/her to respond by localizing the part or limb stimulated. The child learns to sort similar and dissimilar objects: rank objects from softest to roughest as he develops cognitively (Jones, 1988, 102–103).

**Texture Tub Activities** (Phillips and Drain, 1979, 10) assist the child in refining discrimination skills. A plastic basin or container is partially filled with one or more of the following textures: popcorn, rice, macaroni, cornmeal, sand (wet/dry), oatmeal, gravel, water (soapy and clear), dry beans. Using small toys or objects such as spoons, measuring cups, squeeze toys, balls, paper cups assist the child in playing. "Pour the material over the child's hands and assist the child in scooping, filling, and dumping containers with the material." Bury objects partially and totally, encouraging the child to find them.

Styrafoam "worms" and other unique shapes in various colors, also, make very interesting items with which to experiment. It is fun for the child to fill a box with the styrafoam shapes and get in. The little "worms" can be thrown in the air or "poured" on the child's head and allowed to roll down his body.

**Sand/Water Play Areas** (Bailey and Wolery, 1984) or "tub" centers with varying activities and schedules; for example, Monday-water, Tuesday-sand, Wednesday-water with food coloring, Thursday-dry beans and noodles, Friday-water with soapsuds provide interesting opportunities for discrimination. Provide a variety of textured materials (e.g., macaroni, salt, noodles, shells, dried beans, leaves, styrafoam) and tools (e.g., cans, sponges, shovels, floating and sinking objects, boats, toy mixers and beaters, funnels, squeeze bottles, straws, and buckets). Object permanence can be encouraged through partially or completely burying objects under dry materials or water. Means-ends is facilitated through experiences with tool use (e.g., beaters, cups, funnels).

**Hand, Body, and Feet Activities** can be used to promote recognition and discrimination of tactile-kinesthetic-vestibular stimulation. Additional tactile-kinesthetic-vestibular activities include the following:

HAND ACTIVITIES:

- finger painting with shaving cream, pudding, cereal
- building a tower with finger jello
- squeezing and mashing bananas
- playing with playdough and clay
- manipulation of opposites: rough/smooth, soft/hard, etc.

BODY ACTIVITIES:

- rolling up in a blanket or on the carpet
- playing inside a carpeted barrell
- message with vegetable oil

FEET ACTIVITIES:

- walking barefooted in grass, sand, etc. (Jones, 1988, 104).

**Orientation in Space Activities. Movement toys** of all kinds provide many opportunities for the child to practice balance and orientation in space activities. Examples of Tactile-Kinesthetic-Vestibular Activities at the orientation in space level are provided as follows:

- hitting a punching bag or tether ball
- throwing items through space (balls, bean bags)
- stringing beads
- kicking large balls
- jumping on an air-mattress
- playing with inner tubes
- rolling on mats
- rocking on a hobby horse
- swinging on a swing
- riding on a merry-go-round, tricycle, skateboard, etc. (Jones, 1988, 105).

**Fine Motor Activities**

Fine motor skills involve the development of the efficient and accurate use of the hands and fingers. "The primary fine motor skills to be developed during the sensorimotor stage include the following skills: (1) grasp and release, (2) finger control, (3) eye-hand coordination, and (4) arm movements while grasping, which can be facilitated by a wide variety of activities" (Jones, 1988, 158–159). Examples of sensorimotor stage fine motor activities are included in TABLE 5. Refer to previous activities for other examples of fine and gross motor play skills of young children.

**Activities, Art and Music**

The development of body image can be facilitated in numerous ways through activities and games, art and music. The teacher's imagination is the only limitation to what can be done. ENCOURAGING A POSITIVE BODY IMAGE (TABLE 6) provides additional ways to enhance the development of body image and the self.

## Encouraging a Positive Image of the Social Self

"When children are socially competent, they are basically 'Fit to live with' (Hendrick, 1990, 196). Socially competent children possess feelings of self-worth, are usually able to control their aggressive impulses, know and use a number of methods of obtaining what they want from other children, are able to form friendships, and understand what constitutes acceptable behavior in various settings (Hendrick, 1990). "A child feels more comfortable and has a greater sense of control over his environment when he feels he interacts well with others, that he engages in appropriate social behaviors, and that people like and accept him" (Yawkey, 1980, 59).

ENCOURAGING A POSITIVE SOCIAL IMAGE (TABLE 7) includes some activities for enhancing the image of the social self.

## Encouraging a Positive Image of the Emotional Self

The emotional growth and development of a child does not occur in isolation. A child expresses emotional skills at play, and in interactions with other children and adults. "Curriculum for the emotional self

## TABLE 5

## FINE MOTOR ACTIVITIES

| GRASP AND RELEASE ACTIVITIES | FINGER CONTROL ACTIVITIES |
|---|---|

Fill N' Dump Activities:
    6-12 Months use containers with large opening(milk carton, coffee can, oatmeal box) and small objects to place in containers and dump (spools, measuring spoons, clothespins, corks, poker chips).
    12-24 Months decrease size of container and opening (plastic milk bottle).

Water Play: Use warm water and many items--sponges, and shampoo bottles for squeezing, spoons, bowls, containers with/without spouts, eggbeaters, cups, tubes, straws, funnels, water toys.

Sand Play: Use many of the water toys plus shovels, spoons, buckets.

Animal Cage: Put spring type clothespins around rim of a box to make a cage.

Squeeze nerf balls and squeeze toys.

Pickup Small Items such as raisins and put in bowl.

Play Dough: Good for poking, pinching, grasping, squeezing, holding, rolling.

Finger Paint: With pudding, with vaseline on waxed paper.

Gadet Board: manipulate locks, plugs, latches, zippers, levers, snaps, buttons

Finger Play: "Itzy Bitzy Spider".

Easel Painting

Opens &Closes Containers: Opens & closes match boxes, crayon boxes, plastic refrigerator containers, bandaid boxes, unscrews lids.

Presses Buttons with Thumb

Turns Knobs

Winds Up Toys & Music Boxes

Rings Small Bells

Finger Puppet Games

Unwraps Small Packages and wrapped candy.

## ARM MOVEMENTS WHILE MAINTAINING GRASP ACTIVITIES

Eye-Hand Coordination

Place objects in container.

Puts rings on a stick.

Strings large beads.

Puts pegs in pegboard.

Scribbles with large crayon.

Make Music: Hit drum with sticks, play tambourine (pie tin with pop bottle caps), shake string of bells.

Tear paper/cloth.

Use cookie cutters to cut out play dough, finger jello, etc.

Shake small marshmallows from a can.

TABLE 5 (Continued)

| | |
|---|---|
| Pours from one container to another | Pour tinted water from plastic syrup bottle into large mixing bowl. |
| Build block, box tower (attach velcro to blocks/ boxes to help stack. | Stack empty boxes/empty cans. |
| Sand/Water play. | |
| Cut stiffened jello into squares with dull knife/ spatula. | |
| Make Collage Activities (paste, tear, place, pat). Materials--paper plates, foam meat trays, egg cartons, pictures, yarn, buttons, foam bits, wood pieces, beans, macaroni, etc. | |
| Pop beads. | |
| Build with magnetized marbles. | |

SOURCE: Jones, C. (1988, 160).

involves the planning of experiences that inspire trust, autonomy, and initiative and that teach children to remain in contact with their feelings" (Hendrick, 1990, 3). Competencies included in a curriculum for developing and enhancing emotional competence include the following: (1) Help the child learn to separate from the family, (2) Foster basic attitudes of trust, autonomy, and initiative in the child, (3) Help the child remain in contact with her feelings while learning to control what she does about them, (4) Help the child learn to use play and creative materials to resolve emotional problems, (5) Help the child learn to face reality, (6) Help the child cope with crisis situations, (7) Help the child begin to build empathy for other people (Hendrick, 1990).

Yawkey (1980, 141–142) suggests the following: (1) Give honest compliments for the good things the child does, (2) Let the child choose between two things (activities, vegetables, shirts, books) when possible, (3) Listen carefully when the child is talking, (4) Encourage the child to assist you (taking care of baby, watering plants), (5) Let the child do a task his way (peel carrots, set table), (6) Ask for the child's suggestions and

## TABLE 6

### ENCOURAGING A POSITIVE BODY IMAGE

| ACTIVITIES | ART | MUSIC |
|---|---|---|
| Name body parts. | Draw self & name parts. | Rhythm band. |
| Keep chart of height growth. | Provide a mirror and draw on face. | Use body to express rhythm. |
| Use photos of child and discuss characteristics. | Trace around child's body and let him color it. | Sing songs--wash our face, Thumpkin. |
| Tape record a conversation and discuss voice. | Make collage from photos of self. | Play musical games: |
| Teach basic relaxation techniques. | Make plaster of Paris handprints. | Farmer in the Dell, Ring around the Rosie, Did you ever see a Lassie? |
| Play games using body in space: Freeze, Simon Says, Imitation. | Make dolls & dress in own clothes. | Hokey Pokey, Drop the Handkerchief |
| Be quiet & listen to sounds of the body. | Fingerpaint. | London Bridge, Musical Chairs, |
| Play games:<br>• Head, Hands, Fingers, Toes<br>• Show me your "Nose"<br>• Statues | Draw pictures of nurses, doctors, carpenters, etc. of different races. | Jack-in-the Box |
| Discuss likenesses and differences from peers. | Draw pictures of handicapped/ ethnically different children. | |
| Use children's names when addressing them. | Make Booklets: My Favorite Things | |
| Use name tags (parties, etc.) | Make book prints in snow; footprints in sand. | |
| Discuss color differences--eyes, hair, skin | Flannel board body parts-- both sexes, culturally different and handicapped. | |
| Playing house--change roles. | Finger painting with pudding. | |

REFERENCES: Yawkey, 1980; Samuels, 1987.

TABLE 7

ENCOURAGING A POSITIVE SOCIAL IMAGE

| INTERACTIONS WITH PEOPLE | INTERACTIONS WITH THE ENVIRONMENT |
|---|---|
| Promote interactions with children of various ages, nationalities, handicapping conditions, etc. | Teach to use the magic words: "please" and "thank you". |
| Expose to people with various lifestyles. | Discuss appropriate behavior in various settings. |
| Involve in a variety of community activities. | Emphasize appropriate behavior. |
| Field trips to offices, fire station, band, etc. | Discuss social behaviors in library and on playground. |
| Promote positive self statements. | Discuss social behaviors at school to children as their "jobs". |
| Pretend by trading roles with child. | Discuss differences among cultures, ie. Navajo children are not encourged to compete. |
| Guests from different careers visit class and talk about their jobs. | Children of other cultures and lands: clothing food, music, history. |
| Guest from various ethnic, racial, & cultural backgrounds & talk about themselves and family. | Discuss ownership--"Teacher's things", "My things", "School's things", etc. |
| Handicapped guests (VI,HI, PI) talk about their conditions. | Field trip to museum. |
| Discuss roles of family members; all kinds of families (e.g., one-parent, foster parent, etc.) | Engage in cooperative activities in classroom and on playground. |
| Roles of family members in colonial times. | Learning abour sharing and empathy. |
| Make cards/gifts for Grandparents, Mother's Day, Father's Day, birthdays, etc. | Develop responsibility through classroom jobs. |
| Promote relationships with peers (Choice & assigned) in various activities. | Practicing school bus safety. |
|  | Waiting patiently for a drink, etc. |
| Role play to understand feeling of someone"teased", "not included", etc. | Building inner controls--handling aggression, anger, etc. |
|  | Foster social skills in cafeteria, and at snack time. |

REFERENCES: Hendrick, 1990; Samuels, 1987; Yawkey, 1980.

use them when possible, (7) Remind the child how much better he can do things now than previously, (8) Let the child help with various duties (dusting, sweeping), (9) Avoid competition with other children, (10) Encourage children to play cooperatively together, (11) Help the child develop a code of ethics, (12) Be empathetic when appropriate.

Hendrick (1990) suggests additional activities for learning to deal with emotions: (1) Use pretend play; (2) Encourage storytelling by children; (3) Use aggression-relieving activities, such as: mud, sand, and water activities; jumping hard on a mattress; throwing bean bags; dancing; hammering (peg and hammer set); beating a large drum; swinging and rocking; fingerpainting; (4) Accepting what cannot be changed; (5) Developing coping skills; (6) Bibliotherapy (in advance); (7) Find security in routine activities; (8) Self-expressive materials. "The emphasis of curriculum for the emotional self should be on helping children become as resilient as possible by using everyday life situations as the medium for teaching" (Hendrick, 1990, 191).

### Encouraging a Positive Image of the Cognitive Self

"A child who feels she understands what goes on around her can feel confident and will, as a result, be better able to exert some control over her environment" (Yawkey, 1980, 59).

All previously indicated Early Childhood Activities contribute to cognitive development. Hendrick (1990, 329–341) outlines some basic methods of helping children learn to think for themselves and increase cognitive competence:

(1) **Basic ways to help children enjoy cognitive learning**
   - Keep cognitive learning appropriate to the children's age and abilities
   - Keep cognitive learning a part of real life
   - Keep feelings a part of the experience
   - Model joy and interest in learning yourself
(2) **Help children figure out answers for themselves**
   - When asking questions, keep the pace reasonably slow
   - Encourage children to ask questions themselves
   - Use children's questions to help them learn
(3) **Ask children to think of ways to solve problems; propose alternative solutions**

- Reinforce the production of creative ideas by recognizing their value

(4) **Help children learn facts; use the facts to practice thinking and reasoning**

(5) **Set up a science table that encourages thinking**
   - Introduce children to the scientific method
   - Organize Let's-Find-Out Tables (e.g., How do volcanoes work?)

Yawkey (1980, 59–60) suggests the following: (1) Arrange for as large a variety of age-appropriate learning experiences as possible (e.g., trips to the library, a fish hatchery, a farm, a museum); (2) Provide materials so s/he can create products of his/her own design—paste or glue, scissors, crayons, magazines, textured papers, pine cones, sand, flour, leaves, etc.; (3) Encourage child to engage in pretend activities; (4) Provide books on many topics, filmstrips, etc.; (5) Encourage perceptive questioning—"That's a good question, Bobby!"

## Encouraging a Positive Self-Concept

"A healthy self-concept is derived from the affirmation of others. A child feels loved, wanted, and capable as he basks in the presence of someone who, by word and action, is telling him he is all these things" (Yawkey, 1980, 12). Teachers need many techniques for helping children develop healthy self-concepts including the following: knowledge of child development, classroom management, individualization, use of positive feedback, well-designed teaching plans, collaboration with other professionals and parents, and self-analysis of their own teaching (Robinson, 1977). "If a child is to achieve a healthy self-concept, all parts of his being need to be challenged and developed. . . . Play is one of the easiest, most inexpensive, and most accessible ways to promote a healthy self-concept" (Jensen, 1980, 147).

Activities to promote a positive self-concept include all of the previously mentioned techniques to enhance the body image, the social self, the emotional self, and the cognitive self. McDonald (1980, 54–57) suggests additional strategies: (1) Recognize, respect, and encourage individual differences; (2) Teach children to be pleased about the good fortune of others; (3) Capitalize on the child's strengths; (4) Provide a comprehensive range of activities; (5) Separate a child's behavior from the person he is; (6) Keep promises; (7) Never threaten a consequence that you are unwilling to carry out; (8) Provide child appropriate models; (9) Be consistent; (10) Allow a child progressively more autonomy.

*I'm Me, I'm Special* (Hamilton et. al., 1990) is a chapter on self-concept development in *Resources for Creative Teaching in Early Childhood Education.* The basic concepts emphasized include the following: (1) There is no one else just like me; (2) I have some things that belong to me; (3) I belong to someone; (4) My family is special; (5) I live in a special place; (6) I can change by growing; (7) I can change by learning; (8) I can change by pretending; (9) I can change by dressing differently; (10) I can change by getting sick/well; (11) I can change by acting differently; (12) Some things I cannot change. This chapter provides lists of activities and materials for learning centers: Discovery center; Dramatic play center; Learning, language, and readiness materials center; Art center; Book center. The chapter also includes lists of music, poems, records and cassettes, rhythms and singing games, fingerplays and poems, stories, games, large muscle activities, extended experiences, and pages of teacher resources.

*Carolina Early Learning Activities* (Lillie & Sturm, 1987). "The *Carolina Early Learning Activities* is a two-book set of games, crafts, and other learning activities for preschool and kindergarten" (Lillie & Sturm, 1987, iv). This set provides activities in seven learning areas: large motor skills, small motor skills, visual skills, reasoning, listening skills, language skills, and social-emotional development.

> Book One contains 176 activities to develop the skills that three- and four-year-olds need in order to be ready for kindergarten and the grades. Book Two offers 168 activities that will help four- and five-year olds make smooth transitions from the play-oriented environment of preschool to the more demanding first-grade classroom (Lillie & Sturm, 1987, ix).

## ENHANCING SELF-CONCEPTS IN MIDDLE CHILDHOOD AND ADOLESCENCE

This section of the chapter summarizes some of the current psycho-educational interventions utilized during middle childhood and adolescence to enhance the self-concept and academic achievement including the following: cognitive developmental interventions, behavior control interventions, socialization intervention techniques, and academic achievement interventions. Though specific techniques have been categorized under the above headings, there is considerable overlap and many techniques could be categorized logically under several headings.

## Cognitive Developmental Interventions

The cognitive developmental approach is based on information processing theory rather than specific abilities or behavioral models (Reid, 1988). The study of information processing has led to an analysis of the kinds of programs (e.g., plans, strategies, and other control processes) the human mind uses to regulate learning (Reid, 1988, 10). The cognitive developmental approach to learning and instruction identifies the following factors that must be considered in any instructional negotiation: the characteristics of the learners, the learning activities, the criterial tasks, and the materials to be learned (Reid, 1988, 12). The cognitive developmental approach seeks to understand the processes in learning rather than only the products (Reid, 1988).

### Cognitive Behavior Modification

Cognitive behavior modification is a cognitive intervention which analyzes the thinking processes involved in performing a task, and combines behavior modification techniques with self-treatment methods including self-instruction, self-monitoring, and self-evaluation (Mercer & Mercer, 1989). "The cognitive learning techniques include teaching students to stop and think before responding, to verbalize and rehearse what they have seen, to visualize and imagine what they must remember, and to preplan task approaches" (Lerner, 1989, 486).

Meichenbaum, the pioneer of cognitive behavior modification, utilized a four-step process in the self-instructional program including the following: (1) Cognitive Modeling: Adult performs a task while describing the task orally, (2) Overt Self-Guidance: Student performs the same task under the direction of the adult model; (3) Faded-Out Guidance: Student whispers the instructions to self as s/he performs task; (4) Covert Self-Instruction: Student performs task using his/her inner speech to guide performance (Mercer & Mercer, 1989). The basic tenet of this approach is that cognitions including inner speech influence behavior and by modifying cognitions behavior can be changed (Mercer, 1987).

"In the classroom the student might be taught to use the following self-verbalizations: (a) questions about the task ("What does the teacher want me to do?"); (b) answers to the questions ("I'm not supposed to talk out in class."); (c) self-instruction to guide student through the task ("First I raise my hand and wait for the teacher to call on me."); (d) self-reinforcement ("I really did well that time!") (Mercer, 1989, 162).

Cognitive behavior modification has been used successfully to help impulsive students develop self-control, to become more actively involved in learning, to improve attentiveness, to decrease impulsivity, and to improve academics including handwriting, reading comprehension, and arithmetic production (Reid, 1988).

## Instrumental Enrichment

Feuerstein's (1980) *Instrumental Enrichment* is an approach to remediating deficient cognitive functions and training metacognitive skills. Although initially the "content-free process" approach was developed for economically disadvantaged children and youth, its recent application has also been with retarded individuals (Taylor, 1988).

The *Instrumental Enrichment* approach is concerned with remediating the cognitive deficits that occur during information processing (input, elaboration, output) which negatively affect learning. The approach focuses on the training and development of cognitive skills and the development of metacognitive skills that lead to self-regulation and the independent use of cognitive strategies (Taylor, 1988).

The two basic components of the approach are assessment and instruction. The assessment instrument, the *Learning Potential Assessment Device* (LPAD) serves as a stimulus for the mediated learning that is considered to be deficient in the background of environmentally deprived youngsters and at least partially responsible for their deficient cognitive functioning. The instructional approach is called *Instrumental Enrichment* (IE) and consists of fifteen instruments (groups of lessons) that require from 3 to 5 one-hour sessions over the course of two to three years to complete. "In addition to the carefully structured materials, the most critical element of the program is the specially trained teacher, who provides mediated learning experiences" (Lerner, 1989, 192). *Instrumental Enrichment* "if instituted relatively early in the school career, may prevent much of the later educational failure and special education referral and placement now observed with students classified as mildly retarded" (Reschly, 1988, 38).

## Learning Strategies: Strategies Intervention Model

The Strategies Intervention Model (SIM) was designed and tested at the University of Kansas Institute for Research in Learning Disabilities (KU–IRLD) as an instructional alternative for low achieving (e.g., 4th to 5th grade reading level) mainstreamed adolescents to provide them with strategies for learning. A major objective of SIM is to provide direct instruction to strategy deficient adolescents in the metacognitive processes involved in monitoring a problem or task, planning and implementing problem-solving strategies, and evaluating the performance success.

The Strategies Intervention Model has three major components: Strategic Curriculum Component, Strategic Instruction Component, and Strategic Environment Component. The Strategic Curriculum Component specifies **what** will be taught to the low-achieving or at-risk student and consists of four types of strategies: learning strategies, social skill strategies, motivation strategies, and executive strategies. The learning strategies are designed to teach the student how to cope with the academic demands encountered across a variety of school, home, community, and employment settings; and include critical reading, writing, remembering, and test-taking strategies (Lenz et. al., 1988). The social skills strategies are designed to teach the student how to interact appropriately across a variety of situations and settings; and include strategies to resist peer pressure, accept criticism, negotiate, follow directions, and ask for help (Lenz et. al., 1988). The motivation strategies teach the student how to set, monitor, and attain goals related to important areas of his or her life and then communicate these goals to others (Lenz et. al., 1988). The executive strategies are designed to teach the student how to independently solve problems and generalize learning (Lenz et. al., 1988).

The Learning Strategies Curriculum is organized into three major strands (e.g., Acquisition, Storage, Expression and Demonstration of Competence) that correspond to the major demands of the secondary curriculum. The Acquisition strand includes strategies that help students acquire information from written materials: The Word Identification Strategy, The Paraphrasing Strategy, The Self-Questioning Strategy, The Visual Imagery Strategy, The Interpreting Visual Aids Strategy, The Multipass Strategy. The Storage strand includes strategies that enable students to identify and store important information: The First Letter Mneumonic Strategy, The Paired Associates Strategy and The Listening and Notetaking Strategy. The Expression and Demonstration of Competence strand includes strategies that have been designed to enable students to cope with the written expression demands in secondary schools: The Sentence Writing Strategy, The Paragraph Writing Strategy, The Error Monitoring Strategy, The Theme Writing Strategy, The Assignment Completion Strategy, and The Test Taking Strategy.

The Strategic Instruction Component includes procedures for **how** strategies should be taught to students; and procedures for the effective delivery of content to low-achieving and at-risk students. The Strategic Instruction Component includes acquisition procedures, generalization procedures, strategic acquisition devices, and content enhancement procedures. The Strategic Environment Component deals with how to manage and organize educational settings and programs in a manner that will effectively promote and prompt strategic learning and performance.

Teachers need very specialized training in order to implement the Strategies Intervention Model which is provided by Deschler, Schumaker, Clark, Lenz and colleagues at the University of Kansas Institute for Research in Learning Disabilities and by numerous SIM trainers around the country. Teaching materials can only be secured and utilized by SIM trained personnel. A commercial program, Social Skills for Daily Living (Schumaker et. al., 1988) is available through American Guidance Services.

### The Metacognitive Approach to Social Skills Training (MASST)

The Metacognitive Approach to Social Skills Training (MASST) (Sheinker, et. al., 1988) is a program teaching students how to self-direct, self-monitor, self-evaluate, and self-correct to produce appropriate social behaviors. Students are taught to evaluate social situations and generate their own behavioral choices. The program is based on the premise that internal control is necessary to responsible, productive behavior and problem-solving, and that self-knowledge is essential to internal control. The program includes five curriculum segments addressing aspects of metacognition including: (1) self-concept; (2) goal-setting; (3) taking responsibility for achieving those goals; (4) getting friendship, love, and respect; (5) locus of control of feeling, behavior, and success (Sheinker, et. al., 1988).

### Attribution Retraining

There appears to be a relationship between causal attributions and strategic behaviors. Research indicates that attributions about failure appear positively related to persistence in learning disabled students and that children who attributed success to effort were more strategic than those who attributed success to uncontrollable factors such as luck or ability (Kurtz & Borkowski, 1984). Therefore, it appears that in order to retrain self-attributions about the causes of success and failure, a multifaceted approach involving motivation, strategy training, and attributional retraining would empower the student with the skills needed to be successful in the classroom and to transfer the use of strategies in various settings. The Consolidated Method for Independent Learning (Beckman & Weller, 1990) is a technique for attribution retraining paired with motivation and strategy training.

## The Consolidated Method for Independent Learning

The Consolidated Method for Independent Learning (CMIL) (Beckman & Weller, 1990, 26) was "designed to help elementary-age children with learning disabilities believe in themselves as learners and develop a foundation for functional use and generalization of independent learning strategies." This method focuses on fostering metacognitive skills. "CMIL clarifies the learning process for children and increases their sense of responsibility for learning. Through increased motivation, involvement, and productivity and increased self-confidence, children become more willing to attempt tasks they previously might have perceived as too difficult" (Beckman & Weller, 1990, 28).

The CMIL process involves three phases: (1) Developing Self-Efficacy; (2) Using Strategies; (3) Fostering Generalizations. The major purpose of Phase I is to determine one's own learning style including information processing and preferred setting for learning. The purpose of Phase II is fostering independent learning through learning strategies for acquisition and storage of information. Phase III consists of fostering generalizations through drill and practice with a wide variety of materials.

## Behavior Control Interventions

Interrelated factors affecting academic achievement among handicapped students includes inappropriate behavior which reduces engaged learning time or time-on-task which reduces the amount of work completed and the amount learned, and ultimately negatively affects grades. Therefore, it logically follows that if we could help the child control his/her inappropriate behavior and increase engaged learning time that the child/youth would make more academic progress, and ultimately improve his/her grades. Additionally, inappropriate behavior significantly interferes with establishing mutually satisfying social relationships with peers and adults. Thus, assisting the youth in controlling inappropriate behaviors may enhance social relationships as well.

Behavior control interventions are generally concerned with suppressing, controlling, and redirecting misbehaviors in order to have higher levels of engaged learning time. Numerous systems, models, methods, and techniques have been devised to enhance classroom discipline. Behavior control interventions include eight major models of discipline including the three aspects of discipline: (1) Preventive Discipline, (2) Supportive Discipline, (3) Corrective Discipline (Charles, 1989, 5). Behavior control interventions, also, include school-based counseling, stress management techniques, and school survival skills.

## Major Models of Discipline

The eight major models of discipline summarized by Charles (1989) include (1) The Redl and Wattenberg Model, (2) The Kounin Model, (3) The Neo-Skinnerian Model, (4) The Ginott Model, (5) The Dreikurs Model, (6) The Jones Model, (7) The Canter Model, and (8) The Glasser Model.

**The Redl and Wattenberg Model.** This model suggests that effective classroom control requires that teachers understand group dynamics and be aware of the characteristic traits of group behavior (Charles, 1989). They suggest that teachers maintain group control through influence techniques that support self-control, offer situational assistance, appraise reality, and invoke pleasure and pain. Providing cues to assist the child with his own self-control such as sending signals (e.g., eye contact, frowning, head shaking), proximity control (e.g., moving closer to the offender), showing interest in student's work, using humor, and/or ignoring the behavior are supportive discipline techniques designed to control a problem before it becomes serious (Charles, 1989).

Situational assistance provided by the teacher to assist students in regaining self-control may include hurdle help, restructuring or rescheduling the situation, establishing routines, removing the student from the situation, removing seductive objects (Charles, 1989). Appraising the reality of a situation helps students understand the underlying aspects of the situation, the cause-effect aspect of their behavior and that of others in contributing to the outcome of a situation, and assists them in developing values (Charles, 1989). This mental and emotional analysis of a situation enables students to act more appropriately in future situations of a similar nature.

"When behavior problems persist despite the teacher's attempts to support student self-control, provide situational assistance, and appraise reality, it becomes necessary to move to the strongest measure. . . . invoking the pain-pleasure principle" [punishment] (Charles, 1989, 23). "Punishment should consist of planned, unpleasant consequences, the purpose of which is to modify behavior in positive directions. . . . should not be physical, nor should it involve angry outbursts" . . . by the teacher (Charles, 1989, 23). "Punishment does not work well," so should be used only as a last resort (Charles, 1989, 24).

**The Kounin Model.** Kounin's research indicated that a number of teacher variables generally result in appropriate behavior in students. These variables include with-it-ness, overlapping, movement management, group alerting, accountability and format, and avoiding satiation (Polloway et. al., 1989). "With-it-ness, essentially awareness, refers to the teacher's ability to follow classroom action, be aware of possible deviance, communicate awareness to the class, and intervene at the initiation of the problem" (Polloway et. al., 1989, 100). "Overlapping is the ability to attend to two issues at the same time" (Charles, 1989, 31). Teachers frequently find the overlapping technique a necessity while simultaneously conducting small reading groups and managing the rest of the class engaged in seatwork.

"Kounin concluded from his investigations that teachers' ability to manage smooth transitions and maintain momentum was more important to work involvement and classroom control than any other behavior-management technique" (Charles, 1989, 33). Smooth transitions are maximized by routines, clear directions, and completing one task before beginning another.

Group or classroom management is facilitated through grouping procedures, student accountability, attention, and avoidance of satiation. Larger groups allow teachers to call on numerous students during discussions. Ensuring that each student is accountable or responsible for learning keeps students on-task. For example, during a lesson expect all students to provide an answer on their magic slate or individual chalkboard and hold it up for teacher to see. Common mistakes made by teachers during group lessons include (1) teacher focusing on one student at a time, and (2) teacher calling on students in a predictable sequence; these teacher behaviors may result in off-task and inappropriate student behavior (Charles, 1989).

Facilitation of group or classroom management includes avoiding satiation on instructional activities. Satiation causes careless work that results in increased errors, and an increase in off-task behaviors. This can be avoided by changing the level of intellectual challenge; alternating reading, discussion activities, creative production, and independent tasks; changing materials, and restructuring groups (Charles, 1989). Kounin's suggestions for maintaining a good learning environment are primarily preventive in nature and are included in most of the discipline systems used today (Charles, 1989).

**The Neo-Skinnerian Model.** The various applications of Skinner's work to classroom practice involve the principles of operant conditioning and are commonly called behavior modification (Kaplan, 1991).

"Behavior modification works even when done sporadically, but is best approached in a systematic way . . . The multitude of systems fit roughly into five categories: (1) informal **"Catch 'em Being Good"**; (2) **Rules-Ignore-Praise** (RIP); (3) **Rules-Reward-Punishment** (RRP); (4) **Contingency Management**; and (5) **Contracting**" (Charles, 1989, 47). The **Catch 'em Being Good** approach rewards students for doing what is expected and is highly effective with primary grade (K–3rd) students. **Rules-Ignore-Praise** (RIP) approach involves ignoring inappropriate behavior, but praising and rewarding the appropriate behavior of a student sitting nearby (Charles, 1989). This system works relatively well at the elementary level where there are no serious behavior problems. The **Rules-Reward-Punishment** (RRP) approach incorporates limitations and consequences into the behavior modification technique. "As with RIP, RRP begins with rules and emphasizes rewards, but it does not ignore inappropriate behavior. The added factor of limits and consequences makes this approach especially effective with older students and with students who have behavior problems" (Charles, 1989, 49).

**Contingency Management** is based on the Premack Principle which " . . . asserts that a low-probability activity can be increased in frequency when paired with a high-probability activity" (Polloway et. al., 1989, 105). Thus, completing a page of long division problems can be encouraged by giving rewards (e.g., candy, free time) for completion and accuracy. Contingency management often involves an elaborate system of tangible reinforcers such as token economies in which tokens are given to a student immediately following the occurrence of a target behavior.

"A **token economy** is based on items symbolizing actual reinforcers, much like the monetary reward system of free enterprise" (Polloway et. al, 1989, 106). "The tokens may be exchanged for tokens of higher value or cashed in for prizes such as food, toys, comic books, magazines, badges, privileges, and other activities" (Charles, 1989, 49).

**Contingency Contracting** is a form of contingency management in which contracts, oral or written, are prepared stating "the work assignment the learner has contracted to complete and the consequences that the instructor will provide on completion" (Polloway et. al., 1989, 105). Contingency contracting, thus, is a motivational technique to promote social and academic goals by involving the student in managing his own behavior (Mercer, 1989).

**The Ginott Model.** This model of classroom discipline "deals with methods of communication that maintain a secure, humanitarian, and productive classroom environment" (Charles, 1989, 56). The Ginott Model emphasizes the role of the teacher in classroom discipline, focusing on the teacher's own self-discipline and the teacher's use of sane messages when correcting misbehaving students. "Teachers with self-discipline do not lose their tempers, insult others or resort to name calling. They are not rude, sadistic, or unreasonable. Rather, they strive to model the behavior they expect of their students" (Charles, 1989, 65).

Teachers should express anger and displeasure without damaging the character of their students. Teachers should focus on how they feel using I-messages (e.g., "I am angry."), rather than You-messages (e.g., "You are a bad boy."). "I-messages tell how the teacher feels about the situation. You-messages attack the student" (Charles, 1989, 59). "Ginott urges teachers to invite cooperation rather than demand it. . . . Teachers who do not invite cooperation must use ordering, bossing, and commanding. Ginott stresses the need to avoid direct commands, which frequently induce hostility" (Charles, 1989, 60). Thus, Ginott's model stresses appropriate teacher behavior and communication as preventive discipline by setting an environment of respect among teacher and students.

**The Dreikurs Model.** Dreikurs contends that "All students want recognition, and most behavior occurs from their attempts to get it. When unable to get the recognition they desire, their behavior turns toward four "mistaken goals" which teachers must recognize and deal with" (Charles, 1989, 70). The four major goals of misbehavior include attention-getting, power seeking, revenge seeking, and assumed disability (Dreikurs et. al., 1971). "These four goals of disturbing behavior can be observed in young children up to the age of ten. It is difficult for parents and teachers to recognize that the child's disturbing behavior is directed against them" (Dreikurs et. al., 1971, 17).

**Attention-Getting Behavior.** Attention-seeking children do not care whether they get negative or positive attention as long as they are getting attention. "They disrupt, ask special favors, continually need help with assignments, refuse to work unless the teacher hovers over them, or they ask an irrelevant question" (Charles, 1989, 74). The adult can use two fairly reliable means of determining if the child is engaged in attention-getting behavior: (1) the adult feels annoyed with the behavior, not angry, but just tired of the continual annoying behaviors of the child, and (2) when corrected if the student stops the behavior at least for a brief time before re-engaging in the behavior, the student's motive is attention-getting (Dreikurs et. al., 1971).

**Power Seeking Behavior.** If attention-getting does not provide the students the recognition they seek, they will seek power to force the desired attention. Power-seeking students feel that defying adults is the only way they can get what they want. A need for power is expressed by arguing, contradicting, lying, temper tantrums, stealing, cheating, hostility, using both verbal and physical aggression against the adult and/or his possessions (Dreikurs et. al., 1971).

An adult can diagnose a power struggle with a student by self analysis, if the adult feels threatened and thinks "Who does that kid think s/he is, I'm the adult here and I'm the one in charge," then a power struggle is already in progress. If the student's reaction to correction is to refuse to stop the misbehavior or increases the misbehavior, a power struggle is in process.

**Revenge Seeking.** "The goal of revenge is closely related to the goal of power. Some students feel they should be allowed to do whatever they please and they consider anyone who tries to stop them as an enemy. These students are very difficult to deal with because they do not care about consequences" (Charles, 1989, 78). Revenge on the part of the child will be more probable if the teacher responded to his bid for power with punishment. "Coping with a child bent on revenge constitutes one of the most serious problems for a teacher. Such a child is almost inaccessible to reason" (Dreikurs et. al., 1971, 202). If the teacher feels hurt by the child and upon attempts to correct, the child becomes violent or hostile, the student's goal is revenge. "Underneath their bravado these individuals are deeply discouraged. Their behavior only elicits more hurt from others. They feel totally worthless and unlovable, and these feelings cause them to withdraw to the next mistaken goal—displaying inadequacy" (Charles, 1989, 75).

**Assumed Disability.** Students who assume disability feel helpless, discouraged, and total failures. "In almost all poor performances, be they academic or social, the child expresses his discouragement. An assumed or real disability or inadequacy is used by the child to protect himself against the demands of life. The child employs a cloak of inadequacy in order to be left alone" (Dreikurs et. al., 1971, 208). "Their mistaken belief is: If others believe I am inadequate they will leave me alone. Students with this goal play stupid. They refuse to respond to motivation and passively refuse to participate in classroom activities" (Charles, 1989, 75). Teachers diagnose assumed disability by their feelings of helplessness and total powerlessness to reach the child or to help the child as s/he assumes the role of "a blob" refusing to cooperate, participate, or interact (Dreikurs, 1971).

**Natural and Logical Consequences.** Dreikurs (1971) suggests the use of a democratic classroom, and natural or logical consequences in preventing and correcting misbehavior. Natural consequences occur when a parent or teacher does not intervene in a situation but allows the situation to teach the child (Polloway et. al., 1989). For example, if a student refuses to complete his math homework he may fail math; or if a child persists in running into the street he may get hit by a car. Frequently natural consequences are considered too harsh or harmful to the safety and well-being of the child, then logical consequences must be used. Logical consequences are prearranged results that follow certain behaviors and allow students to make their own choices about how they want to behave. For example, students who do not complete their math assignment by morning recess must work on math during morning recess. "Consequences should relate as closely as possible to the misbehavior, so students can see the connection between them" (Charles, 1989, 84).

Natural and logical consequences will be effective only if they are applied consistently, and work best with attention-getting students (Dreikurs et. al., 1971). Teachers and parents should withdraw from power struggles and refuse to participate; later discuss the situation with the student. The Dreikurs Model aims to have students assume greater responsibility for their own behavior and learning through operating in a democratic classroom. "Overall, Dreikurs' greatest contribution lies not in how immediately to suppress undesired behavior, but in how to build, in students, an inner sense of responsibility and respect for others" (Charles, 1989, 86).

**The Jones Model.** This model focuses on the role of the teacher as a facilitator to assist students in learning and practicing self-control. Three techniques that teachers should use in assisting students in building personal responsibility for their own behavior include using (1) effective body language; (2) incentive systems; and (3) efficient methods of providing individual help during independent work time. "Good classroom discipline results mainly from the first technique—effective body language, which includes posture, eye contact, facial expressions, signals, gestures, and physical proximity" (Charles, 1989, 89).

Jones' (1987) Classroom Management Training Program is composed of three major skill clusters: Skill Cluster #1: Body Language; Skill Cluster #2: Incentive Systems; and Skill Cluster #3: Providing Efficient Help. The training program concentrates on helping teachers learn to use their physical mannerisms to set and enforce behavior limits. "Few physical acts are more efficient than eye contact for conveying the impression of being in control" (Charles, 1989, 91). "Teachers who need to deal with minor misbehavior are instructed to move near the offending student, establish brief eye contact, and say nothing. The student will usually return immediately to proper behavior" (Charles, 1989, 92).

Teachers should use incentive systems that have educational value such as free time to read, work on other assignments, do art work, pursue personal interests (Charles, 1989). The incentives should be ones that can be earned by all students of all ability levels in the classroom. When at all possible, teachers should avoid tangible reinforcers, but often they need to begin at that level and move toward intangible rewards.

> Jones described independent seat work as having four inherent problems: (1) i sufficient time for teachers to answer a l requests for help; (2) wasted student time; (3) high potential for misbehavior; and (4) the perpetuation of dependency. . . . Jones determined that all four problems could be solved through teaching teachers how to give help more efficiently (Charles, 1989, 98–99).

Among Jones' (1987) suggestions for giving help more efficiently was organizing the classroom seating so that students are within easy reach of the teacher; using graphic reminders such as models or charts that provide clear examples and instructions; and learning to cut to a bare minimum the time used to give individual help (e.g., 20 seconds or less).

The Jones Model primarily focuses on preventive behavior control techniques.

**The Canter Model.** "The main focus of Canter's Model is on assertively insisting on proper behavior from students with well-organized procedures for following through when they do not. It provides a very strong system of corrective discipline" (Charles, 1989, 104). The basis of this assertive position is caring about oneself to the point of not allowing students to take advantage and caring about students to the point of not allowing them to behave in ways that are damaging to themselves and their peers (Canter et. al., 1986).

Canter indicates that teachers should eliminate nonassertive and hostile interactions with misbehaving students, and use an assertive response style instead. Appropriate behavior is rewarded with positive personal attention by the teacher, positive notes to parents, special awards, material awards, home rewards, and/or group rewards (Canter et. al., 1986). The consequences for misbehavior are clearly spelled out, posted in the classroom, and consistently applied. Canter et. al. (1986) suggests the following consequences: 1st misbehavior—teacher writes name on the board (a warning); 2nd misbehavior—check by name (15 minutes detention after or in-school); 3rd misbehavior—2nd check by name (30 minutes detention after or in-school); 4th misbehavior—3rd check (30 minutes detention, student phones parents and explains); 5th misbehavior—4th check (30 minutes detention; student phones parents, explains, and meets with principal); and 6th misbehavior—student suspended; taken home by principal or representative (Charles, 1989). Each day the student begins with a clean record; no checks from the previous day.

**The Glasser Model.** During the middle-to-late 1960's, Glasser focused on reality therapy as a means to manage behavior by teaching the child to behave responsibly and to face reality. Since good behavior is caused by making good choices and bad behavior is caused by making bad choices, the role of the teacher is to help students learn to make good choices by forcing them to acknowledge their behavior and make value judgments about it. "Glasser stresses that reasonable consequences must follow whatever behavior the student chooses" (Charles, 1989, 125).

The Glasser Model Pre-1985 is a preventive discipline model based on creating a classroom environment and curriculum that meets students' basic needs for belonging: power, fun, and freedom as a means of motivating students (Charles, 1989). The classroom meeting or democratic classroom is considered a prerequisite to a good system of discipline in which students help each other solve social problems, educational and learning problems, etc. through discussions (Charles, 1989).

The Glasser Model Post-1985 proposes that classrooms be organized into small cooperative learning groups in order to provide students a sense of belonging, to increase their motivation, and to free them from overdependence on the teacher (Charles, 1989). "Glasser advocates learning teams because they can better meet students' needs and therefore increase work output while reducing discipline problems" (Charles, 1989, 129).

## School-Based Counseling

School-Based Counseling consists of techniques utilized in the classroom by the classroom teacher to assist the child in learning about his/her behavior, their role in precipitating the events that follow, and what the child can do to prevent the situation from being repeated, and/or to deal with the current situation.

**Life-Space Interviewing (LSI) (Redl, 1959).** The concept of life-space interviewing was developed by Fritz Redl (1959) to be used with emotionally disturbed students in managing a classroom crisis or an everyday problem and to provide the student with insights into their behavior on the spot in their natural setting where the blow-ups occur (Mercer & Mercer, 1989). During life space interviews, an effort is made to determine how the child perceives the problem, discussions are usually private or only with concerned parties, and the focus is on sorting out the issues and preventing future problems rather than on determining punishment (Epanchin, 1991, 438). The purpose of the LSI is to make the students aware of their feelings and motivations, realize how this has been affecting their lives, and how to break this cycle (Morgan & Rinehart, 1991).

The interview is designed to be free of judgment; the teacher is simply a listener and helper for the student as he makes decisions about how to handle problems (Mercer & Mercer, 1989, 165). The teacher's best use of LSI is to provide emotional first aid on the spot at times of unusual stress to reduce the child's frustration while supporting him during the emotional situation, to reinforce behavioral and social rules, and to assist the child to solve his own everyday problems (Mercer & Mercer, 1989).

The LSI requires utilization of the cognitive skills of modeling, comparison, abstraction, projection, and prediction, thus, it is most useful with older elementary and secondary aged students (Morgan &

Rinehart, 1991). Since primary grade children do not have the sophisticated cognitive skills or well developed language skills, and weak abilities to compare, abstract, project, and predict, their responses to their feelings are primarily behavioral reactions (Morgan & Rinehart, 1991). Effective life-space interviewing requires training and practice on the part of the teacher. Life-space interviewing is a behavior control intervention requiring schoolbased counseling skills. It "lends itself to dealing with attributional biases and to teaching problem solving and consequential thinking" (Epanchin, 1991, 339).

**Reality Therapy.** Reality therapy is a school-based counseling technique developed by Glasser (1965) which is used to manage behavior by teaching the child to behave responsibly and to face reality (Mercer & Mercer, 1989). This interview technique, similar to life-space interviewing, attempts to help the student make sound decisions when confronted with a problem (Mercer & Mercer, 1989).

When the student is involved in misbehavior, the teacher helps the student define the problem by asking "what and where" types of questions (e.g., "What are you doing?"). Then the teacher calls for a value judgment by the student, asking questions such as "Is that helping you or the class?" or "Is that behavior against the rules?" (Charles, 1989). Lastly, the teacher and student develop a plan to help the student behave appropriately and follow the rules. If the student does not adhere to the plan, the teacher assigns "time-out." The "student is not allowed to participate with the group again until making a commitment to the teacher to adhere to the plan. If a student disrupts during time-out, he is excluded from the classroom" (Charles, 1989, 124). The principal notifies the parents to pick up the student. "Students who are repeatedly sent home are referred to a special school or class, or to a different community agency" (Charles, 1989, 124).

## The School Survival Skills Curriculum

The School Survival Skills Curriculum (Silverman, et. al., 1983) is divided into three strands (Behavior Control, Teacher-Pleasing Behaviors, and Study Skills) which focus on skills that seem to be lacking in high school students with learning problems. The Behavior Control strand of the curriculum is designed for students who do not appear to understand the role they play in precipitating their problems. Components of the Behavior Control strand include behavior awareness, impact of behavior, behavior consequences, behavior options, behavior change, practicing change, and exerting control. "In the Behavior Control strand the goal is to help the students alter their locus of control and regain control over their environment. Students learn that they can change consequences because they can control their own antecedent behaviors" (Silverman, et. al., 1983, 169).

The Teacher-Pleasing Behaviors strand provides support to students who have difficulty coping with the demands of the classroom. Components of this strand include identifying classroom rules (overt and covert) and requirements for each class, identifying appropriate classroom behaviors, behavior change, using teacher-pleasing behaviors in the classrooms. Many students with learning problems do not learn "that their classroom behaviors have an impact on how the teacher responds to them, and that, depending on the behaviors they display, the teacher's response will be positive or negative" (Silverman, et. al., 1983, 169).

The goals of the Study Skills strand are to teach students "systematic methods for approaching classroom tasks and strategies for compensating for deficiencies in basic skills" (Silverman, et. al., 1983, 169). The components of the strand include organizing assignments and study time, following written and oral directions, listening for information from lectures, locating information in a text, taking notes from a text, preparing for tests, and taking tests. Instruction in the School Survival Skills Curriculum is provided in a weekly small-group meeting. "Peers interacting together, supporting one another, learning from one another are the backbone of the school survival skills lessons" (Silverman et. al., 1983, 170).

### Teacher Effectiveness Training

"Teacher Effectiveness Training offers a model for effective relationships in classrooms so that the time of both teachers and students is spent more profitably and with a greater sense of satisfaction and achievement for both" (Gordon, 1974, 42). Teacher effectiveness during problem situations requires that the teacher determine, "Who owns the problem?" The inappropriate behavior is the teacher's problem only if it "tangibly and concretely interferes with his or her teaching activities" (Gordon, 1974, 46). If the student owns the problem, the role of the teacher is to help the student solve his problem, but not solve it for him.

Teacher effectiveness is predicated upon good communication and the kinds of messages they send to their students. Teachers should avoid communicating unacceptance with the following types of messages:

(1) ordering, commanding, directing; (2) warning, threatening; (3) moralizing, preaching; (4) advising, offering solutions or suggestions; (5) teaching, lecturing, giving logical arguments (Gordon, 1974). Teachers should avoid messages that communicate judgments or put-downs such as (1) judging, criticizing, disagreeing, blaming; (2) name-calling, stereotyping, labeling; (3) interpreting, analyzing, diagnosing (Gordon, 1974).

Effective teachers use listening strategies (active and passive) as a critical component assisting students to solve their own problems. Passive listening includes silent listening, consisting of verbal or nonverbal acknowledgment responses (e.g., nods, smiles, "Uh-huh") and additional encouragement responses (e.g., "That's interesting." "Do you want to talk about it?") (Gordon, 1974). "Active listening is the process of decoding a student's uniquely coded message and then trying to give feedback" (Epanchin, 1991, 440). Active listening facilitates problem solving by the student by helping students talk and think out loud (Gordon, 1974).

Teacher Effectiveness Training focuses on avoiding power struggles and confrontation with students by using I-messages rather than You-messages. I-messages specify a description of what is causing the problem, a description of the tangible effect of the behavior, and identification of the resulting feelings (Gordon, 1974). Then the teacher must engage in active listening for a positive outcome. Therefore, T.E.T. is known as an "I Win-You Win" method or a "No-Lose" method of managing behavior and resolving conflicts.

**Stress Intervention**

The literature contains considerable evidence that anxiety and stress interfere with intellectual functioning abilities such as accuracy, spontaneity, and expressiveness; and with cognitive processes such as problem-solving, incidental learning, and verbal communication skills (Levitt, 1980; Silverstein, 1966). Additionally, Jones (1985) indicated that handicapped students experienced significantly more anxiety than nonhandicapped students. Anxiety and stress negatively impact the self-esteem. Anxiety prone individuals have chronically low self-esteem, and low self-esteem creates anxiety (Coopersmith, 1959). "Students with an external locus of control will probably tend to experience more stress than their more internal peers simply because they believe they have less control over the stressors they encounter in their lives" (Kaplan, 1991, 193). In order to assist students in increasing their self-concept, it is important to reduce anxiety and stress.

**Psychoeducational stress interventions** include techniques and procedures concerned with prevention and/or reduction of excessive anxiety and stress. Since school and school-related activities frequently are significant causes of stress and anxiety for children and youth, teachers may play a significant role in stress reduction. "Proactive teacher interventions are directed at generating and maintaining coping behavior processes in children in order to foster adaptation to difficult life situations and potential future stressful life events of high frequency" (Blom et. al., 1986, 151). Thus, proactive techniques focus on prevention of future stress and dealing with current stressful situations.

Blom et. al. (1986) suggest a number of psychoeducational programs both student-centered and teacher-centered to prevent and reduce stress. A number of the previously mentioned student-centered behavior control techniques assist children in dealing with stress and anxiety including the following: (1) The Classroom Meeting: Deals with classroom problems (Glasser, 1969); (2) Magic Circle: Teaches about emotions and emphasizes self-awareness, mastery, and social interaction (Palomares & Rubini, 1974); (3) Self-Esteem Education; Emphasizes locus of control and responsibility for one's actions (Coopersmith, 1975); (4) Cognitive Behavior Modification: Student is taught to use role playing, visual imagery, body relaxation, prompting, rehearsing and verbal mediation in reducing anxiety and stress (Mercer & Mercer, 1989). Additionally, a number of teacher focused strategies and techniques for stress prevention and reduction include the following: (1) Congruent Communication: Teachers address the emotional situation without judging the child's character or personality (Ginott, 1972); (2) Life-Space Interview: Teachers provide support for emotionally experienced stress involving the child's school experiences (Redl, 1959); (3) Logical Consequences; Avoids teacher punishment by substituting logical and natural consequences, and learning alternatives to maladaptive behavior (Dreikurs, et. al., 1971); (4) Teacher Effectiveness Training: Proposes strategies of student-teacher interaction that avoid win-lose confrontations, and encourage the child to solve his/her own problems (Gordon, 1974).

**Stress management techniques** are numerous including relaxation, exercise, positive mental attitude, cognitive understanding, recreation, general fitness, biofeedback, social support, assertiveness, effective planning, stress awareness, and good nutrition" (Blom, et. al., 1986, 181).

Relaxation Training is intended to help students monitor and regulate their physiological responses to stressors (Maher & Springer, 1987).

Generally, relaxation training involves instruction in progressive relaxation (the alternate tensing and relaxing various muscle groups) and/or instruction in guided imagery. "Relaxation appears to be an effective adjunct to other forms of intervention for the alleviation of some behavior problems and for anxiety reduction" (Maher & Springer, 1987, 109).

**Holistic approach to stress management** described by Kaplan (1991) considers stress management from three perspectives: (1) somatic-physiological interventions, (2) cognitive-psychological interventions, and (3) social-behavioral interventions. "Somatic-physiological stress coping skills produce a direct effect on the body. They are the easiest to learn and they produce the fastest results" (Kaplan, 1991, 195). The major somatic-physiological stress coping skills include diaphragmatic breathing, progressive relaxation training (PRT), both effective before, during, or after stress experiences; and exercise, especially aerobic exercise, which is most beneficial as a preventive or after experiencing a stressor.

Cognitive-psychological coping skills involve learning how one's beliefs and attitudes contribute to their anxiety and how they can modify these debilitating emotions by disputing irrational beliefs and generating rational self-talk (Kaplan, 1991). Cognitive-psychological coping skills also focus on learning proficiency in problem solving to reduce stress levels by feeling more in control of situations or stressors and the outcomes (Kaplan, 1991). Social-behavioral coping skills include all of the verbal and other overt behaviors required by the student to manage stress through the manipulation of his or her environment (Kaplan, 1991). Several of these coping skills include acting assertively in response to criticism, and time management.

## Socialization Intervention Techniques

Many students served in special education programs appear to lack the ability to process or interpret their social experiences, thus display social skills deficits. Since social skills are learned behaviors, many deficits in social skills can be remediated through imitation, modeling, and role playing. Three major emphases in socialization training include social competence, social skills, and social problem-solving. Minimally, a socially competent person must possess a number of specific social skills including the following:

(1) Social Communication: Interpreting facial expressions, body language, social and interpersonal cues, and voice intonation;

(2) Social Problem-Solving: understanding social rules and expectations, tactful negotiation; identify the problem, determine alternatives, predict consequences, evaluate new behaviors;

(3) Social Interactions: initiating appropriate social interactions, establishing and maintaining friendships, social perspective-taking;

(4) Social Maturity: control of oneself when upset or angry, present self in an appropriate manner, be acceptant and tolerant of oneself, value ethical behavior (Epanchin, 1991; Geston et. al., 1987).

Many of the previously discussed cognitive interventions and behavior control interventions including stress reduction techniques, also, have significant positive impact on the social acceptability of students to peers and adults. Most cognitive-based interventions focus on increasing social behaviors through utilization of metacognitive skills.

## Operant Conditioning and Social Learning

Operant conditioning and social learning are the two major training methods used with persons who are mentally retarded. Generally, approaches that incorporate social learning theory are used more often with persons who have greater intellectual abilities; the more severely intellectually impaired are more likely to be treated with operant conditioning methods (Matson & Ollendick, 1988).

"The social learning approach puts particular emphasis on modeling and role playing" (Matson & Ollendick, 1988, 49). This approach is particularly valuable in teaching mildly mentally retarded children and youth such social skills as eye contact, appropriate content of speech, sharing, helping others, controlling voice volume, and interacting with peers.

Lerner (1989) indicates that social skills training should include the following activities: (1) Judging behavior through stories and films, (2) Grasping social situations through pictures, (3) Grasping social situations on films, (4) Telling time, (5) Distinguishing reality from make-believe, (6) Learning to generalize newly acquired social behaviors, (7) Learning conversational skills, and (8) Friendship skills.

## Social Communication

Handicapped children and adolescents experience difficulty with pragmatics or the social use of communication because they do not appropriately interpret voice intonation, body language, and facial expressions. Many handicapped children, also, lack referential communication or "the ability to use descriptors and referents that enable one to be understood. Children who lack referential communication skills are unable to assess the informational needs of others" (Epanchin, 1991, 421). For younger children training activities in the use of pragmatics may often be included in language development and in activities.

## Skill Streaming the Elementary School Child (McGinnis & Goldstein, 1984).

Skill Streaming is a comprehensive social skills program which incorporates an emphasis on appropriate use of language in several areas:

(1) Classroom Survival Skills: asking for help, saying thank-you, offering to help an adult, asking a question;
(2) Friendship-Making Skills: introducing yourself, beginning and ending a conversation, asking a favor, giving and accepting a compliment, apologizing;
(3) Skills for Dealing with Feelings: expressing your feelings, expressing concern for another, expressing affection;
(4) Skill Alternatives to Aggression: Asking permission, responding to teaching, negotiating;
(5) Skills for Dealing with Stress: making and answering a complaint, saying no.

## Skill Streaming the Adolescent (Goldstein et. al., 1980), also, focuses on improving social skills including socially appropriate conversation. These commercial programs, also, involve training in appropriate social interactions and in social maturity or control of oneself in various social situations.

## Social Problem-Solving

School-based interventions are designed to help students (a) to understand the social consequences of their misbehavior and to plan more appropriate problem-solving actions, (b) to develop more appropriate social interaction skills so that socially inept behaviors are not perceived by teachers as misbehavior, and (c) to apply self-monitoring strategies that encourage acceptable behavior and interfere with or interrupt unacceptable behavior (Knoff, 1987, 120).

Social problem-solving incorporates interrelated skills used to resolve conflicts that require either initiation of action or reaction to the response of others (Geston et. al., 1987). The ability to understand and solve social problems enables one to behave in a socially appropriate manner and to predict behavioral outcomes. "This model diverges from other models in that general principles are being taught rather than discrete skills" (Matson & Ollendick, 1988, 45). The teaching process involves four steps: (1) problem definition and formulation: discussions of a number of problem situations that the child is likely to encounter, the identification of feelings and the behaviors that can produce feelings; (2) determining alternatives to the problematic social behaviors: use of specific problem situations and pictorial presentations to explain behavior alternatives; (3) predicting consequences: discussions and examples of how one's behavior affects others; (4) evaluation of new behaviors: guided practice using self-evaluation to evaluate new behavior (Matson & Ollendick, 1988).

> A number of curricula have been developed with the purpose of promoting social and moral reasoning and problem solving. These programs involve teaching the child or the class how to solve problems. A step-by-step problem-solving strategy is taught, and once it is mastered, it is used during subsequent lessons and whenever problems arise. Most programs approach the task by exposing the child to real-life dilemmas and helping the child think through the problem (Epanchin, 1991, 427).

## Social Maturity

An important aspect of social maturity is self-management in terms of completion of academic tasks, decreasing inappropriate behaviors and increasing prosocial behaviors, improving interactions with peers and adults. Self-Management may be implemented as a cognitive-behavioral model or operant model of self control which includes the following major components: (1) self-monitoring, (2) self-evaluation, (3) self-reinforcement, (4) self-instruction (Mace et. al., 1987). The self-monitoring step involves self-observation and self-recording (e.g., operant model-data sheets, grids; CBM- mental notes). Self-evaluation involves comparing dimensions of their behavior against criteria in order to determine adequacy of performance (Mace et. al., 1987). Self-reinforcement occurs when the student awards himself with points, privileges, material goods, etc. "The purpose of self-instruction is to change the student's thoughts about solving specific problems, by means of modeling and fading control of verbalizations from teacher to student" (Mace et. al., 1987, 170). Thus, "self-instructional statements lead to changes in cognitions, which lead to changes in overt behavior, which lead to self-evaluation, and ultimately lead to self-reinforcement or punishment, which strengthens or weakens the target behavior" (Mace et. al., 1987, 170).

## Academic Achievement Interventions

The academic achievement interventions summarized focus on techniques which are designed to increase the students' positive self-attributes, peer interactions, academic achievement, and ultimately enhance his/her self-concept. They are meant to provide a sample of the information available rather than exhaustive coverage. Some of these academic achievement interventions are study skills training, and various peer-influenced academic interventions including cooperative learning, peer tutoring, jigsaw learning, and team-assisted individualization (TAI).

### Study Skills Training

"Academic achievement and autonomy in learning...might best be enhanced by applying a combination of study skills techniques and self-management strategies to reduce anxiety and increase students' personal involvement in the educational process" (Wise et. al., 1987, 67). Numerous study skills interventions have already been presented as Cognitive Developmental Interventions (e.g., Cognitive Behavior Modification, Instrumental Enrichment, Learning Strategies: Strategies Intervention Model, The Consolidated Method for Independent Learning); and Behavior Control Interventions (e.g., The School Survival Skills Curriculum, Stress Management Techniques). Self-Management techniques have been discussed under Behavior Control Interventions including the Behavior Control Strand of The School Survival Skills Curriculum, and Cognitive Behavior Modification; and Socialization Interventions including *Skill Streaming the Elementary School Child* (McGinnis & Goldstein, 1984). and the cognitive-behavioral and operant models of self-control training.

The major emphases to emerge from all of the study skills interventions are as follows: (1) Teach specific study and test-taking strategies and techniques, and (2) Teach self-management skills which address the needs of students to control and regulate themselves in the environment—anxiety management, concentration, time management (Wise et. al., 1987).

### Peer Influenced Academic Achievement Interventions

"The term peer-influenced academic interventions represents a variety of structured interactions between two or more students, designed or planned by a school staff member to achieve academic (primary) and social-emotional (secondary) goals" (Miller & Peterson, 1987, 81). Some of these academic interventions include the following: Cooperative learning, peer tutoring, jigsaw learning, TAI, integrated groups, and Sponge PATs.

**Cooperative Learning.** "The way in which teachers structure interdependence among students learning goals determines how students interact with each other, in turn, largely determines cognitive and affective outcomes of instruction" (Johnson et. al., 1986, 3). Teachers can structure classrooms or lessons in three basic ways: Competitively, individually, or cooperatively. Competitive situations pit students against each other to achieve a goal that only one or a few students can attain. During individual learning situations students work to accomplish learning goals that may be unrelated to those of the other students. Cooperative learning requires students to work together to accomplish shared goals.

Cooperative learning provides students opportunities to develop and to practice social and problem-solving skills (Miller & Peterson, 1987). Research indicates that cooperative learning has positive effects on self-esteem, locus of control, time-on-task, liking class or school, feelings about classmates, and perspective-taking (Slavin, 1983).

Cooperative learning involves more than just assigning students to a group to complete a project or assignment. Cooperative learning requires that the interaction among the students must include five basic elements: (1) positive interdependence, (2) face-to-face interaction, (3) individual accountability, (4) interpersonal and small group skills, and (5) time and procedures to process how well they worked together (Johnson et. al., 1986, 8). "Positive interdependence is the essence of cooperative learning" (Johnson et. al., 1987, 71). Teachers can structure positive interdependence through goals, rewards, resources, roles, tasks, fantasy, and the environment. The classroom teacher must integrate the components of the cooperative task so that students are individually responsible for their components that will be culminated into the whole project, as well as for learning all of the project or assignment.

Since many handicapped elementary and secondary students lack basic social skills such as correctly identifying the emotions of others and appropriately discussing an assignment, such skills will probably need to be taught and role played. Few students have had very much experience with cooperative projects requiring input by all. It should be expected that handicapped students may initially experience difficulty until they learn what is expected of them.

**Jigsaw Techniques.** "Jigsaw is a method of cooperative learning that is particularly applicable to classroom research projects and committee work" (Geston et. al., 1987, 145). "In the jigsaw strategy, students on a team are responsible for learning an integrated body of knowledge; each student on a team is assigned one component of that larger body. Each student is then responsible for teaching that part to others . . . " (Kauchak & Eggen, 1989, 393).

Initially, the class is organized into 5 or 6 groups of equal numbers of students, approximately 5–6 students. The teacher organizes the research project into 5 or 6 content component areas corresponding to the number of members on each team (Geston et. al., 1987). For example, if the class is studying South Carolina, the content component areas might be physical features, climate, peoples, economy, and history. Each student in a group is given a different content component area. These original groups will later serve as "integration groups."

Research groups or "expert groups" will be formed by grouping together all children assigned physical features, climate, etc. The "expert group" researches their assigned area, discusses the information, and prepares a report. Group investigation, like most cooperative learning models, has been consistently found to improve such social variables as intergroup relations and preference for cooperation (Sharon et. al., 1984). Each research group student takes his report and returns to their original group. It is then his/her responsibility to teach his specific content to the other students in his/her group. All students take an examination on the information from all content areas.

"Students are rewarded as a group based on the achievement of all group members on the final quiz on all topics. This gives students an incentive to make certain that their group mates have learned the material they are presenting" (Slavin, 1987, 156). However, the success of cooperative learning methods that use group rewards for individual learning led to a conclusion that two elements were needed to make cooperative learning methods effective for academic achievement: group rewards and individual accountability" (Slavin, 1987). For example, students are individually quizzed and the results of these individual assessments are summed to form scores or a grade given for the group report (oral or written) as an incentive to students to help one another learn.

**Team Assisted Individualization (TAI)** (Slavin, 1987). TAI was developed as a means of solving the problem of student heterogeneity in the cooperative learning of math.

> In TAI, students work in four-or-five member heterogeneous teams on self-instructional math units appropriate to their level of achievement. Students within the teams check each other's work, help one another with problems, and take care of almost all clerical activities, freeing the teacher to work with homogeneous teaching groups drawn from the different teams (Slavin, 1987, 159–160).

Team Assisted Individualization appears to be an effective way to mainstream handicapped students into regular education classes. It provides support, encouragement, and peers to provide information on class routine and help with academics. TAI is by far the most successful of the cooperative learning methods for increasing achievement. TAI has also had positive effects on student self-esteem, race relations, and attitudes toward mainstreamed students (Slavin, 1987).

TAI is the most structured of the cooperative methods. Unlike other cooperative learning methods, TAI prescribes a specific set of learning materials and a structured way of using them to strike a balance between direct instruction from the teacher, individualization, mastery learning, and cooperative activities (Slavin, 1987).

**Sponge Preferred Activities (Sponge PATs)** (Hunter, 1976).

Many teachers have discovered ways, using both enrichment and drill, to use transition times to increase learning. These slack times occur frequently after students have finished assignments or work contracts. Sponge PATs are sponge preferred activities that "soak up" time for learning and help to prevent discipline problems as well by keeping students actively involved. Sponge PATs must involve minimal planning, no set up, and almost no effort on the part of the teacher, and do not distract the teacher and other students as they finish the instructional period.

Suggestions for Sponge PATs include the following (teacher and students' imaginations are the only limitation: (1) Projects that set students free to be creative; (2) Keep project box with ideas and tools; (3) Tempra-paint mural across chalkboard (seasonal, social studies); (4) Science displays/projects; (5) Interest centers; (6) Learning games; (7) Stained glass windows from colored cellophane and electrician's tape (Hunter, 1976); (8) Peek boxes (book reports, science, social studies); (9) Writing activities (poems, creative stories, various story frames, cards and letters to pen pals—elderly, foreign countries, etc.); (10) Modeling figures (clay, fine wire, etc.).

## Self-Concept Enhancement Ideas from Classroom Teachers

Classroom teachers continually use numerous techniques, strategies, motivation, and behavior management procedures in encouraging cooperative harmony and self-concept building within their classrooms. This section of the chapter includes ideas contributed by teachers that have been implemented successfully in their classrooms.

### Behavior Management

**Quiet Area:** For students who often disturbed others, I had an area in the classroom, normally used to store an unused desk, that I referred to as the REST AREA. I told a student who was disturbing others that I really felt s/he was tired and should go to the REST AREA until they felt like doing their work. They could stay as long as they felt it necessary to become "refreshed." Only one student at a time is allowed in the area. This year my REST AREA has been renamed QUIET AREA. This idea has solved several problems: (1) It isolates the trouble-maker without a lot of fuss and the student completes assignments; (2) "Time-Out" is viewed as a choice place to work; (3) It can also be used as a reward if students prefer to study there (Joan Cook, Elementary LD/EMR resource teacher, Cumberland County, Fayetteville, NC).

**Daily Reinforcement Calendar.** On the first day of the month, each primary grade student receives a blank calendar which s/he completes with correct numerals, month's name, etc. The sticker for rewarded behavior is pasted on the appropriate date. This method serves the dual purpose of a daily reinforcement (sticker) that is charted on the individual calendar. The calendars help to develop awareness of time—months, days, seasons (Gail Johnson, K–5 EMR/LD Resource Room, Scotland County School District, NC).

**Land of OP:** Using a wallet-sized photo of each student, I cut out the face and attach it to a wall adhesive paper holder to make a game-board marker. Each face (student) has the opportunity to travel the "Yellow Brick Road" (a teacher-made trail game board hanging on the wall) to the Land of Op (Opportunity). Each student is allowed to progress one step each day that they come to class prepared (homework assignment), displayed appropriate behavior, and completed the daily assignment. Upon completion of their individual journeys to the Land of Op, they each receive a small reward (e.g., pencil, bookmark, eraser) (Gail Johnson, K–5 EMH/LD Resource Room, Scotland County School District, NC).

**Holiday Bulletin Boards:** My students last year liked to complete bulletin boards. As a reward for good behavior, they were able to do bulletin boards for various teachers and organizations in school, such as the Student Council bulletin board. They completed the Christmas bulletin board in the school cafeteria. Many teachers dropped notes in my mailbox complementing the class on their good work. This motivated the class to work harder so they could do the Easter bulletin board (James Baugus, SLD/EMR Resource Room, Pine Forest Junior High, Fayetteville, NC).

**Classroom Pet:** A classroom pet is often a good incentive to keep the noise level down and "goofing off" movements to a minimum. One year I had an Iguana in a terrarium on the cabinet in view of all students. When the noise level was too high, the Iguana got nervous and expanded the red balloon pouch on his chest. Students were very concerned that we were "humane" to the Iguana and allowed to keep him in class. So when students saw the Iguana's "red balloon," they quietened down right away (Carroll Jones).

Some teachers use classroom rabbits to calm students. The rabbit is allowed to hop freely about the classroom, however, quick or loud noises or movements frighten him and he'll hide. As the rabbit hops near students they are allowed to quietly and gently reach down and pet him. Students particularly enjoy floor games and activities when the bunny hops among them. During creative writing time, students always have a topic if they can think of nothing else (Betty Jo Henderson, Woodfields Elementary, Greenwood, SC).

**Behavior Interventions.** During a Seminar in Application of Consultation Skills at Fayetteville State University, May 1989, the participants outlined behavior interventions for classroom teachers to use in preventing and controlling inappropriate behavior. The following outline includes some of those strategies:

A. Role Playing: Act out appropriate and inappropriate behaviors with natural consequences;

B. Student Oriented Problem-Solving: Helping students work through the problems that they encounter in classes using the following: (1) Coping Strategies, (2) Role Playing, (3) Counseling (private/group), (4) Brainstorming;

C. Fine Arts Therapy: Using music, dance, drama, art, and other creative expressions to facilitate learning: (1) Use music to create/demonstrate feelings/mood, (2) Use role playing to demonstrate expected behaviors, (3) Drama therapy, (4) Art therapy, (5) Dance therapy;

D. Modified Environment: Arrange the classroom in such a way as to reduce distractions and enhance learning: (1) Move the Student's desk, (2) Use study carrels, (3) Rearrange the seating;

E. Awareness of Clues and Cues: Give student and teacher a brief language of cues, using body language, to reinforce good behavior or provide silent warning before a consequence is invoked;

F. Negotiation Training: Teach students negotiation skills as a method of problem-solving with their peers;

G. Behavioral Training: Teach students the social and classroom behaviors expected in class;

H. Observing/Giving Feedback: An observer gives feedback regarding student's needs or behavior such as proximity to board, classroom distractions, and neighbors which may be provocative. This feedback may be given teacher to teacher regarding the following: (1) Provocative neighbors, (2) Inappropriate seating chart, (3) Traffic patterns, (4) Tantalizing objects;

I. Developing Plans: Work with teacher to develop a cooperative plan for each student by anticipating problems, rewards, and consequences in advance: (1) Use rules with naturally occurring consequences, (2) Create charts and graphs to monitor student progress and to provide feedback (Dickens et. al., 1989)

## Enhancing Academics

**Pass to Another:** Class discussions with learning disabled and educable mentally handicapped students may be very stressful, especially if the student called on does not know the answer. This procedure helps to reduce anxiety and embarrassment. When I ask oral questions, I call on students by name with the understanding that after thinking a second or two and the answer does not come to mind (they don't know), the student may say "Pass to _____" (names another student). I feel that I accomplish several things including the following: (1) I have gotten the student to respond in some way rather than sitting quietly uninvolved, (2) The student may be helped to overcome shyness or embarrassment during class discussions, (3) The student feels more comfortable when asked the next question, (4) The student learns the answer because s/he will listen to what the selected student has to say because s/he chose them to respond (Joan Cook, Elementary LD/EMR Resource Room Teacher, Cumberland County, Fayetteville, NC).

**Super Star:** Students who score 100% on their work will have their paper displayed on the "Super Star" bulletin board. At the end of the month the student with the most 100s will get a special cash award (one for each grade level). The student's name will be placed on the "Super Star Winner of the Month" Chart with a gold star. At the end of the year the student with the most stars will be presented an award at the Award Day Program (Minnie Spates, 11–15 year old EMH Resource, Language Arts & Math, Roseboro-Salemburg School, Roseboro, NC).

**Spelling Bubble Gum Machines:** Students cut out a picture of a bubble gum machine (8 × 11 ½ sheet of paper), and color the picture. Post the bubble gum machines on the wall or bulletin board with each student's name underneath. Each time the student spells correctly 9 out of 10 spelling words s/he earns a paper gumball to paste or tape on their machine. The first person to fill their machine is given a reward. The machines are then "emptied" and we begin again (Ginger Naylor, TMR, Sampson County Schools, Laurinburg, NC).

**Magic Slates:** In an attempt to involve 100% of the students in class activities, an effective method of eliciting responses is by using "magic slates." After asking the class a question, each student writes his/her answer on a slate and holds it up for me to see. This allows for immediate feedback and reinforcement (Sandra Hunt, Foreign Language Instructor, Georgetown H.S., Georgetown, SC).

**Academic Interventions:** During the previously mentioned Seminar in Application of Consultation Skills at Fayetteville State University, May 1989, the participants also outlined academic interventions/strategies for classroom teachers to use in enhancing the academic functioning and self-concept of students. The following outline includes some of those strategies:

A. Modifying/Substituting Assignments: Modifying, changing, or substituting difficult assignments so that credit may still be earned (1) Shortened assignments, (2) Lower the reading level;

B. Modifying Grading Criteria: Grading students on their effort in light of their ability rather than a class norm including the following: (1) Oral vs. Written Book Reports or presentations, (2) Special Projects, (3) Current Events—TV News/newspaper articles, (4) Give grade for effort, (5) Give grade for class participation;

C. Monitoring Assignments: Assisting students as needed in the progress or completion of assignments: Homework sheet/booklet, Contracts: Assignment sheets, Budgeting work;

D. Learning Centers and Modules: Creating learning packages/areas for concept units: Listening Center, Viewing Center, Learning Activity Packages, Reading Nook with bean-bag chairs, Free Time Activity Center;

E. Buddy System: Arranging for a "buddy" to assist a target student in such activities as reading from the board, getting assignments, and giving behavioral cues;

F. Compensatory Devices: Teaching students to use devices or techniques to enhance specific skills including the following: calculators, tape recorders, typewriters, language masters;

G. Life Skills: Use actual real-life reading examples to enhance academic progress including the following: coupons, labels, newspapers, food cans and boxes, menus, survival signs, etc.;

H. Survival Folder: Compile individual student folders containing reference and resource items the student can refer to daily including the following: Math facts, mini-dictionary, vocabulary words, measurement units;

I. Career Education: Educational methods designed to help students make a smooth adjustment from a school environment to adult life includes the following skills: 1. Interviewing Skills, 2. Money Management Skills, and 3. Finding and Using Resources;

J. Self-Correcting Materials: Use materials relating to the topic being taught or areas of weakness for the student which may be completed without assistance including the following: Worksheets with answers on the back, Folders with answer sheets in the room, Puzzles that must match front and back (Dickens et. al., 1989)

## Motivation

**Race Track:** Using pictures of sports cars from magazine car advertisements, I cut out the cars and make game-markers for the "Race Track" gameboard. At the end of each successful class period as a reward for good behavior, students rolled one die to determine the number of spaces his/her car could travel along the race track. This activity provided a game-like atmosphere for unmotivated students. Their work or behavior and overall motivation improved immensely (Gail Johnson, K–5, EMH/LD Resource Room, Scotland County School District, Laurinburg, NC).

**Personal Interview:** When I was first assigned to a classroom of BEH adolescents in October, five teachers had already left this classroom. I had a personal interview with each student and began keeping a behavior record. I discovered that many of the students lacked the personal attention and concern of an adult. Each week I selected a "Student of the Week" whom the Principal wrote a success story about and placed it on the cafeteria bulletin board (Sylvester Mack, BEH Adolescents, Whiteville City Schools, Whiteville, NC).

**Hey Lolly:** As a beginning circle time activity each day, we sing "Hey Lolly." Each child's name and photo are held high as we sing, "I know a boy whose name is E R I C, hey lolly lolly lo—E R I C spells Eric" . . . etc. Students love the recognition and learn each others names. (Patricia Wheeler, 6–12 year old TMR students, Scotland County Schools, Laurinburg, NC).

**Mickey's Candyland:** To motivate my 1st–8th grade LD/EMR Resource students I turned the classroom into a business operation. The name of the business is Mickey's Candyland. The students have jobs or duties to complete. Transactions are done each day. If students complete the transactions correctly, they receive a reward. The transactions required using and developing math skills, reading, and survival skills (e.g., making change, etc.) (Doris Dockery, 1st–8th Resource EMR/LD, Old Dock Elementary, Whiteville, NC).

**Motivation Through Dancing:** During a nine month course, students work on mastering technique, balance, muscle control, remembering sequences of variations and timing. Older students enjoy leading classes of younger students in drills and activities, which helps them practice skills as well. Their final learning experience is a large production on stage in front of an audience with costuming and make-up. The students help select the theme, the music, and the costumes. The production is filmed, and following the performance, we have a big cast party and watch ourselves on TV (Dorothy Davis, Dance Instructor, Fayetteville School of Dance Arts, Fayetteville, NC).

**Homework Brick House:** To encourage students to complete homework quickly and without reminders, give each student a copy of a hand drawn brick house. Students earn a brick (initialed and dated by parents) for each 5 minutes of homework, limited to 3 bricks per night. When the student returns to school with his/her homework, the teacher verifies the earned brick(s) by initialing, and the student colors the brick. When each brick has been colored, the student chooses a prize from the Treasure Box (Janet Struk, 2nd grade teacher, Portland, Oregon).

**Secondary Level Self-Monitoring System:** Develop a system that allows students to monitor their own progress. A self-monitoring system should provide students with a way to keep track of the daily progress in their academic and behavioral grades throughout each grading period. The students can be issued a form each grading period on which they are to record a predetermined number of points as they complete various instructional tasks, including tests, homework, quizzes, and class participation. A similar form can be issued for students to record points for following appropriate standards of behavior in various areas including attendance, punctuality, entry and dismissal behavior, bringing materials, work habits, and clean up (Levine, 1989, 331).

**Classroom Money Economy:** One way to teach students about our economic system and the value of money is to use a full class token system, imitating our monetary system using laminated copies of coins and bills. Each assignment is given a value depending on difficulty level; for example, math review sheet: A = 5, B = 4, etc. A predetermined value structure for misbehavior is posted and discussed. For each misbehavior, the teacher collects a predetermined amount of class money (response cost).

Students may use their "money" daily, weekly, monthly to purchase a wide variety of "extras" including the following: extra time on the computer; extra library time; a homework "free" night; watching TV, filmstrips; listening to literature story tapes; doing art, etc. extra time activities. The imaginations of the teacher and students are the only limitations on "rewards."

Once per month or bimonthly, the class has "store"; and students take turns being storekeeper. Students use their "money" to purchase items at the store including teacher, student, and parent donated items. Students can also purchase a wide variety of extras around their school.

**More About Me:** There are numerous ways to assist students in feeling self pride using art, music, drama, creative writing, etc. in the following activities: Personal journal, autobiography, personal timelines, personal coat-of-arms, personal flag, collage of self, "Proud of" bulletin boards, twenty things I like to do, family tree (Canfield & Wells, 1976).

**Running Errands.** Trainable mentally retarded students are taught to "run errands" to various areas of the school (e.g., attendance cards to the office, notes to other teachers, lunch reports to the cafeteria). Students earn this privilege by doing a good job on all assigned work for two consecutive days. They often ask, "Doing a good job?" and are frequently given positive feedback. (Sara Crawford, Teacher of 6–10 year old, ungraded TMR students, Greenwood District #50, Greenwood, SC).

### Enhancing Affective Abilities

**"What's it like to be hearing impaired?":** For hearing impaired students who are mainstreamed for part of the day, I visit regular classes and conduct a lesson on "What's it like to be hearing impaired?" I include a short lesson on what causes hearing loss, differences and similarities between hearing and deaf people, and even show samples of auditory trainers and personal hearing aids. This makes both hearing and hearing impaired children feel at ease with each other (Ellen Smith, Elementary (K–5 and High School 9–12, Hearing Impaired, Scotland County School District, Laurinburg, NC).

**Songs in Sign Language:** During special times of the year, I try to visit regular classes where hearing impaired children are mainstreamed to teach simple songs in sign language. This is a great "lift" to my hearing impaired students as they get to help teach the songs to their classmates. (Ellen Smith, Elementary K–5 and High School 9–12, Hearing Impaired, Scotland County School District, Laurinburg, NC).

**Fantasy Reading:** The importance of self-esteem is explained through the experiences of Wilbur in *Charlotte's Web.* Charlotte, a spider, befriends the self-pitying pig and encourages him to stand on his own four feet. Bilbo Baggins in *The Hobbit* finds his identity after he accepts a challenge from the wizard Gandalf. Students are more apt to learn the importance of such traits in the framework of fantasy. (Dr. Roberta Herrin, East Tennessee State University, The Fayetteville Times, June 7, 1989 newspaper article, 'Fantasy Hobbit 'Webs' Learning").

# SUMMARY

Developing and enhancing the self-concepts of students should be at the center of each teacher's curriculum and concern. Research has consistently shown that students who feel positively about themselves and their skills and abilities, approach tasks more positively and make more progress than anxiety ridden students who expect failure. The "sky is the limit" for ideas used by creative teachers to motivate students and to make learning more interesting and rewarding. This chapter touched the surface of the many self-concept enhancement possibilities from psychology, sociology, and educational theory; from Early childhood, middle childhood, and adolescence experts in the areas of cognition, behavior, socialization, and academics; and practical daily procedures used in the classrooms of many teachers.

"Teachers have the potential to greatly enhance or seriously limit their students' feelings of self-worth, achievement, and behavior" (Gearheart et. al., 1988, 96–97).

> Every teacher is in his own way a psychologist. Everything he does, says, or teaches has or could have a psychological impact. What he offers helps children to discover their resources and their limitations. He is the central figure in countless situations which can help the learner to realize and accept himself or which may bring humiliation, shame, rejection, and self-disparagement (Jersild, 1952, 139).

# BIBLIOGRAPHY

Achenbach, T.: *Revised Child Behavior Checklist.* Burlington: University of Vermont, 1982, 1983.

Achenback, T. & Edelbrock, C.: *Manual for the Child Behavior Checklist and Revised Child Behavior Profile.* Burlington, VT: Queen City Printers, 1983.

Alley, G. & Deshler, D.: *Teaching the Learning Disabled Adolescent: Strategies and Methods.* Denver: Love, 1979.

American Speech-Language-Hearing Association: Definitions: Communicative disorders and variations. *ASHA,* 24: 949–950, 1982.

Ames, L. & Haber, C.: *Your Seven-Year-Old.* New York: Dell, 1985.

Ames, L., Ilg, F. & Haber, C.: *Your One-Year-Old.* New York: Dell, 1982.

Ames, L. & Ilg, F.: *Your Two-Year-Old.* New York: Dell, 1976a.

Ames, L. & Ilg, F.: *Your Three-Year-Old.* New York: Dell, 1976b.

Ames, L. & Ilg, F.: *Your Four-Year-Old.* New York: Dell, 1976c.

Ames, L. & Ilg, F.: *Your Five-Year-Old.* New York: Dell, 1976d.

Ames, L. & Ilg, F.: *Your Six-Year-Old.* New York: Dell, 1979.

Andrews, R.: The self-concepts of good and poor readers. *Slow Learning Child: The Australian Journal of Education of Backward Children,* 18: 160–167, 1971.

Asher, S. & Renshaw, P.: Children without friendships: Social knowledge and social skill training. In S.R. Asher & J. Gottman (Eds.), *Development of Children's Friendships.* New York: Cambridge University Press, 1981.

Bailey, D. Jr. & Wolery, M.: *Assessing Infants and Preschoolers with Handicaps.* Columbus, OH: Merrill, 1989.

Ballif, B.: The significance of the self-concept in the knowledge society. Paper presented at Self-Concept Symposium, Boston, 1978.

Barker, W. & Doeff, A.: *Preschool Behavior Rating Scale.* New York, NY: Child Welfare League of America, 1980.

Barraga, N.: *Visual Handicaps and Learning.* Austin, TX: Educational Resources, 1983.

Battle, J.: Enhancing self-esteem: A new challenge to teachers. *Academic Therapy,* 16(5): 541–550, May 1981.

Battle, J.: *Enhancing Self-Esteem and Achievement.* Seattle: Special Child Publications, 1982.

Beckman, P. & Weller, C.: Active independent learning for children with learning disabilities, *Teaching Exceptional Children, 22 (2):* 26–27, Winter 1990.

Beers, C. & Wehman, P.: Play skill development. In. N. Fallen & W. Umansky, *Young Children with Special Needs.* Columbus, OH: Merrill, 1985.

Berger, K.: *The Developing Person Through Childhood and Adolescence.* New York: Worth, 1986.

Biehler, R. & Hudson, L.: *Developmental Psychology.* Boston: Houghton-Mifflin, 1986.

Biehler, R. & Snowman, J.: *Psychology Applied to Teaching (5th ed.).* Boston: Houghton Mifflin, 1986.

Bley, N. & Thornton, C.: *Teaching Mathematics to the Learning Disabled.* Rockville, MD: Aspen, 1981.

Blom, G., Cheney, B. & Snoddy, J.: *Stress in Childhood: An Intervention Model for Teachers and Other Professionals.* New York: Teachers College Press.

Bloom, R., Shea, R. & Eun, B.: The Piers-Harris Self-Concept Scale: Norms for behaviorally disordered children. *Psychology in the Schools, 16 (4):* 483–486, 1979.

Boersma, F. & Chapman, J.: *The Perception of Ability Scale for Students.* Los Angeles: Western Psychological Services, 1988.

Borkowski, J. & Varnhagan, C.: Transfer of learning strategies: Contrast of self-instructional and traditional formats with EMR children. *American Journal of Mental Deficiency, 83:* 369–379, 1884.

Borys, S.: Factors influencing the interrogative strategies of mentally retarded and nonretarded students. *American Journal of Mental Deficiency, 84:* 280–288, 1979.

Bowerman, M.: Semantic factors in the acquisition of rules for word use and sentence construction. In D. Morehead & A. Morehead (Eds.), *Directions in Normal and Deficient Child Language.* Baltimore: University Park Press, 1976.

Brazelton, T.B.: The truth about child development. *Family Circle, 103(1):* 72–74, 1990.

Brigance, A.: *BRIGANCE Diagnostic Inventory of Early Development.* Allen, TX: Teaching Resources/Developmental Learning Materials, 1983.

Brookover, A. & Erikson, E. L.: *Society, Schools, and Learning.* Boston: Allyn & Bacon, 1962.

Brown, A.: The role of strategic behavior in retardate memory. In N.R. Ellis (Ed.) *International Review of Research in Mental Retardation,* Vol. 7. New York: Academic Press, 1974.

Brown, L. & Hammill, D.: *Behavior Rating Profile.* Austin, TX: Pro-Ed, 1983.

Bruininks, R., Woodcock, R., Weatherman, R. & Hill, B.: *Scales of Independent Behavior: Woodcock-Johnson Psycho-Educational Battery* (Part 4). Allen, TX: DLM Teaching Resources, 1984.

Bruno, R., Johnson, J. & Simon, S.: Perception of humor by regular class students and students with learning disabilities or mild mental retardation, *Journal of Learning Disabilities, 20:* 568–570, 1987.

Bryan, T.: Learning disabled children's comprehension of nonverbal communication. *Journal of Learning Disabilities, 10:* 501–506, 1977.

Bryan, T. & Bryan, J.: *Understanding Learning Disabilities, 3rd Ed.* Palo Alto, CA: Mayfield, 1986.

Campbell, K.: *The New Science: Self-Esteem Psychology.* Lanham, MD: University Press of America, 1984.

Campione, J. & Brown, A.: Memory and metamemory development in educable retarded children. In R.V. Kail, Jr. & J.W. Hagen (Eds.), *Perspectives on the Development of Memory and Cognition.* Hillsdale, NJ: Erlbaum, 1977.

Canfield, J. & Wells, H.: *100 Ways to Enhance Self-Concept in the Classroom: A Handbook For Teachers and Parents.* Englewood Cliffs, NJ: Prentice-Hall, 1976.

Cantor, N., Markus, H., Neidenthal, P., & Nurius, P.: On motivation and the self-concept. In R.M. Sorrentino & E. T. Higgins (Eds.), *Handbook of Motivation and Cognition: Foundations of Social Behavior,* New York: Guilford Press, 1986.

Carter, J.: Intelligence and reading achievement of EMR in three educational settings. *Mental Retardation, 13 (5):* 26–27, 1975.

Cartledge, G. & Milburn, J.: *Teaching Social Skills to Children.* New York: Pergamon, 1986.

Cartwright, G., Cartwright, C. & Ward, M. *Educating Special Learners, (3rd Ed.)* Belmont, CA.: Wadsworth, 1989.

Chapman, J.: Cognitive-Motivational characteristics and academic achievement of learning disabled children: A longitudinal study, *Journal of Educational Psychology, 80 (3):* 357–365, 1988.

Chapman, J. & Boersma, F.: *Projected Academic Self-Concept Scale.* Unpublished instrument, University of Alberta, Edmonton, Alberta, Canada, 1978.

Charles, C.: *Building Classroom Discipline From Models to Practice (3rd Ed.).* New York: Longman, 1989.

Cheek, H. Jr., Flippo, R. & Lindsey, J.: *Reading for Success in Elementary Schools.* Fort Worth, TX: Holt, Rinehart & Winston, 1989.

Christopherson, V.A.: The family as a socialization context. In T. Yawkey & J.E. Johnson (Eds.): *Integrative processes and socialization: Early to middle childhood,* 123–138, 1988.

Cole, M. & Cole, S.: *The Development of Children.* New York: W. H. Freeman, 1989.

Coleman, J. et. al.: *Youth: Transition to Adulthood.* Report of the Panel on Youth of the President's Science Advisory Committee. Chicago: University of Chicago Press, 1974.

Combs, A.: Teachers too are individuals. In D. E. Hamachek (Ed.), *The Self in Growth, Teaching, and Learning.* Englewood, NJ: Prentice Hall, 1965.

Combs, A. & Gordon, I.: Attitudes and behavior of biological science curriculum study special materials classes in two Florida counties 1965–66. Final report to Biological Science Curriculum Study Director, Boulder, CO, 1967.

Combs, A. and Snygg, D.: *Individual Behavior, 2nd Ed.* New York: Harper & Row, 1959.

Coopersmith, S.: *The Antecedents of Self-Esteem.* San Francisco: W. H. Freeman, 1967.

Coopersmith, S.: *Coopersmith Self-Esteem Inventories.* Monterey, CA: Publishers Test Service., 1981.

Copeland, R.: *Piagetian Activities: A Diagnostic and Developmental Approach.* Eau Claire, WI: Thinking Publications, 1988.

Crandall, V.: *Intellectual Achievement Responsibility Questionnaire.* Yellow Springs, OH: FELS Research Institute, 1965.

Cullinan, D. & Epstein, M.: Behavior disorders. In N. Haring & L. McCormick

(Eds.). *Exceptional Children and Youth: An Introduction to Special Education, (5th Ed.)* Columbus, OH: Merrill, 1990.

Daehler, M.W. & Bukatko, D.: *Cognitive Development.* New York: Knopf, 1985.

Derr, A.: How learning disabled adolescent boys make moral judgments, *Journal of Learning Disabilities, 19:* 160–164, 1986.

Deshler, D. & Schumaker, J.: Social skills of learning-disabled adolescents: A review of characteristics and intervention, *Topics in Learning and Learning Disabilities, 3:* 15–23, 1983.

Dewey, D.: Motivational patterns of retirement-aged adults participating in college. *Dissertation Abstracts International, 39:* 1433A, 1978.

Dion, K., Berscheid, E. & Walster, E.: What is beautiful is good. *Journal of Personality and Social Psychology, 24:* 285–290, 1972.

Dodge, K. & Frame, C.: Social cognitive biases and deficits in aggressive boys. *Child Development, 53:* 620–635, 1982.

Doll, E.: *Vineland Social Maturity Scale.* Circle Pines, MN: American Guidance Service, 1985.

Douglas, V.I.: Attentional and cognitive problems. In M. Rutter (Ed.), *Developmental Neuropsychiatry.* New York: Guilford Press, 1983.

Drew, C., Logan, D. & Hardman, M.: *Mental Retardation: A Life Cycle Approach, 4th Ed.* Columbus, OH: Merrill, 1988.

Dunn, L. (Ed.): *Exceptional Children in the Schools: Special Education in Transition, 2nd Ed.* New York: Holt, Rinehart, & Winston, 1973.

Dweck, C.: Motivational processes affecting learning. *American Psychologist, 41:* 1040–1048, 1986.

Edgerton, R. (Ed.): *Lives in Process: Mentally Retarded Adults in a Large City.* Washington, DC: American Association on Mental Deficiency, 1984.

Edwards, J. & Edwards, D.: Rate of behavior development: Direct and continuous measurement. *Perceptual & Motor Skills, 31:* 633–634, 1970.

Eklof, A.: Validation of a component theory of motivation to achieve in school among adolescents. *Dissertation Abstracts International, 33 (7):* 3375A, 1973.

Elder, G.H.: Structural variations in the child-rearing relationship, *Sociometry, 25:* 241–262, 1962.

Elkind, D.: *Children and Adolescents: Interpretative Essays on Jean Piaget.* New York: Oxford University Press, 1970.

Ellis, N.: Memory processes in retardates and normals. *International Review of Research in Mental Retardation, 4,* 1970.

Englert, C. & Thomas, C.: Sensitivity to text structure in reading and writing: A comparison of learning disabled and nondisabled students, *Learning Disabilities Quarterly, 10:* 93–105, 1987.

Epanchin, B.: Aggressive behavior in children and adolescents. In B. Epanchin & J. Paul (Eds.) *Emotional Problems of Childhood and Adolescence: A Multidisciplinary Perspective.* Columbus, OH: Merrill, 1987.

Epstein, S.: The self-concept revisited: Or a theory of a theory. *American Psychologist, 28:* 404–416, May 1973.

Epstein, M., Polloway, E., Patton, J., & Foley, R.: Mild retardation: Student characteristics and services. *Education & Training of the Mentally Retarded, 24* (1): 7–16, 1989.

Erikson, E.H.: *Identity: Youth and crisis.* New York: Norton, 1968.

Fallen, N. & Umansky, W.: *Young Children With Special Needs,* 2nd ed. Columbus, OH: Merrill, 1985.

Farls, R.: High and low achievement of intellectually average intermediate grade students related to the self-concept and social approval. *Dissertation Abstracts. 28:* 1205A, 1967.

Federal Register: Implementation of Part B of the Education of All Handicapped Children Act, 42, August, 23, 1977.

Fewell, R.: *Play Assessment Scale.* Seattle: College of Education, University of Oregon, 1986.

Fischer, K.: Learning as the development of organized behavior. *Journal of Structural Learning, 3:* 253–267, 1980.

Flavell, J.H.: *Cognitive Development, 2nd Ed.* Englewood Cliffs, N.J.: Prentice-Hall, 1985.

Fontana, A.: Toward the measurement of self-esteem. *Perceptual and Motor Skills. 23:* 607–612, 1966.

Fowler, J.W.: Stages in Faith: The structural developmental approach. In F. Hennessey (Ed.) *Values and Moral Development and Behavior: Theory, Research, and Social Issues.* New York: Holt, Rinehart & Winston, 1976.

Frankenburg, W., Dodds, J., & Fandal, A.: *Denver Developmental Screening Test.* Denver: LADOCA Project & Publishing Foundation, 1981.

Gardner, W.: Mental retardation: A critical review of personality characteristics. In P. Browning (Ed.), *Mental Retardation Rehabilitation and Counseling.* Springfield, IL: Thomas, 1974.

Gearheart, B., Weishahn, M. & Gearheart, C.: *The Exceptional Student in the Regular Classroom 4th Ed.,* Columbus, OH: Merrill, 1988.

Gergen, K.: *The Concept of Self.* New York: Holt, Rinehart & Winston, 1971.

Germann, G. & Tindal, G.: An application of curriculum-based assessment: The use of direct and repeated measurement. *Exceptional Children, 52* (3): 244–265, 1985.

Geston, E., Weisberg, R., Amish, P., & Smith, J.: Social problem-solving training: Skills based approach to prevention and treatment. In C. Maher & J. Zins (Eds.), *Psychoeducational Interventions in the Schools.* New York: Pergamon, 1987.

Gickling, E. & Thomas, V.: A personal view of curriculum-based assessment. *Exceptional Children, 52* (3): 205–218, 1985.

Ginnott, H.: *Teacher and Child.* New York: Macmillan, 1972.

Glasser, W.: *Reality therapy: A new approach to psychiatry.* New York: Harper & Row, 1965.

Goetz, T. & Dweck, C.: Learned helplessness in social situations. *Journal of Personality and Social Psychology, 39:* 246–255, 1980.

Gordon, T.: *T.E.T.: Teacher Effectiveness Training.* New York: Wyden, 1974.

Greenspan, S.: Defining social competence in children: A working model. In B. K. Keogh (Ed.). *Advances in Special Education (Vol. 3): Socialization Influences On Exceptionality.* Greenwich, CT: JAI Press, 1981.

Gresham, F.: Social competence and motivational characteristics of learning disabled students. In M. Wang, M. Reynolds, & H. Walberg (Eds.), *Handbook of Special Education: Research and Practice, Vol. 2, Mildly Handicapped Conditions.* New York: Pergamon, 1988.

Gresham, F. & Elliott, S.: *Social Skills Rating System.* Circle Pines, MN: American Guidance Service, 1990.

Gresham, F. & Reschly, D.: Social skills and peer acceptance differences between learning disabled and nonhandicapped students, *Learning Disability Quarterly,* 9:23–32, 1986.

Griffin, G.: Childhood predictive characteristics of aggressive adolescents. *Exceptional Children,* 54 (3): 246–252, 1987.

Grossman, H. (Ed.): *Manual on Terminology and Classification in Mental Retardation.* Washington, DC: American Association on Mental Deficiently, Special Publication No. 2, 1973 and 1977.

Grossman, H. (Ed.): *Classification in Mental Retardation.* Washington, DC: American Association on Mental Deficiency, 1983.

Guralnick, N. & Groom, J.: The peer relations of mildly delayed and nonhandicapped preschool children in mainstreamed play groups. *Child Development, 58:* 1556–1579, 1987.

Hallahan, D. & Kauffman, J.: *Exceptional Children: Introduction to Special Education,* 4th Ed., Englewood Cliffs, NJ: Prentice-Hall, 1988.

Hallahan, D., Kauffman, J. & Lloyd, J.: *Introduction to Learning Disabilities, 2nd Ed.,* Englewood Cliffs, NJ: Prentice-Hall, 1985.

Hamilton, D.S., Flemming, B.M., Hicks, J.D.: *Resources for Creative Teaching in Early Childhood Education, 2nd Ed.* New York: Harcourt Brace Jovanovich, 1990.

Hansen, J. & Maynard, P.: *Youth: Self-Concept and Behavior.* Columbus, OH: Merrill, 1973.

Hardt, J.: How passive-aggressive behavior in emotionally disturbed children affects peer interactions in a classroom setting. (ERIC Documents ED297518), 1988.

Haring, N. & McCormick, L.: *Exceptional Children and Youth, 5th Ed.,* Columbus, OH: Merrill, 1990.

Harter, S.: Effectance motivation reconsidered: Toward a developmental model. *Human Development, 21:* 34–64, 1978.

Harter, S.: *Perceived Competence Scale for Children.* Denver: University of Denver, 1980.

Harter, S.: Competence as a dimension of self-evaluation: Toward a comprehensive model of self-worth. In R. Leahy (Ed.), *The Development of the Self.* Orlando: Academic Press, 1985.

Harter, S.: Processes underlying the construction, maintenance and enhancement of the self-concept in children. In J. Suls & A. Greenwald (Eds.), *Psychological Perspectives On the Self.* (Vol. 3, 136–182). Hillsdale, NJ: Erlbaum, 1986.

Harter, S.: Developmental processes in the construction of the self. In T. Yawkey & J.E. Johnson (Eds.), *Integrative Processes and Socialization: Early to Middle Childhood.* Hillsdale, NJ: Erlbaum, (1988).

Harter, S. & Pike, R.: The pictorial Scale of perceived competence and social acceptance for young children. *Child Development, 55:* 1969–1982, 1984.

Hartup, W.W.: Peer relations. In E.M. Hetherington (Ed.), *Socialization, personality, and social development.* Vol. 4 of P.H. Mussen (Ed.), *Handbook of Child Psychology (4th Ed.)* New York: Wiley, 1983.

Havighurst, R.: *Developmental Tasks and Education.* New York: Longmans, Green, 1952.

Hawaii Transition Project: [Transitional Resources] Honolulu: University of Hawaii, Department of Special Education, 1987.

Helms, D. & Turner, J.: *Exploring Child Behavior.* Philadelphia: Saunders, 1982.

Helton, G.: Guidelines for assessment in special education. In E. Meyen, G. Vergason, & R. Whelan, *Effective Instructional Strategies for Exceptional Children.* Denver: Love, 1988.

Hendrick, J.: *Total Learning: Developmental Curriculum for the Young Child* (3rd Ed.). Columbus, OH: Merrill, 1990.

Heward, W. & Orlansky, M.: *Exceptional Children, (3rd Ed.).* Columbus, OH: Merrill, 1988.

Hill, W. & Ruhe, J.: *Comparative Self-Esteem of Blacks and Whites in Segregated and Integrated Dyads.* Technical Report No. 73-1, National Technical Information Service, Springfield, VA, 1977.

Hollingshead, A.B.: *Elmtown's Youth and Elmtown Revisited.* New York: Wiley, 1975.

Horney, K.: *Neurosis and Human Growth.* New York: W.W. Norton, 1950.

Horrocks, J.E. & Jackson, D.W.: *Self and Role: A Theory of Self-Processes and Role Behavior.* Boston: Houghton Mifflin, 1972.

Howes, C.: Peer Play Scale as an index of complexity of peer interaction. *Developmental Psychology, 16:* 371–372, 1980.

Hresko, W. & Brown, L.: *Test of Early Socio-Emotional Development.* Austin, TX: PRO–ED, 1984.

Hunter, M.: Teacher competency: Problem, theory, and practice, *Theory into Practice, 15* (2): 162–167. (ERIC Documents Reproduction No. EJ149074), 1976.

Hutton, J. & Roberts, T.: *Social-Emotional Dimension Scale.* Austin, TX: Pro-Ed, 1986.

Jensen, M.: The young child's rudimentary self. In T. Yawkey (Ed.). *The Self-Concept of the Young Child.* Salt Lake City: Brigham Young University Press, 1980.

Jersild, A.: Self-understanding in childhood and adolescence. *American Psychology, 6:* 122–126, 1951.

Johnson, D., Johnson, R. & Holubec, E.: *Circles of Learning: Cooperation in the Classroom* (Revised). Edina, MN: Interaction Book Company, 1986.

Johnson, D. & Blalock, J.: *Young Adults with Learning Disabilities.* New York: Grune & Stratton, 1987.

Jones, C.J.: Analysis of the self-concepts of handicapped children, *Remedial and Special Education, 6:* 32–36, Sept./Oct. 1985.

Jones, C.J.: *Evaluation and Educational Programming of Deaf-Blind/Severely Multihandicapped Students: Sensorimotor Stage.* Springfield, IL: Charles C Thomas, 1988.

Joseph, J.: *Joseph Preschool and Primary Self-Concept Screening Test.* Chicago: Stoetling Co., 1979.

Jurkovic, G. & Şelman, R.: A developmental analysis of intrapsychic understanding:

Treating emotional disturbances in children. In R.L. Selman & R. Yando (Eds.), *New Distinctions for Child Development, No. 7, Clinical-Developmental Psychology.* San Francisco: Jossey-Bass, 1980.

Kaplan, B.: Anxiety: A classroom close-up. *The Elementary School Journal, 71:* 70–77, Nov. 1970.

Kaplan, J. with Drainville, B.: *Beyond Behavior Modification: A Cognitive-Behavioral Approach to Behavior Management in the School, 2nd Ed.* Austin, TX: PRO–ED, 1991.

Kauffman, J.M. & Kneedler, R.D.: Behavior disorders. In J.M. Kauffman & D.P. Hallahan (Eds.) *Handbook in Special Education.* Englewood Cliffs, NJ: Prentice-Hall, 1981.

Kazden, A.E.: *Conduct Disorders in Childhood and Adolescence.* Beverly Hills, CA: Sage, 1987.

Keating, D.: Four faces of creativity: The continuing plight of the intellectually underserved. *Gifted Child Quarterly, 24:* 56–61, 1980.

Kegan, R.: The loss of Pete's dragon: Developments of the self in the years five to seven. In R. Leahy (Ed.) *The Development of the Self.* Orlando: Academic Press, 1985.

Kehle, T. & Barclay, J.: Social and behavioral characteristics of mentally handicapped children. *Journal of Research and Development in Education, 12* (4): 46–56, 1979.

King, R.: Differentiating conduct disorder from depressive disorders in school age children. Paper presented at the Annual Meeting of the American Educational Research Association (70th, San Francisco, CA. (ERIC Document Number: ED269683), April 16–20, 1986.

Kirk, S. & Gallagher, J.: *Educating Exceptional Children (6th Edition).* Boston: Houghton Mifflin, 1989.

Kneeder, R.: The use of cognitive training to change social behaviors. *Exceptional Children Quarterly, 1:* 65–73, 1980.

Knight-Arest, I.: Communicative effectiveness of learning disabled and normally achieving 10- to 13-year old boys, *Learning Disability Quarterly, 7:* 237–245, 1984.

Knobloch, H. & Pasamanick, B.: *Developmental Diagnosis.* New York: Harper & Row, 1974.

Knoff, H.: School-based interventions for discipline problems. In C. Maher & J. Zins (Eds.), *Psychoeducational Interventions in the Schools.* New York: Pergamon, 1987.

Kohlberg, L.: Moral stages and moralization: The cognitive developmental approach. In T. Lickona (Ed.) *Moral Development and Behavior: Theory, Research, and Social Issues.* New York: Holt, Rinehart, & Winston, 1976.

Kohn, M., Parnes, B. & Rosman, B.: *Kohn Social Competence Scale.* New York: Martin Kohn Publisher, 1979.

Kramer, J. & Engle, R.: Teaching awareness of strategic behavior in combination with strategy training: Effect on children's memory performance. *Journal of Experimental Child Psychology, 32:* 513–530, 1981.

Kramer, J., Nagle, R. & Engel, R.: Recent advances in mnemonic strategy training with mentally retarded persons: Implications for educational practice. *American Journal of Mental Deficiency, 85:* 306–314, 1980.

Kramer, J., Piersel, W. & Glover, J.: Cognitive and social development of mildly retarded children. In M. Wang, M. Reynolds, & H. Walberg (eds.). *Handbook of Special Education: Research and Practice, Volume 2 Mildly Handicapped Conditions.* Oxford: Pergamon, 1988.

Krasnor, L. & Rubin, K.: Preschool social problem solving: Attempts and outcomes in naturalistic interactions. *Child Development. 54:* 1545–1558, 1983.

Kruger, D.: *An Introduction to Phenomenological Psychology.* Pittsburgh: Duquesne University, 1979.

Kurtz, B. & Borkowski, J.: Children's metacognition: Exploring relations among knowledge, process, and motivational variables. *Journal of Experimental Child Psychology, 37:* 335–354, 1984.

LaBenne, W. & Greene, B.: *Educational Implications of Self-Concept Theory.* Pacific Palisades, CA: Goodyear, 1969.

Lanyon, R. & Goodstein, L.: *Personality Assessment,* 2nd Ed., New York: John Wiley, 1982.

Lawrence, E. & Winschel, J.: Locus of control: Implications for special education. *Exceptional Children, 41:* 483–490, 1975.

Leahy, R.L. & Shirk, S.R.: Social cognition and the development of the self. In R. Leahy (Ed.), *The Development of the Self.* Orlando: Academic Press, 1985.

Lecky, P.: *Self-Consistency: A Theory of Personality.* New York: Island Press, 1945.

Lenz, B.K., Clark, F., Deshler, D. & Schumaker, J.: *The Strategies Intervention Model Training Package.* Lawrence, KS: The University of Kansas Institute for Research in Learning Disabilities, 1988.

Lerner, J.: *Learning Disabilities: Theories, Diagnosis, and Teaching Strategies, 5th Ed.,* Boston: Houghton Mifflin, 1989.

Lerner, J., Mardell-Czudnowski, C. & Goldenberg, D.: *Special Education for the Early Childhood Years, (2nd Ed.).* Englewood Cliffs, NJ: Prentice-Hall, 1987.

Lerner, R. & Shea, J.: Social behavior in adolescence. In B. Wolman, ed., *Handbook of Developmental Psychology.* Englewood Cliffs, NJ: Prentice-Hall, 1982.

Levine, J.: *Secondary Instruction: A manual for Classroom Teaching.* Boston: Allyn & Bacon, 1989.

Levine, M.: *Developmental Variations and Learning Disorders.* Cambridge, MA: Educators Publishing Service, 1987.

Levitt, E.: *The Psychology of Anxiety, 2nd Ed.* Hillsdale, NJ: Earlbaum, 1980.

Lewis, M. & Michalson, L.: *Scales of Socio-Emotional Development.* New York: Plenum, 1983.

Lillie, D. & Sturm, T.: *Carolina Early Learning Activities.* New York: Walker, 1987.

Lloyd, J.: Academic instruction and cognitive behavior modification: The need for attack strategy training. *Exceptional Education Quarterly, 1:* 53–64, 1980.

Logan, D. & Rose, E.: Characteristics of the mentally retarded. In P.T. Cegelka & H.J. Prehm (Eds.), *Mental Retardation: From Categories to People.* Columbus, OH: Charles E. Merrill, 1982.

Longhurst, T. & Berry, G.: Communication in retarded adolescents: Response to listeners feedback, *American Journal of Mental Deficiency, 80:* 158–164, 1975.

Loper, A.: Metacognitive development: Implications for cognitive training. *Exceptional Education Quarterly, 1:* 1–8, 1980.

Lovitt, T.: *Introduction to Learning Disabilities.* Boston: Allyn & Bacon, 1989.

Luchow, J. et. al.: Learned helplessness: Perceived effects of ability and effort on academic performance among EH and LD/EH children. Paper presented at the Annual Convention of the Council for Exceptional Children (63rd, Anaheim, CA, April 15–19, 1985). (ERIC Reproduction No. ED257264), 1985.

Luftig, R.: *Assessment of Learners with Special Needs.* Boston: Allyn & Bacon, 1988.

Lunn, J.: *Streaming in the Primary School.* Stough: NFER, 1970.

Lyon, V.: Personality tests with the deaf. *American Annals of the Deaf, 79:* 1–4, 1934.

Maccoby, E.: *Social development.* New York: Harcourt Brace, 1980.

Mace, F., Brown, D. & West, B.: Behavioral self-management in education. In C. Maher & J. Zins (Eds.), *Psychoeducational Interventions in the Schools.* New York: Pergamon, 1987.

MacMillan, D.: *Mental Retardation in School and Society* (2nd ed.). Boston: Little, Brown, 1982.

MacMillan, D. & Morrison, G.: Correlates of social status among mildly handicapped learners in self-contained classes. *Journal of Educational Psychology, 72:* 437–444, 1980.

Maher, C. & Springer, J.: School-based counseling. In C. Maher & J. Zins (Eds.), *Psychoeducational Interventions in the Schools.* New York: Pergamon, 1987.

Manaster, G.J.: *Adolescent Development: A Psychological Interpretation.* Itasca, IL: F.E. Peacock, 1989.

Mann, L. & Sabatino, D.: *Foundations of Cognitive Process in Remedial and Special Education.* Rockville, MD: Aspen, 1985.

Mann, P., Beaher, J., & Jacobson, M.: The effect of group counseling on educable mentally retarded boys' self-concepts. *Exceptional Children, 35* (5): 359–366, 1969.

Mardell-Czudnowski, C. & Goldenburg, D.: *Developmental Indicators for the Assessment of Learning-Revised.* (*Dial-R*). Edison, NJ: Childcraft Education Corp., 1983.

Margalit, M. & Zak, I.: Anxiety and self-concept of learning disabled children. *Journal of Learning Disabilities, 17* (9):537–539, Nov. 1984.

Maslow, A.: *Motivation and Personality.* New York: Harper, 1954.

Matson, J. & Ollendick, T.: *Enhancing Children's Social Skills Assessment and Training.* New York: Pergamon, 1988.

McCandless, B.: *Children: Behavior and Development.* New York: Holt, Rinehart, & Winston, 1967.

McDonald, K.: Enhancing a child's positive self-concept. In T. Yawkey (Ed.) *The Self-Concept of the Young Child.* Salt Lake City: Brigham Young University Press, 1980.

McGinnis, E. & Goldstein, A.P.: *Skillstreaming the Elementary School Child: A Guide for Teaching Prosocial Skills.* Champaign, IL: Research Press, 1984.

McNelly, F. Jr.: *Development of the Self-Concept in Childhood.* ED 086 318, Dec. 1972.

Mercer, C.: *Students with Learning Disabilities, 3rd Ed.,* Columbus, OH: Merrill, 1987.

Mercer, C. & Mercer, A.: *Teaching Students with Learning Problems, 3rd Ed.,* Columbus, OH: Merrill, 1989.

Mercer, C. & Snell, M.: *Learning Theory Research in Mental Retardation: Implications for Teaching.* Columbus, OH: Merrill, 1977.

Miller, J. & Peterson, D.: Peer-Influenced academic interventions. In C. Maher & J. Zins (Eds.) *Psychoeducational Interventions in the Schools.* New York: Pergamon, 1987.

Mitchell, J. (Ed.): *The Ninth Mental Measurement Yearbook.* Lincoln, NE: University of Nebraska Press, 1985.

Morgan, S.: Locus of control in children labeled learning disabled, behaviorally disordered, and learning disabled/behaviorally disordered. *Learning Disabilities Research, 2* (1): 10–13 (ERIC Reproduction No. ED350866), 1986.

Morgan, S.: Responses to feelings and emotional well-being. In S. Morgan & J. Rinehart (Eds.), *Interventions for Students with Emotional Disorders.* Austin, TX: PRO–ED, 1991.

Morrison, G.: Mentally retarded. In E. Meyen & T. Skrtic (Eds.) *Exceptional Children and Youth: An Introduction,* 3rd Ed. Denver: Love, 1988.

Mussen, P., Conger, J., Kagan, J., & Huston, A.: *Child Development & Personality, 7th Ed.,* New York: Harper & Row, 1990.

Neisworth, J. & Bagnato, S.: *The Young Exceptional Child: Early Development and Education.* New York: Macmillan, 1987.

Nihira, K., Foster, R., Shellhaas, M. & Leland, H.: *AAMD (Adaptive Behavior Scale — School Edition.).* Washington, DC: American Association on Mental Deficiency, 1981.

Nowicki, S. & DiGirolamo, A.: The association of external locus of control, nonverbal processing difficulties, and emotional disturbance. *Behavioral Disorders, 15* (1): 28–34, 1989.

Nowicki, S. & Strickland, B.: A locus of control scale for children. *Journal of Consulting and Clinical Psychology, 40:* 148–154, 1973.

Oden, S.: Alternative perspectives on children's peer relationships. In T. Yawkey & J.E. Johnson (Eds.), *Integrative Processes and Socialization: Early to Middle Childhood.* Hillsdale, NJ: Erlbaum, 1988.

Ollendick, H., Balla, D. & Zigler, E.: Expectancy of success and the probability learning performance of retarded children. *Journal of Abnormal Psychology,* (77) 275–281, 1971.

Oyer, H., Crowe, B. & Hass, W.: *Speech, Language, & Hearing Disorders: A Guide for the Teacher.* Boston: Little, Brown, 1987.

Palincsar, A. & Brown, D.: Enhancing instructional time through attention to metacognition. *Journal of Learning Disabilities, 20* (2): 66–75, 1987.

Palomares, U. & Rubini, T.: *Magic Circle.* La Mesa, CA: Human Development Training Institute, 1974.

Pascarella, E., Pflaum, S., Bryan, T., & Pearl, R.: Interaction of internal attribution for effort and teacher response mode in reading instruction: A replication note. *American Educational Research Journal, 5:* 173–176, 1983.

Patton, J., Beirne-Smith, A., Payne, J.: *Mental Retardation, 3rd Ed.* Columbus, OH: Merrill, 1990.

Patton, J. & Polloway, E.: Mild mental retardation. In N. Haring & L. McCormick (Eds.) *Exceptional Children and Youth: An Introduction to Special Education,* 5th Ed. Columbus, OH: Merrill, 1990.

Paul, J.: Defining behavioral disorders in children. In B. Epanchin & J. Paul (Eds.) *Emotional Problems of Childhood and Adolescence: A Multidisciplinary Perspective.* Columbus, OH: Merrill, 1987.

Pearl, R., Donahue, M. & Bryan, T.: Social relationships of learning disabled children. In J. Torgensen & B. Wong (Eds.), *Psychological and Educational Perspectives on Learning Disabilities.* New York: Academic, 1986.

Perna, S. et. al.: The relationship of internal locus of control, academic achievement, and IQ in emotionally disturbed boys, *Behavioral Disorders, 9* (1): 36–42, 1983.

Peterson, N.: *Early Intervention for Handicapped and At-Risk Children.* Denver: Love, 1987.

Piers, E. & Harris, D.: *Piers-Harris Children's Self-Concept Scale (The Way I Feel About Myself).* Los Angeles: Western Psychological Services, 1969 and 1984.

Politino, V.: Attitude toward physical activity and self-concept of normal and emotionally disturbed children. *Dissertation Abstracts International, 40* (8A): 4476, Feb. 1980.

Polloway, E., Epstein, M., Patton, J., Cullinan, D. & Luebke, J.: Demographic, social and behavioral characteristics of students with educable mental retardation. *Education and Training of the Mentally Retarded, 21:* 27–34, 1986.

Polloway, E., Patton, J., Payne, J. & Payne, R.: *Strategies for Teaching Learners with Special Needs, 4th Ed.* Columbus, OH: Merrill, 1989.

Polloway, E. & Smith, J.: Current status of the mild mental retardation construct: Identification, placement, and programs. In M. Wang, M. Reynolds, & H. Wahlberg (Eds.), *The Handbook of Special Education: Research and Practice.* Oxford: Pergamon, 1987.

Pray, Jr., B.S., Kramer, J. & Camp, C.: Training recall readiness skills to retarded adults: Effects on skill maintenance and generalization. *Human Learning, 3:* 43–51, 1984.

Pullis, M.: Affective and motivational aspects of learning disabilities. In D. K. Reid, *Teaching the Learning Disabled A Cognitive Developmental Approach,* Boston: Allyn & Bacon, 1988.

Purkey, W.: *Self-Concept and School Achievement.* Englewood Cliffs, NJ: Prentice Hall, 1970.

Raschke, D. & Dedrick, C.: Earn your fortune: A system to motivate reluctant learners, *Teaching Exceptional Children,* 62–63, Spring 1989.

Redl, F.: The concept of the life space interview. *American Journal of Orthopsychiatry, 29:* 1–18, 1959.

Reid, D.K.: *Teaching the Learning Disabled: A Cognitive Developmental Approach.* Boston: Allyn & Bacon, 1988.

Reschly, D.: Learning characteristics of mildly handicapped students: Implications for classification, placement, and programming. In M. Wang, M. Reynolds, & H.

Wolberg (Eds.), *Handbook of Special Education: Research and Practice. Vol. I, Learner Characteristics and Adaptive Education.* New York: Pergamon Press, 1987.

Rizzo, J. & Zabel, R.: *Educating Children and Adolescents with Behavioral Disorders: An Integrative Approach.* Boston: Allyn & Bacon, 1988.

Robinson, H.F.: *Exploring Teaching in Early Childhood Education.* Boston: Allyn & Bacon, 1977.

Robinson, S. & Deshler, D.: Learning Disabled. In E. Meyen & T. Skrtic (Eds.), *Exceptional Children and Youth: An Introduction 3rd Ed.,* Denver: Love, 1988.

Roessler, R. & Bolton, B.: *Psychosocial Adjustment to Disability.* Baltimore: University Park Press, 1978.

Rogers, C.: *Client-Centered Therapy.* Boston: Houghton Mifflin, 1951; 1959.

Rogers, H. & Saklofske, D.: Self-concepts, locus of control and performance expectations of learning disabled children, *Journal of Learning Disabilities, 18* (5): 273–278, 1985.

Rose-Krasnor, L.: Social cognition. In T. Yawkey & J.E. Johnson (Eds.), *Integrative Processes and Socialization: Early to Middle Childhood.* Hillsdale, NJ: Earlbaum, 1988.

Rosenberg, M.: *Conceiving the Self.* New York: Basic Books, 1979.

Rosenberg, M.: Identity: Summary. In M. Spencer, G. Brookins & W. Allen (Eds.), *Beginnings: The Social and Affective Development of Black Children.* Hillsdale, NJ: Erlbaum, 1985.

Saccuzzo, D. & Michael, B.: Speed of information processing and structural limitations by mentally retarded and dual-diagnosed retarded-schizophrenic persons. *American Journal of Mental Deficiency, 89:* 187–194, 1984.

Samuels, S.: *Enhancing Self-Concept in Early Childhood, Theory and Practice.* New York: Human Sciences Press, 1987.

Santrock, J.: *Adolescence.* Dubuque, IA: Wm. C. Brown, 1990.

Schaefer, P. & Moersch, M.: *Developmental Programming for Infants and Young Children.* Ann Arbor: University of Michigan Press, 1981.

Schloss, P.: Dimensions of students' behavior disorders: An alternative to medical model classification. *Diagnostique, 11* (11): 21–30, Fall 1985.

Schumaker, J. & Hazel, J.: Social skills assessment and training for the learning disabled: Who's on first and what is on second? Part I. *Journal of Learning Disabilities, 17:* 422–431, 1984.

Seligman, M. & Peterson, C.: A learned helplessness perspective on childhood depression. In M. Rutter, C. Izard, & P. Read (Eds.) *Depression in Young People: Developmental and Clinical Perspectives.* New York: Guilford, 1986.

Selman, R.: The child as a friendship philosopher. In S.R. Asher & J.M. Gottman (Eds.), *The Development of Children's Friendships.* New York: Cambridge University Press, 1981.

Shea, T.: *Teaching Children and Youth with Behavior Disorders.* St. Louis: Mosby, 1978.

Shea, T. & Bauer, A.: *Teaching Children and Youth with Behavior Disorders, (2nd Ed.).* Englewood Cliffs, NJ: Prentice-Hall, 1987.

Sheinker, J. & Sheinker, A.: *Study Strategies: A Metacognitive Approach.* Rock Springs, WY: White Mountain Publishing, 1982.

Siegel, M.: *Psychological Testing from Early Childhood Through Adolescence.* Madison, CT: International University Press, 1987.

Silverman, R., Zigmond, N. & Sansone, J.: Teaching coping skills to adolescents with learning problems. In E. Meyen, G. Vergason, & R. Whelan (Eds.) *Promising Practices for Exceptional Children Curriculum Implications.* Denver: Love, 1983.

Silverstein, A.: Anxiety and the quality of human figure drawings. *American Journal of Mental Deficiency, 70:* 607–608, 1966.

Skolnick, A.S.: *The Psychology of Human Development.* San Diego: Harcourt, Brace, Jovanovich, 1986.

Slavin, R.: Cooperative learning: Engineering social psychology in the classroom. In R. Feldman (Ed.) *The Social Psychology of Education: Current Research and Theory.* Cambridge: Cambridge University Press, 1987.

Smilansky, S.: *The Effects of Sociodramatic Play on Disadvantaged Preschool Children.* New York: Wiley, 1968.

Smollar, J. & Youniss, J.: Adolescent self-concept development. In R. Leahy (Ed). *The Development of the Self.* Orlando: Academic Press, 1985.

Snell, M.: Functional reading. In M. Snell (Ed.), *Systematic Instruction of the Moderately and Severely Handicapped 2nd Ed.* Columbus, OH: Merrill, 1983.

Snyder, R., Jefferson, W. & Strauss, R.: Personality variables as determiners of academic achievement of the mildly retarded. *Mental Retardation, 3:* 15–18, 1965.

Song, I. & Hattie, J.: Home environment, self-concept, and academic achievement: A causal modeling approach. *Journal of Educational Psychology, 76,* 6: 1269–1281, 1984.

Sparrow, B., Balla, D. & Cicchetti, D.: *Vineland Adaptive Behavior Scale.* Circle Pines, MN: American Guidance Services, 1984.

Spradlin, J.: Environmental factors and the language development of retarded children. In S. Rosenberg & J. Koplin (Eds.), *Developments in Applied Psycholinguistic Research.* New York: MacMillan, 1968.

Stangvik, G.: *Self-Concept and School Segregation.* Goteborg, Sweden: ACTA, Universitatis Gothoburgensis, 1979.

Stanovich, K.: Cognitive processes and the reading problems of learning disabled children: Evaluating the assumption of specificity. In J. Torgesen & B. Wong (Eds.), *Psychological and Educational Perspectives on Learning Disabilities.* New York: Academic Press, 1986.

Stevenson, D. & Romney, D.: Depression in learning disabled children. *Journal of Learning Disabilities, 17:* 579, 1984.

Stillman, R. (Ed.): *The Callier-Azusa Scale.* Dallas, TX: Callier Center for Communication Disorders, The University of Texas at Dallas, 1978.

Strang, A. & Kirk, S.: The social competence of deaf and hard-of-hearing children in a public day school. *American Annals of the Deaf, 83:* 244–254, 1938.

Swanson, H. & Watson, B.: *Educational and Psychological Assessment of Exceptional Children, 2nd Ed.* Columbus, OH: Merrill, 1989.

Taylor, R.: Psychological intervention with mildly retarded children: Prevention and remediation of cognitive skills. In M. Wang, M. Reynolds, & H. Walberg

(Eds.) *Handbook of Special Education: Research and Practice, Vol. 2, Mildly Handi-capped Conditions.* New York: Pergamon, 1988.

Thomas, C. & Patton, J.: Mild and moderate retardation. In J. Patton, J. Payne & M. Bierne-Smith, *Mental Retardation, 3rd Ed.* Columbus, OH: Merrill, 1990.

Tobias, S.: Anxiety research in educational psychology. *Journal of Educational Psychology, 11:* 573–582, 1979.

Turiel, E., Killen, M. & Helwig, C.C.: Morality: Its structure, functions, and vagaries. In J. Kegan & S. Lamb (Eds.), *The Emergence of Morality.* Chicago: Chicago University Press, 1987.

Unruh, D. et. al.: Locus of control in normal and emotionally disturbed/behavior disordered children. (ERIC Reproduction No. EJ354597), *Child Study Journal, 17* (1): 15–20, 1987.

U.S. Department of Education: To assure the free and appropriate public education of all handicapped children. *Eleventh Annual Report to Congress on the Implementation of the Education of the Handicapped Act.* Washington, DC: Government Printing Office, 1989.

U.S. Department of Education: To assure the free and appropriate public education of all handicapped children. *Tenth Annual Report to Congress on the Implementation of the Education of the Handicapped Act.* Washington, D.C.: Government Printing Office, 1988.

U.S. Office of Education: Education of Handicapped Children. Implementation of Part B of the Education for the Handicapped Act. *Federal Register, Part II.* Washington, D.C.: U.S. Department of Health, Education, and Welfare, 1977.

Videbeck, R.: Self-conception and the reaction of others. *Sociometry, 23:* 351–359, 1960.

Wagner, R.: Human figure drawings of LD children. *Academic Therapy, 16:* 37–41, 1980.

Wahler, R., House, K. & Stambaugh, E.: *Ecological Assessment of Child Problem Behavior: A Clinical Package for Home, School, and Institutional Settings.* New York: Pergamon, 1976.

Walker, H.: *Walker Problem Behavior Identification Checklist.* Los Angeles: Western Psychological Services, 1983.

Wattenberg, W. & Clifford, C.: Relation of self-concept to beginning achievement in reading. *Child Development, 35:* 461–467, 1964.

Weiss, E.: Learning disabled children's understanding of social interactions of peers. *Journal of Learning Disabilities, 17:* 612–615, 1984.

Weller, C. & Strawser, S.: *Weller-Strawser Scales of Adaptive Behavior for the Learning Disabled.* Novato, CA: Academic Therapy, 1981.

Westby, C.: Assessment of cognitive and language abilities through play. *Language, Speech, and Hearing Services in the Schools. 11:* 154–168, 1980.

Whelan, R.: Emotional disturbance. In E. Meyen & T. Skrtic (Eds.) *Exceptional Children and Youth: An Introduction,* (*3rd Ed.*). Denver: Love, 1988.

Whorton, J. & Algozzine, R.: Comparison of intellectual, achievement, and adaptive behavior levels for students who are mentally retarded, *Mental retardation, 16:* 320–321, 1978.

Wiig, E. & Semel, E.: *Language Assessment and Intervention for the Learning Disabled* (2nd. Ed.). Columbus, OH: Merrill, 1984.

Wise, P., Genshaft, J., Byrley, M.: Study skills training: A comprehensive approach. In C. Maher & R. Zins (Eds.) *Psychoeducational Interventions in the Schools.* New York: Pergamon, 1987.

Wylie, R.: *The Self-Concept.* Lincoln: University of Nebraska Press, 1961.

Yamamoto, K.: *The Child and His Image.* Boston: Houghton Mifflin, 1972.

Yawkey, T. (Ed.): *The Self-Concept of the Young Child.* Salt Lake City: Brigham Young University Press, 1980.

Youniss, J.: The nature of social development: A conceptual discussion of cognition. In H. McGurk (Ed.) *Issues in Childhood Social Development.* London: Methuen, 1978.

Zigler, E.: Research on personality structure in the retardate. In N. Ellis (Ed.) *International Review of Research in Mental Retardation, Vol. 1.* New York: Academic Press, 1966.

Zigmond, N.: A prototype of comprehensive service for secondary students with learning disabilities: A preliminary report. *Learning Disability Quarterly, 1:* 39–49, 1978.

Ziller, R., Hagey, J., Smith, M., & Long, B.: Self-esteem: A self-social construct. *Journal of Consulting and Clinical Psychology, 33:* 84–95, 1969.

# INDEX

273